Sex and the Revitalized City

Sex and the Revitalized City

Gender, Condominium Development, and Urban Citizenship

Leslie Kern

UBCPress · Vancouver · Toronto

20 19 18 17 16 15 14 13 12 11 10   5 4 3 2 1

Printed in Canada on FSC-certified ancient-forest-free paper
(100% post-consumer recycled) that is processed chlorine- and acid-free.

Library and Archives Canada Cataloguing in Publication

Kern, Leslie, 1975-
    Sex and the revitalized city: gender, condominium development, and urban citizenship / Leslie Kern.

Includes bibliographical references and index.
ISBN 978-0-7748-1822-3

    1. Women – Housing – Ontario – Toronto – Case studies. 2. Condominiums – Social aspects – Ontario – Toronto – Case studies. 3. Home ownership – Social aspects – Ontario – Toronto – Case studies. 4. Women – Ontario – Toronto – Social conditions – Case studies. 5. Women – Ontario – Toronto – Economic conditions – Case studies. 6. Urbanization – Political aspects – Ontario – Toronto – Case studies. I. Title.

HD7289.42.C3K47 2010   307.3'361608209713541   C2010-900462-0

Canada

UBC Press gratefully acknowledges the financial support for our publishing program of the Government of Canada (through the Canada Book Fund), the Canada Council for the Arts, and the British Columbia Arts Council.

This book has been published with the help of a grant from the Canadian Federation for the Humanities and Social Sciences, through the Aid to Scholarly Publications Programme, using funds provided by the Social Sciences and Humanities Research Council of Canada.

UBC Press
The University of British Columbia
2029 West Mall
Vancouver, BC V6T 1Z2
www.ubcpress.ca

Contents

Acknowledgments

This project has spanned several years, and, throughout that time, I have received amazing support from many wonderful people. Here I wish to thank Gerda Wekerle, who, from the first day we met, has been an invaluable mentor and friend. Stefan Kipfer and Shelley Hornstein have shared their unique perspectives and have greatly enriched my work. My family has shown extraordinary patience during this process, especially Maddy, to whom I owe a great deal of playtime. Numerous academic colleagues have shown me support and inspired me with new ideas. My editor at UBC press, Darcy Cullen, has been a fantastic guide through this process, and two anonymous reviewers made insightful contributions to *Sex and the Revitalized City*. I also owe many thanks to the generous people who agreed to be a part of this research, sharing their time and their thoughts and making this work possible.

Sex and the Revitalized City

Introduction

In 2002, a *Toronto Star* real estate reporter described a revelatory moment among condominium developers and industry analysts:

> As industry insiders sat around marvelling at the seemingly limitless appetite for downtown condominiums in the last few years, it gradually dawned on them that the single woman, as purchaser, was a force to be reckoned with. Buried in the sales data they found evidence of a significant sociological shift. (Cordileone 2002, O1)

While this anecdote evokes an amusing image of smug condominium developers marvelling at their record profits, only to be struck by the deep insight that they may in fact be heralding the dawn of a new age of women's emancipation, the reporter is not completely misguided in attributing the discovery of this significant sociological shift to the condominium industry. This shift has not been reflected upon by urban scholars, despite the questions it raises about the social impacts of gentrification, property redevelopment, and urban revitalization, as well as concerns about women's place in the contemporary postindustrial city.

Even a casual observer of the urban environment could not help but notice the massive transformations in Toronto's physical and social landscapes over the past fifteen years, as vacant lots, brownfield sites, and rezoned lands have spawned hundreds of condominium projects of all forms, and drawn a variety of gentrifier groups into the downtown core, reshaping neighbourhoods old and new. The famous CN Tower is now flanked by dozens of condominium towers along the waterfront; condominium advertisements can be found on billboards, in magazines, and even on television; and major newspapers devote weekly sections to the phenomenon of "condo living." Toronto's evolution into North America's largest condominium market represents a shift in policy and development towards high-rise, high-density urban intensification. While the long-term effects of this boom are yet to be discerned, there are important current issues raised by this particular form of urban revitalization. These include questions about city building processes, about transformations in everyday urban life, and about the definitions of citizen and citizenship mobilized in pursuit of global city status.

These issues are nothing new. However, there is a fresh opportunity here to investigate how condominium development, ownership, and governance affect the daily lives of a distinct group of city dwellers, situated in the context of the broader themes of neoliberal city building and city politics, shifting forms of urban governance, and new constructions of urban citizenship. To do so, I attempt to trace the underlying political-economic rationality behind condominium development as an expression of neoliberal ideology, while simultaneously exploring the ways in which this ideology is filtered through condominium ownership and governance into the daily meanings and practices of urban living for women condominium dwellers. This, I argue, opens a conceptual space within which to understand how people's relationships to the city are being redefined, how opportunities for social justice are shaped in neoliberal times, and what potential exists for democratic citizenship in the revitalized city.

Within the space that this project opens up, I offer some observations on and insights into city building, everyday life, and identity that expand and challenge the received wisdom about women in the city. One of the surprising, and perhaps troubling, aspects to come to light is that, despite the autonomy and freedom experienced by women in the revitalized city, many of the ideologies and discourses at work here reconstitute patriarchal relations and remarkably traditional roles for women, albeit in ways that are flexible enough to fit within the rubric of neoliberal urbanism. For example, condominium ownership seems to offer financial freedom for young women, but it simultaneously draws them into the social, political, and moral structure of private property ownership ahead of, or as a substitute for, marriage or long-term partnership. In a twist on women's historical exclusion from the rights of private property ownership, the contemporary postindustrial city has become a place where private property ownership is positioned as a way of achieving gender equality. However, the financial freedoms offered do not necessarily mean that patriarchal gender ideologies about home, work, family, and the life course are subverted.

Condominiums are often characterized positively as communities. My analysis illustrates how the notion of community may be used to mask or soften the capitalist logic of accumulation, how the logic of highest and best use becomes encoded in community, and how an implicit hierarchy of community posits gentrification as necessary for the creation of community. As self-styled community builders, private city building agents have a central role in shaping the image of the desired urban citizen and urban community. Condominiums, I suggest, create new geographies of inclusion and exclusion that help to define who is thought of as a community member or a fellow citizen. At the same time, the reshaping of public and private space through condominium development creates both constraints and opportunities for citizenship and community engagement, particularly for groups such as women.

Furthermore, the process of urban revitalization seems to promise greater freedom for women in the public realm. I challenge this notion by demonstrating how ideas about women's fear, vulnerability, and need for protection and containment shape the production of contemporary spaces of revitalization. At the same time, the specific contours of urban freedom and its expression are offered to women through a rearticulation of rather traditional feminine bourgeois roles, those of watcher and watched, consumer and consumed. In Figure 1, the advertising billboard invites the consumer to "live in liberty. It's a neighbourhood." Freedom is conflated with the condominium and the city: it is a place that is bought rather than a political concept. Throughout *Sex and the Revitalized City*, I work to unpack the troubling implications of consumer-oriented freedom for women.

Debate about condominium development is polarized in both scholarly literature and mainstream discourse. Condominiums are presented both as the postmodernist version of Jane Jacobs' notion of the "sacking" of the city and as the salvation of the deindustrialized city; as capitalist accumulation gone mad and the solution to the evils of urban sprawl; as the creator of social and economic polarization and the housing equalizer for marginalized groups; as the homogenization of city life and the rebirth of Toronto as a creative city. None of these dichotomous positions captures the complex political, economic, and ideological sources of condominium development, nor do they allow for attention to the ways that condominium ownership and lifestyles affect the daily lives and identities of condominium dwellers. My goal, then, is to present a theoretically informed, empirically grounded,

FIGURE 1   *Live in liberty.* Billboard for Liberty on the Park Condominiums, Liberty
Village, Toronto.

and spatially situated analysis that both deconstructs these polarized views
and advances an understanding of the context-specific effects of neoliberal
urban policies and practices on the ground, tracing the complexities and
contradictions, constraints and opportunities, that are produced in everyday life. In particular, this book emphasizes the issues of tenure and home
ownership; the ways in which condominiums are constituted as communities and how these communities function to redefine or to shift the spaces
and scales of urban governance; and the ways in which condominium living
articulates with a specific vision of city life through the mobilization of particular identities and subject positions.

Focusing on the gendered dimensions of city building processes, and on
the ways in which gender ideologies are embedded in and expressed through
discourses that promote and shape new visions of urban citizens and urban
citizenship, permits a critique of urban revitalization and a more nuanced
reading of the neoliberal city. I argue that neoliberalism comprises sets of
co-evolving discourses and practices that intersect to produce particular,

contextual, on-the-ground effects (Larner 2003). The economic rationality of neoliberalism structures the roll-out (Peck and Tickell 2002) of condominiums as a private, free-market solution to the crises facing postindustrial, globalizing cities. Despite the tendency of neoliberal strategies to subsume the social within the realm of the market and proceed as if blind to social differences, gendered ideas about urban space and urban life are shifted, mutated, redefined, and rearticulated in complex ways within neoliberal agendas. A feminist lens that uncovers the gendered social geographies of the revitalizing city allows us to view the ways in which neoliberalism is constituted through multiple discourses and practices.

One of the challenges in articulating an analysis of condominium development in and through both the frameworks of the neoliberal city and feminist urban theory is that the relevant literatures have not often engaged with one another in a substantive manner. The urban literature that draws on a critique of neoliberal urbanism tends to do so at a relatively high level of abstraction, where the effects of neoliberal political-economic policies and practices are not often traced through the everyday lives of the people they affect (see, for example, Brenner and Theodore's [2002b] edited collection). Feminist urban geography, on the other hand, has been concerned with developing a gendered analysis of social relations as inscribed in, and shaped by, the built environment. Many feminist scholars have maintained a focus on understanding women's everyday experiences around work, family, safety, community activism, and other issues (Bondi and Rose 2003; Darke 1996; Garber and Turner 1995; Miranne and Young 2000; Andrew and Moore-Milroy 1988). Although feminist work has taken on state neoliberalism at various scales (Bondi 2005; Bashevkin 2006; Katz 2005), there is still a need for systematic analyses of the gendered dimensions of city building processes, of the macro-economic forces shaping urban governance, and of issues of land, tenure, and property development in the city (exceptions are Fincher 2004; Kern and Wekerle 2008).

I do not intend simply to use the framework of neoliberal urbanism to understand how condominium development fits into broader city building processes and the framework of feminist urban theory to understand how women experience condominium ownership and condominium lifestyles; rather, I suggest that neoliberal urbanism can and should be traced through everyday life and the ways that people construct their identities in relation to the city. Feminist urban theory can contribute to debates on these city building processes and complicate the neoliberal urbanist story about the capitalist city. Much as socialist feminist work on the city conceptualized the ways in which gendered spatial arrangements were integral to the development of the Fordist economy (Mackenzie and Rose 1983), it is now time for an integrated approach that draws on feminist theory and critiques of neoliberal urbanism in order to illuminate the new kinds of gendered policies and ideologies that are shaping the postindustrial city in ways that articulate with, or contradict, neoliberal rationality.

A central question for this project is: To what extent, and how, do condominiums filter, reflect, or reproduce neoliberalism in a particular urban context? Answering this question involves laying out a basic framework for understanding neoliberalism and the role that it plays in contemporary city building, its effects on everyday life, and its role in mobilizing particular identities and subject positions. Although specific manifestations of neoliberal strategies are always context-specific and show a high degree of variation, they draw on certain central ideological components. In his lectures on bio-politics at the Collège de France in 1978 and 1979, philosopher Michel Foucault (1991) described the development of neoliberal thought from German post-First World War Ordoliberalism through the Chicago School of neoliberalism in the United States. He noted that the American version of neoliberalism consistently expanded the economic domain to include the social sphere, viewing social issues as fundamentally economic problems (see Lemke [2001] for a further analysis of Foucault's thought on US neoliberalism). The scope of the economic order is expanded in such a way that all human action and behaviour fall within its realm. Although traditional liberal capitalism also subordinated society to the laws of the free market, a regulatory and protectionist response arose to mitigate the harsher inequities of the market system (Polanyi 2001). Neoliberalism seeks to dismantle these regulations and protections (what we know as the welfare state), and redefines the relationship between the state and the market such that the market becomes the organizational principle for the state and society, and the basis of government becomes the rational, entrepreneurial, economic individual. To operationalize this philosophy, the neoliberal state produces specialized apparatuses for controlling individuals; however, simultaneously, it evades becoming responsible for them.

Neoliberalism is, in large part, a language of property, one that reinvigorates traditional liberalism wherein private property functions as the foundation for individual self-interest (Blomley 2004; Harvey 2005). The focus on private property and rights exercised through the free market is particularly intense in cities, where downtown areas have become sites of massive re-investment, including residential investment and repopulation. Urban housing markets are becoming key sites for neoliberalization as the welfare state withdraws and policies such as rent control and funding for social housing are increasingly abandoned.

Cities are key geographical sites for the implementation of neoliberal policies and practices. Political geographers Neil Brenner and Nik Theodore (2002a) note that the retrenchment of national welfare state regimes imposes tight fiscal constraints on cities that produce intense conflicts over how to sustain local economies. The "shock treatment of deregulation, privatization, liberalization, and enhanced fiscal austerity" (368) is administered through urban neoliberal policy experiments, including place marketing, tax incentive schemes, public-private coalitions, property redevelopment plans, and enterprise zones. The results of these practices at the urban level are the manifestations of what geographer and gentrification scholar Neil Smith (1996) calls the revanchist city. He suggests that, increasingly, cities are spaces where the poor and other marginalized populations are punished through criminalization, stigmatization, and displacement as white middle-class gentrifiers reclaim urban space from the demonized underclass. The results are an uneven valorization/devalorization of places and people and new geographies of centrality and marginality (Sassen 1998).

Under the rubric of a critique of neoliberal urbanism and the revanchist city, city building through condominium development can be understood as an economic strategy for increasing the spaces available for capital investment and accumulation, which subsumes the social functions of cities under an economic logic. Individual freedom and fulfillment will be achieved by providing opportunities for investment, entrepreneurialism, and wealth accumulation. While the specific contours of this process in Toronto are traced in much greater detail in the following chapters, I note here that the social aspects of this mode of city building (particularly those dealing with social exclusions) have been primarily examined in relation to class, while gender and race have largely been sidelined (but see Hubbard 2004; Fincher 2004; Freeman 2006; Z. Newman 2002).

Of particular interest to me are the ways in which neoliberal urban development processes also work to reconfigure everyday life by producing new living spaces and reshaping the meanings associated with the spaces of everyday life. In using the phrase "everyday life," I recognize and invoke urban philosopher Henri Lefebvre's (1991a, 1996) understanding of the phrase – inhabiting the city, working in the city, creating the city – as the basis for claiming a right to the city as well as his notion that everyday life forms spaces of representation (the lived in, appropriated spaces of the city). However, I am also drawing upon a specifically feminist understanding of how the seemingly mundane, routine daily tasks and processes that people (particularly subjugated people) engage in are tied to macro-political and economic forces (D. Smith 1988). Feminist urban scholars share with Lefebvre a belief that the spaces of the everyday are both the sites and the stakes of socio-political struggles. The mundane spaces of women's everyday lives are always relevant to the real world of social struggle, despite their exclusion from much social science research and theory (Little, Peake, and Richardson 1988; D. Smith 1988). In *Sex and the Revitalized City*, I explore how women's everyday lives – daily meanings and practices revolving around home, family, work, leisure, and other activities – are structured in and through condominium living in ways that express (and may, at times, reproduce or challenge) neoliberal ideas about the privatization and commodification of the social realm.

In attempting to link everyday life to neoliberal urban governance, I ask how condominium living, and its attendant discourses, articulate with neoliberal ideals around self-governance, autonomy, and entrepreneurialism. Can condominium development be understood as part of a broader shift away from state responsibility for social and economic well-being and towards community, household, or individual responsibility? Michel Foucault (1990, 1991) contextualized his observations about neoliberalism within his broader argument about the demise (or reformulation) of sovereign power and the need for and development of a new form of power, a new way of governing. The shift away from oppressive sovereign power (the power to take life and let die) is marked by the growth of technologies of power that do not rely on the threat of death; rather, they rely on the exercise of tactics and the construction of knowledge about, and managing of, individuals and populations (Rutherford 2007). Foucault (1990, 139) wrote: "The disciplines of the body and the regulations of the population constituted the two poles around which the organization of power over life was deployed." Both are made the objects of knowledge for government and governed via the construction of dominant truths, normalizing powers, regulatory apparatuses, and disciplining tactics and discourses that involve not just the top-down power of the state but also the governance of the self as a social body.

Neoliberalism is a particular manifestation of this new modality of rule, one that operates on both the individual and the population. Under neoliberal urban governance, the techniques and focus of government have proliferated outwards from state-run institutions onto an array of self-governing entities that are expected to assume the role (or some of the roles) of the state. In this context, the political apparatus of the state is merely one partner in a web of governmental technologies that disperse power by engaging in governance at a variety of scales (Osborne and Rose 1999). Government is thus continuously reinvented through the policies of downsizing, privatizing, decentralizing, and downloading.

Neoliberalism also works upon the individual, invoking and mobilizing a particular vision of the self, or of the ideal citizen. Foucauldian scholar Nikolas Rose (1996) argues that the political and economic rationalities of neoliberalism have structured the rise and dominance of the regime of the free, autonomous self. Mobilizing specific identities is an integral part of the process of governance; in the context of neoliberalism and the wider shift away from sovereign power, the power to govern increasingly works through, rather than against, the subject (Foucault 1990).

In order to develop a framework that tries to connect the underlying political-economic rationality behind condominium development to the production of particular identities and their potential impact on the meanings and practices of urban citizenship, I draw upon Foucault's concept of governmentality. Rather than simply invoking neoliberalism as both the cause and endgame of all processes of political and economic restructuring (Larner 2003), governmentality, as an analytical tool, helps to illuminate the ways that neoliberalism is translated into specific modes of governance that shape the conduct of individuals and thus redefine contemporary democratic citizenship. Foucault (1991) defined government broadly as the conduct of conduct. Governmentality scholar Mitchell Dean (1999, 10) expands on this statement, describing government in the Foucauldian sense as "any attempt to shape with some degree of deliberation aspects of our behaviour according to particular sets of norms and for a variety of ends." This broad definition includes all acts of self-governance as well as the governance of others. Governmentality, or the thought and rationality behind modes of rule, draws attention to specific mentalities, arts, and regimes of governance, questioning both how we are governed and how we govern as well as the relationship between the governing of ourselves, of others, and of the state (Foucault 1991).

Particular forms of governance constitute and transform the subject in ways that effectively engage the contemporary political rationality at the heart of those forms of governance. However, regimes of government do not absolutely determine forms of subjectivity: "They elicit, promote, facilitate, foster and attribute various capacities, qualities and statuses to particular agents" (Dean 1999, 32). Foucault (1990) viewed this as the primary form of power in contemporary liberal democracies: power does not function to control individuals but, rather, to produce subjects that actively control themselves.

In the context of the neoliberalization of the city, I am interested in how this concept of the human subject is appropriated into urban revitalization policies and how this might shape a rearticulation of what it means to be a city dweller or an urban citizen. Who are the new subjects of the city and how are these subjects being mobilized? What are the sources of this re-invented notion of city life? Here, of course, I explore the gendered dimensions of the particular identities that are promoted through condominium advertisements, by developers, through condominium ownership and governance, and through the everyday lifestyles created at the nexus of condominium and downtown living. My objective is to investigate the reworking of gendered subject positions in contemporary spaces and discourses of revitalization. In identifying and critiquing the kinds of citizen subjectivities that arise from this process, I am also concerned to note the exclusion and silencing of other urban identities. Promoting the desirability of a specific type of city dweller certainly means that there are many city dwellers who will not be seen as essential or desirable in the revitalization project. This discursive exclusion has significant effects on vulnerable populations, who find themselves literally, as well as symbolically, marginalized by redevelopment and gentrification.

In the context of condominium development, a subject position that is frequently invoked through advertising and news media, and by developers, planners, and condominium purchasers, is that of the independent, self-sufficient, urban professional woman. This trope seems to draw upon a feminist understanding of the city as a space that is potentially liberatory, recognizing that the spaces of the metropolis have provided a degree of freedom from patriarchal norms that is essential to the development of autonomous female subjectivity (Werbner and Yuval-Davis 1999; Wilson 1991). In *Sex and the Revitalized City*, however, I also read the development of autonomous subjectivity through the lens of neoliberal governmentality and the mobilization of entrepreneurial subjects. I draw on feminist literature on women and the city to suggest that an extremely narrow and exclusionary vision of women's emancipation is invoked by this subjectivity, one that does not coincide with feminist struggles for improved quality of life and the right to participate in urban life.

In exploring the ways in which condominium development in Toronto expresses, filters, or translates neoliberal ideology, I hope to make a broader argument about the reshaping of urban citizenship in democratic societies under advanced liberalism. Political theorists James Holston and Arjun Appadurai (1996) argue that cities remain a strategic arena for the development of citizenship because they engage the tumult of citizenship through the concentration of difference and the availability of public space. They also suggest that cities are significant because place is still fundamental to the problems of membership in society. Until new formations beyond the nation-state gain more relevance, cities may still be the most important sites through which we rethink citizenship; indeed, the spaces of the city – such as the public street and the square – may still be necessary (if not sufficient) for the development of true democratic citizenship. Political theorist Susan Bickford (2000) also maintains that we need to expand the focus on the public sphere to include the built environment as a space that shapes our sense of what people, perspectives, and problems are present in the democratic public.

Cities, however, are contradictory spaces for democracy. The liberal conception of municipal government constituted the city as a space of both government and liberty (Isin 1999). Drawing on sociologist Zygmunt Bauman, urban scholar Engin Isin (1999, 167) argues that the "chaos, ambiguity and disorder of everyday life in the city were always subjected to the will to spatial order, the will to govern." This repression of disorder through the will to govern can lead to intolerance, fear, and resentment of strangers, and thus cities become places of exclusion, segregation, and repression. Current city building practices increasingly work towards the privatization, surveillance, and control of so-called public spaces (Mitchell 2003; Flusty 2001). Bickford (2000, 358) argues that "the possibility of achieving a genuine public realm inhabited by multiple 'we's' is blocked through these practices ... They produce the illusion of safety for some at the expense of actual danger and discomfort for others."

Given the critical issues raised by the neoliberalization of cities, it is timely to investigate some crucial questions about the role of condominium development in the reconstitution of citizenship and citizenship subjectivities. Are condominiums inserted into an urban context that is already hollowed out as a space of democracy? Do condominiums mobilize the consumer citizen, reflecting neoliberal ideals of the autonomous self-governing subject? Do they create a hostile built environment that limits the potential for democratic politics? Do condominiums challenge the gendered spatial arrangement of cities by redefining spaces of public and private life in ways that are potentially emancipatory for women? Are condominiums contradictory sites for citizenship, encouraging participatory democracy but within a framework based on rights, status, and entitlement?

These questions imply a concern with the potential for social justice in the city in neoliberal times. I cannot suggest that neoliberal urban agendas have created persistent social injustices such as homelessness, violence against women, and racial segregation in Toronto: these problems are unfortunately not new and pre-date even the flaws of the welfare state. However, neoliberal rationality structures a new set of responses to urban problems that serves not only to exacerbate these inequalities but also to rein in the potential for social justice-oriented remedies (Peck 2006; Mitchell 2003). I understand social justice in the urban context as centred on both a logic of representation and the direct struggle against injustice (Young 1990). I also agree with geographer Don Mitchell (2003) that there is an inherently geographical character to the normative notion of social justice, which is not only a concept but also a practice that requires a space of representation and struggle. Thus, social justice implies a "right to the city"; the crucial importance of public space, action, and connection; and a sense of order that is progressive and democratic rather than repressive and oppressive.

Under neoliberal regimes, the cornerstones of social justice are chipped away through a rationality that reduces social problems to market-based, individual problems with, naturally, market-based and individual solutions. As geographer Jamie Peck (2006) argues in his critique of post-9/11, post-Katrina American urban policy agendas, neoliberal rationality attempts to tackle urban problems through the increased moral and penal regulation of marginalized groups and the reclaiming of the city for business, the market, and the middle class. Moments of crisis – 9/11, Hurricane Katrina, the current economic recession – precipitate the roll-out of fear-mongering discourses that call for regressive social, moral, and spatial ordering in cities. In this climate, the social justice call for redistribution, representation, and rights is trampled by what Peck calls a First World form of structural adjustment. The market governance of cities under neoliberal "shock treatment" (Brenner and Theodore 2002a) profoundly limits the potential for spaces of representation to develop. In Canadian cities like Toronto, the fear of failure in the ostensibly crucial global inter-urban competition legitimates the purification of urban space in the name of capital investment.

In *Sex and the Revitalized City*, in an attempt to challenge the politics of neoliberal urban revitalization on a broader scale, I situate Toronto as an exemplary case study. More specifically, I offer an analysis of condominium development as a critical process through which the gendered power relations of the neoliberal city are made visible and, literally, built into the urban landscape. Toronto, as Canada's global city, is driven to compete for a place in the global urban hierarchy as a financial centre, cultural capital, and tourist destination. However, Toronto's history as a liveable, diverse, and progressive city has not been erased, meaning that the process of revitalization, and its injustices, do not proceed uncontested. The power to define and produce spaces do not solely rest with dominant forces and influential agents. Although this struggle is increasingly marginalized by city politics that place private, corporate interests above broad-based, inclusive democratic decision-making processes, I suggest that perhaps it is in the spaces, meanings, and practices of everyday life that cracks in the revitalization narrative will appear, opening sites for struggle and resistance.

Sex and the Revitalized City is organized into six parts. Chapter 1 uses the lens of neoliberal urbanism to interrogate the discourses that shape urban revitalization in Toronto, and it develops a framework for a gendered analysis of urban revitalization policies. Chapter 2 delves into the issue of tenure, arguing that the home ownership element of condominiums reflects a neoliberal expansion of the spaces of capital accumulation in the city and that discourses around condominium ownership are structured, in part, through a conflation of gendered freedom with financial security that reflects neoliberal ideals of autonomy and self-governance. Chapter 3 explores the construction of condominiums as communities, looking at the continuities and discontinuities between the high-rise building boom of the 1960s and 1970s and the condominium boom of today in terms of gender-related issues such as social networking, community formation, and governance. I suggest that, although many of the social concerns of earlier decades are re-invoked today, these concerns are subsumed within an inherently capitalistic logic that sees condominiums primarily as sites for capital accumulation. Chapter 4 continues a focus on the notion of community by unpacking condominium security as a site that reveals a gendered tension between ideals of community and the dynamics of freedom and fear. Chapter 5 seeks to deconstruct the gendered dimensions of the "myth of urbanity" as it is sold through condominium development and to explore how everyday urban life for women is increasingly constituted through notions of the consumer citizen. The Conclusion draws out some of the key themes that emerge from these discussions, connecting my interpretations to a broader concern with the dimensions of urban citizenship for women in the contemporary postindustrial city.

1

Growing Up
Toronto's Condominium Boom and
the Politics of Urban Revitalization

*We have become a nation living in concrete boxes, thrust
into the sky. More than 17,000 new condos sold in Greater
Toronto last year – the most ever in the history of the
area. And we don't take a back seat to any place else on
the continent.*

— Tony Wong, "Is the Sky the Limit for Condos?"
Toronto Star, *25 May 2006*

In 2006, Toronto surpassed other major North American condominium markets such as Chicago and Miami in the construction and sales of new condominiums. But as the rather poetic comments from *Toronto Star* real estate reporter Tony Wong suggest, the scale and intensity of the condominium boom comprise just one of the significant dimensions of this story.

Wong hints at one of these dimensions with his use of the term "nation," through which he implies that condominium dwellers constitute a community based on some shared identity or interests. This is a claim worth unpacking. Do Toronto's condominium owners share common interests or lead similar lives? Is this new nation within the city a political, social, or cultural force that will effect changes in policy, lifestyle, and demographics? The answers to these questions are highly relevant in terms of the potential role of condominium dwellers in producing urban space and influencing urban politics.

Wong's comments also suggest that the move towards a particular *form* of city living is significant. The "concrete boxes, thrust into the sky," represent a

shift away from low-density, low-rise suburban homes in the Greater Toronto Area (GTA) towards high-density, high-rise urban living. This is not
the first time, though, that there has been a high-rise building boom in Toronto and in its suburbs. The 1960s and 1970s saw major construction of
rental and some condominium buildings throughout the city (Wekerle et al.
1980). So what are the underlying reasons for the current wave of high-rise
construction, and how do these differ from those shaping the first wave?
Wong notes that condominium sales are at an all-time high, a trend that
could be shaped by a number of factors, such as a widespread change in lifestyle preferences, a downturn in the economic fortunes of potential single-
family homebuyers, the increased cost of suburban homes and suburban
living, and, of course, low interest rates. The underlying political-economic
forces that have structured the condominium boom have not been probed
in detail, nor have the social and economic consequences of a rapid increase
in high-density living been questioned by critical scholars.

Wong's brief narration also draws attention to the fact that condominiums are indeed *sold*. In the 1960s and 1970s, the goal of increasing density
was met by high-rise construction; however, this wave consisted primarily
of rental buildings and also included alternative tenures such as co-op. Various levels of government also subsidized this construction. Thus, the condominium boom is not simply the result of a resurgence of interest in
apartment-style living: it is also representative of a culture of property that
heavily values home ownership (Blomley 2004; Choko and Harris 1990).
Condominium development is a rather efficient means of rapidly increasing
the percentage of homeowners in the downtown area and drawing people
into the social, economic, and political structures of private property ownership. However, there is a need to understand how these property relations
affect the meanings and practices of urban life for city dwellers. By placing
condominium development within the context of broader urban agendas,
this chapter attempts to frame the themes through which, I argue, we can
begin to advance an understanding of the ways in which contemporary city
building processes shape the daily lives of particular city dwellers.

"R" Words

> A successful city is one with a competitive advantage
> over others locally, nationally and internationally. It has
> a quality of life that will attract and retain people who
> have capital, skills, knowledge, ingenuity and creativity.

> *A successful city with an enviable quality of life is*
> *diverse, equitable and inclusive; it astonishes with its*
> *human-made and natural beauty; it thrives on making*
> *connections and it inspires great leadership and*
> *stewardship.*
>
> – *City of Toronto*, Official Plan, 2002

Like so many other postindustrial cities seeking an advantage in the competition for global capital, knowledge workers, and tourist dollars (Evans 2003;
Short 1999), Toronto has embarked upon a plan for urban revitalization
that is centred upon property redevelopment, aestheticization, and branding strategies designed to attract investment and new middle-class residents
(Kipfer and Keil 2002). Urban revitalization policies (sometimes relying on
other names, such as renaissance, regeneration, or reurbanization) have become commonplace with the decline of manufacturing sectors in the urban
regions of Western nations and the rise of a multi-tiered global economy in
which cities function as key nodes in a complex network of production, consumption, and exchange (Lees 2000). The so-called global cities concen-
trate these functions by serving as command centres for multinational
corporations, homes for highly skilled knowledge workers, centres for financial markets, and hubs of specialized services (Sassen 1998). Toronto is
Canada's global city in that it is deeply interconnected with other global
cities through the stock market, multinational corporations, cultural exchanges, and, of course, its high immigrant population. Toronto, though, is
feeling the pressure of inter-city competition, the crisis of fiscal constraints
as the provincial and federal governments download costs and services to
the municipality, the wear and tear of aging infrastructure, and the shame
of crumbling, polluted industrial sites. In this context, the city has encouraged property redevelopment schemes, commissioned new place marketing campaigns, and declared its revitalization objectives in its new *Official
Plan* (Lehrer and Laidley 2008; City of Toronto 2002).

The central motif of the *Official Plan* is successful competition at regional, national, and international levels. The overarching goal is to create a successful, competitive city that retains a high quality of life. Some of the
specific objectives include the development of spectacular spaces and attractions, the revitalization of major mixed-used urban corridors, the redevelopment of the waterfront, and the creation of globally competitive
employment districts. The answer to the question of how to successfully

compete is found under the label of reurbanization: "Toronto's future is one of growth, of rebuilding, of reurbanizing and of regenerating the City" (City of Toronto 2002, 9). "Reurbanization" is Toronto's current word of choice for promoting growth through intensification.

The city wants to encourage new commercial, retail, and leisure development along major avenues designated as high-density, mixed-use zones rather than expanding through continued suburban development. There is also a major focus on residential intensification. The *Plan* recognizes that the city will attract over half a million new residents through national and international migration within the next twenty-five years. Over the past fifteen years, high-density residential development has been the primary engine of growth through intensification, dubbed "smart growth" in planning and popular discourse. How has this been accomplished in a local culture that, since the 1950s, has valued single-family home ownership, low-density suburban sprawl, and suburban ways of life? In other words, how is reurbanization organized and rationalized in Toronto?

There are several co-evolving and interconnected discourses and policies that have shaped the logic and practice of reurbanization in the Toronto context. These comprise key themes that emerge within various discourses, including (1) the city's need to improve its financial circumstances by increasing its property tax base; (2) the desire to maintain employment levels in the central city; (3) the need to increase transit use and make use of other existing physical infrastructure; and (4) the desire to attract knowledge workers for the postindustrial economy. There are three major discursive formations within which these themes are situated: antisprawl/environmental, economic, and socio-cultural. Each of these discourses has found expression in provincial and municipal policies that pave the way for intensification to form the backbone of Toronto's revitalization strategy. Toronto is certainly not unique, however, in its pursuit of success through intensification, and critical geographers have challenged the discourses and policies of urban revitalization, linking them to a wider revanchist urban strategy and the neoliberalization of urban governance and urban life (MacLeod 2002; N. Smith 2002; Davidson and Lees 2005).

The Environmental Case for Residential Intensification

> *A co-ordinated approach to the redevelopment of land*
> *within the existing urban fabric to accommodate regional*
> *growth is known as reurbanization. By improving and*

> *making better use of existing urban infrastructure and*
> *services before introducing new ones on the urban fringe,*
> *reurbanization helps to reduce our demands on nature*
> *and improve the liveability of the urban region.*
>
> – *City of Toronto*, Official Plan, 2002

The current provincial government in Ontario, under the leadership of Liberal premier Dalton McGuinty, was elected in 2003, in part, because of its promise to halt rapid development in ecologically sensitive areas north of Toronto (such as the Oak Ridges Moraine). Despite its unsuccessful attempt to literally stop the bulldozers in mid-dig, the provincial government passed the Greenbelt Act in 2005, legislation designed to limit exurban development and to encourage intensification in the core areas of the cities of the GTA. The Ontario Places to Grow Act complemented this legislation, defining zones for urban growth and intensification and limiting suburban sprawl. These policies give a regional justification to the city's reurbanization plan and serve as a legislative backbone for high-density development, which is often controversial in a region that has experienced most of its growth through suburbanization.

Although these policies respond to growing public concern over the ecological consequences of sprawl, this issue has gained solid political traction by emphasizing sprawl's troubling economic factors, such as the high costs of land, gasoline, highway infrastructure, and public transit beyond city limits. The *Official Plan* suggests that residential intensification will help to combat pollution and greenhouse gas emissions, reduce dependence on fossil fuels, mitigate the rising cost of electricity, lower the stress of commuting, and relieve the pressure to expand roads and transit. The theme of increasing our reliance on the existing infrastructure of central city areas emerges in this discourse. The city's election (in 2003 and again in 2006) of downtown-focused mayor David Miller, who has lobbied the provincial and federal governments for public transit funding and other money for cities (known as *The New Deal for Cities*), suggests that Torontonians are increasingly in support of municipal policies that favour intensification.

The extent to which Toronto's intensification policies are truly motivated by environmental concerns is questionable, however, in the context of an urban agenda focused on growth and competition. Environmental geographer Susannah Bunce's (2004, 180) analysis of the language of smart growth and reintensification in Toronto's *Official Plan* and other recent planning documents suggests that "the environmental problems of regional sprawl serve as a public rationale for the primary municipal goal of increasing Toronto's economic and land-use development through private-sector investment and the attraction of skilled, professional labour to the city." Other local critics agree that ecological concerns are instrumentalized to the wider goal of opening up space, in the context of land scarcity, for increased capital investment (Bourne 2001; Desfor and Keil 2003; Bunce and Young 2003). In this way, a neoliberal rationality – one that subsumes all concerns, including environmental concerns, within an economic logic – emerges from an ostensibly environment-focused discourse.

In practice, the outcomes of this rationality are shaped by legislation and zoning. The province's Greenbelt legislation limits the potential for developers to buy exurban land cheaply by imposing restrictions that make this land supply more scarce. The low-density zoning regulations in suburban areas also mean that developers must apply for rezoning to build high-density projects in single-family home neighbourhoods. While condominiums are popping up in many suburban cities, the existing zoning imposes an additional obstacle for developers seeking to maximize their profits through increased density. These difficulties have been mitigated by a developer-friendly municipal planning approval and appeals board (the Ontario Municipal Board [OMB]), the rezoning of industrial and commercial lands downtown, and negotiable height and density restrictions, making urban property development highly attractive. The mobilization of an environmentally based, anti-sprawl rhetoric in support of these policies means there is a broad-based consensus around intensification that is difficult to challenge without taking the politically untenable position of seeming to be in favour of suburban sprawl (Desfor, Keil, Kipfer, and Wekerle 2006). In this way, the economic logic shaping the anti-sprawl discourses remains invisible.

Toronto's environmental discourse and policy can be read as part of the neoliberalization of governance, wherein the state enacts various policy prescriptions designed to open up particular markets to increased penetration by capital. In this case, the state has not fully withdrawn from the control of land supply and development, indeed the state appears to be taking an active role in conserving and protecting vulnerable land, but it has reorganized its interventions in ways that free up other spaces for massive redevelopment. The greenwashing of intensification means that critical questions about the process and outcomes of urban redevelopment are effectively evaded. Few are challenging the city's reliance on the small group of powerful decision makers who shape land-building markets to spearhead the capitalist restructuring of the city, meaning that both the resulting forms of redevelopment and the process itself will likely reflect the interests and ideals of a particular set of stakeholders, while excluding the needs of others (Fainstein 2001; MacLaran 2003). In Toronto, there has been very little attempt to move outside the parameters of the sprawl versus intensification debate in order to question the underlying rationality that shapes reurbanization or to critically examine the potential social impacts. This situation stands in contrast to public discourse in Toronto during the first major high-rise construction boom of the 1970s, when the potential social consequences of tall buildings were hotly debated in city politics, local newspapers, and academic sources (Wekerle et al. 1980; Conway 1977; "Battle in the Sky" 1971; Worthington 1973; Stoffman 1973).

Revitalization by Design

> Great cities do not happen by accident – they are
> designed and orchestrated so that individual private
> and public developments work together to create cohesive
> blocks, neighbourhoods and districts ... good urban design
> is good business and good social policy.
> – *City of Toronto*, Official Plan, *2002*

These anti-sprawl and pro-intensification discourses and policies have emerged co-constitutively with a strategy designed to reuse or build anew upon spaces that have fallen into disuse as Toronto's manufacturing economy has declined in importance. As Toronto seeks to position itself as an entrepreneurial, competitive, and attractive centre of global finance and international culture, the visible image of the city becomes central. The *Plan* (City of Toronto 2002, 20) states, "building a high-quality public realm ... is essential to attract businesses, workers, residents and shoppers." The strategy includes waterfront revitalization plans; major renovation of old, and construction of new, cultural institutions; preservation and reuse of historical buildings; and construction of retail, sports, and leisure complexes. A common theme in the media is that Toronto has not lived up to its architectural potential (Kingwell 2004; Pooley 2005). As such, the city has formed private partnerships with investors and spent hundreds of millions of dollars on several high-profile redevelopment projects, including major cultural institutions redesigned by celebrity architects, such as the Art Gallery of Ontario designed by Frank Gehry and the Royal Ontario Museum designed by Daniel Libeskind. These projects proceed through the belief that Toronto will create for itself a Bilbao effect, attracting investors, tourists, and new residents, and securing its place as a destination city (Lehrer 2006; Lehrer and Gamsby 2007; Evans 2003; Pooley 2005).

Although the spectacular and controversial projects noted above have garnered a great deal of attention, architectural critics have not ignored the most common form of infill and redevelopment in Toronto: the condominium. For example, the *Toronto Star* runs a weekly column critiquing new condominium developments on their architectural merits. As such, the lexicon of urban design has entered into the public consciousness to some extent and has led to popular debate on the form and future of the city. However, structuring this debate around a good design/bad design binary hides the underlying economic logic of revitalization, eliding issues such as the decision-making processes that shape development or the deep-rooted liberal assumptions about why and how property *should* be redeveloped. The logic behind residential redevelopment in particular remains unquestioned when condominium developments are judged and debated based on their height, style, and scale.

What is this logic? Critical urban scholars argue that revitalization through the redevelopment of urban property represents a new and powerful wave of gentrification (N. Smith 1996; Lees 2000; Lees, Slater, and Wyly 2008). This wave differs from traditional modes of gentrification in that large-scale property redevelopment is led by capital rather than by individual homeowners and is often facilitated by state interventions (Hackworth and Smith 2001). Gentrification through redevelopment is a global urban strategy increasingly shaped by global capital (N. Smith, 2002). Neil Smith (1996) has argued that residential intensification is the leading edge of the class remake of the central urban landscape. Unlike previous rounds of gentrification, under the rubric of revitalization, the state actively removes the legislative and zoning barriers that were set up to limit the redevelopment of vulnerable neighbourhoods or to protect public space (Hackworth and Smith 2001). Revitalization through better design and new development functions, in effect, to revitalize urban capital accumulation strategies by opening new sites for investment despite a relative scarcity of land. The beneficiaries of revitalization are landowners, financiers, developers, investors and builders, and the middle class and elite to whom the redeveloped city caters (Lees 2000).

Critics of contemporary redevelopment plans tie these tactics to re-vanchist urban agendas that operate through an abstract view of property, seeing it solely in terms of its exchange value rather than its use value. Blomley (2004, 84) notes that the rise of contemporary urban neoliberalism "has increasingly embraced the principle of highest and best use as a metric for urban land use and planning decisions, abandoning a logic of community and neighbourhood." He critiques the logic of the highest and best use of land, which, under advanced liberalism, means private ownership, private development, and the potential for profit. Discourses of urban renaissance and revitalization position gentrification as a necessary step based upon the assumption that middle-class interests constitute the highest and best use of urban space. These discourses also appear to take an interest in public space, while actually facilitating the growth of privatized spaces that are defined by exclusive boundaries or geared solely to consumption activities (Zukin 1998; Graham and Marvin 2001; Soja 2000). Revitalization through re-development and redesign facilitates capital's return to the city (N. Smith 1979), resulting in the over-valorization of spaces of the middle class (Sassen 1998). While Toronto's image makeover is more than purely aesthetic, the discourse of image and design shapes the contours of the debate over the form of the city in highly limiting ways.

If You Build It ...

> Downtown will continue to evolve as a healthy and
> attractive place to live and work as new development
> that supports the reurbanization strategy ... is attracted
> to the area.
>
> – *City of Toronto,* Official Plan, *2002*

> Today, the real competitive advantage for urban
> economies lies in the foundations that support growth
> [including] ... a well-educated, highly-skilled labour force.
>
> – *City of Toronto,* Official Plan, *2002*

Reurbanization is meant to create the kinds of neighbourhoods, social infra-structure, and lifestyle spaces that are believed to appeal to the professional, cultural, and knowledge workers who will fuel Toronto's postindustrial economy. In one sense, intensification is an attempt to capitalize on the demographic effects of urban restructuring, which has produced an increasingly polarized labour force based upon both low-wage, deskilled service-sector labour on the one hand and highly professionalized labour in the advanced tertiary and quaternary sectors on the other (Bourne and Rose 2001; Ley 1996). While the deskilled labour force and new immigrants are · increasingly settling (sometimes by choice, sometimes by necessity) in peripheral areas (Siemiatycki and Isin 1997), the new middle class formed by these changes has stimulated demand for new housing and services in the city. Demands include inner-city housing options such as condominiums as well as consumer services, leisure activities, and recreational spaces. These demands are fulfilled through redevelopment agendas.

A background study for the *Official Plan* prepared by geographer Larry Bourne (2000a), entitled "Downtown Toronto as Living Space," lists the suspected advantages of downtown population growth: to improve the economic vitality of the core and the region, to improve the image of the city, to contribute to the local tax base, to support local businesses, to reduce inbound commuting, and to reduce crime levels through the principle of eyes on the street. But how will the city attract the new middle class? Recently, Toronto has begun to use the rhetoric of Richard Florida's (2002, 2008) creative class/creative cities theory to legitimize spending on entertainment, aesthetics, and redevelopment. This theory asserts that professionals in the new knowledge economy embody certain tastes and desires that must be catered to in order to draw in this highly mobile group. This group is believed to value the proximity of work, home, and leisure spaces; thus, intensification is a natural solution for a city that fears a brain drain or the loss of skilled professionals and creative people to other, more desirable, locations. Similarly, the construction of several "new urbanist" developments within the city seems to support the belief that people increasingly favour walkable neighbourhoods that are close to public transit, with homes on smaller lots in close proximity to neighbours. The anti-sprawl rhetoric is interconnected with this discourse in that part of the desire for integrated urban neighbourhoods is believed to stem from public distaste for the consumerist and environmental excesses of suburban life.

The bid to capture and retain the creative class is, in a sense, nothing new – geographer David Harvey (1989) noted this feature of interurban competition when addressing the rise of entrepreneurial urban governance during the 1980s. Harvey warned that such strategies may experience short-lived success and that their failure could trigger a cycle of rather expensive and

ultimately futile competitive behaviour. Nonetheless, contemporary revitalization politics centre on the need to attract people with capital, knowledge,
skills, ingenuity, and creativity (Peck 2005). What is not often discussed in
mainstream debate is the extent to which the state must intervene in coercive ways to facilitate this process.

Urban political theorists Stefan Kipfer and Roger Keil (2002) assert that
Neil Smith's (1996) description of the revanchist city, wherein large-scale
redevelopment projects reclaim the city for the middle class and lead to the
eviction or marginalization of poor, racialized, and vulnerable groups, can
now be applied to Toronto. They note several features of urban revanchism
in Toronto, including workfare implementation, a law-and-order agenda,
target policing, harassment of street people, raids of gay bars, and the criminalization of youth of colour. While there are few studies documenting the
effects of revitalization policies on Toronto's vulnerable populations, recent
research suggests that the benefits of reurbanization are limited to a select
group of city dwellers who are part of the overall economic vision of competition and growth (Slater 2004a; Khosla 2003; Gordon 2005).

The organization and rationale of reurbanization in Toronto suggest that
revitalization can be read as a strategy to facilitate the takeover of the city by
capital and the middle class. In Toronto, co-evolving discourses and policies
structured around the issues of sprawl, urban design, and the role of the new
middle class position reurbanization as the city's best strategy when faced
with the disciplining and coercive force of interurban competition (Peck
2005). A neoliberal rationality runs through the heart of these policies,
which are designed to open the city to flows of capital investment with little
state regulation, to encourage new heights of consumption, and, above all,
to create a widespread consensus that urban revitalization through intensification is a natural, beneficial, and effective solution for Toronto's current
challenges.

As geographer Alan Latham (2003) points out, urban political econo-
mists have effectively deconstructed the underlying rationalities behind
urban revitalization policies but have been less successful in understanding
everyday relationships and practices or in rethinking the relationship between the economic and the cultural in daily urban life. Moreover, gender
is often a sidelined category in studies of urban revitalization. This resonates with feminist analyses that have begun to address the gender dimensions of contemporary urban transformations (Bashevkin 2006). But despite
the growth of a very large and complex body of work on the neoliberalization of the city, and a substantial amount of feminist urban research over

the past three decades, there is relatively little feminist or gender-focused work directly interrogating the discourses, policies, and outcomes of revitalization politics or the gendered implications of specific processes such as intensification.

Sex and the Revitalized City?

Feminist and critical urban scholars have addressed gender in the context of entrepreneurial urban restructuring across themes such as the reshaping of urban governance and urban citizenship, gentrification, sexuality and urban space, and property development. Popular sources such as the news media have also identified gender as a salient dimension of recent urban trends. In her early review of feminist analyses of urban restructuring, geographer Geraldine Pratt (1990) suggested that geographers had tended to ignore and under-theorize the links between urban restructuring and the gendered division of labour; moreover, feminists argued that geographers often subsumed cultural processes into economic ones, marginalizing theoretical and epistemological issues around the ways in which gender, as a social construct, is produced in and through urban restructuring and the ways that it is co-constituted with other systems of privilege and oppression, such as class, sexuality, and race (Mackenzie 1988). These issues continue to be significant ones for feminist analyses of urban restructuring under more entrepreneurial forms of governance. Feminist urban scholar Sue Brownill's (2000) analysis of regeneration policies in Britain makes a strong argument about gender-blindness and blatant sexism (i.e., blaming single mothers for urban problems) in regeneration discourses. However, there are still few projects addressing either the construction of gender (in relation to other socially produced differences) through contemporary neoliberal urbanism or the ways in which neoliberal urbanism is itself shaped by gender. I propose here several key steps towards developing a feminist approach to entrepreneurial urban restructuring.

Power and Policy Making

Critical urban scholars question the rise of public-private partnerships, the courting of private investment, the narrowing of the definition of stakeholder in this process, and the resurgence of business and trade organizations that seek to influence policy making (Kipfer and Keil 2002; Tickell and Peck 1996). These concerns have been taken up by feminists who have examined the regendering of local governance that occurs as decision-making power is increasingly transferred from the local state to various other decision-making structures and agents (i.e., Abrar, Lovenduski, and Margetts 1998; Kern and Wekerle 2008; Chouinard 1996). Political scientist Sylvia Bashevkin's (2006) study contrasting local state restructuring and its gendered consequences in Toronto and London attempts to place changes in policy and planning within the context of neoliberal ideologies. Her work shows that the specific, contextual manifestations of neoliberalization can lead to particular gendered outcomes – for example, the total dismissal of gender issues from city planning in Toronto. Massive redevelopment projects such as London's Docklands/Canary Wharf site have been characterized by Brownill (2000) as a man-made world, where the "thrusting" towers of Canary Wharf link male corporate power to their domination of the landscape. Similarly, urban scholar Susan Fainstein (2001) has pointed out that the privatization of urban space through massive redevelopment projects effectively reinforces the power and vision of the white men who control such projects, resulting in a city that symbolizes masculine power (see also Dolores Hayden's notion of "skyscraper rape" [1977]).

These studies point to the need to question the underlying process through which a particular vision of revitalization is imagined and implemented. Within entrepreneurial urban regimes, male-dominated boards centred on growth and business agendas can work to ghettoize women into the "soft" areas of social policy and community building (Tickell and Peck 1996). A feminist perspective must, therefore, challenge both the exclusion of women from decision-making bodies and the feminization of social issues as a way of removing those issues from the revitalization agenda. Feminist analyses of neoliberal urbanism can examine the (re)organization of masculinism, as an ideology justifying and naturalizing male power, in and through narratives and policies of revitalization.

Gendering Highest and Best Use

In the on-the-ground process of redevelopment and reurbanization, there are specific decisions made about what kinds of spaces will be redeveloped, preserved, reused, or renovated. Feminists must continue to challenge the masculinist vision of how, where, and why the city should be redeveloped or revitalized. For example, the preservation, adaptive reuse, or wholesale imitation and reconstruction of industrial buildings for commercial, cultural, or residential use implies a desire to venerate a male-centred history of the city as a place of work and industry. In Toronto, the institutions of high art and culture, such as the ballet, opera house, museum, and art gallery, have received massive funding for redesign by (male) celebrity architects (Kingwell 2004); the fact that these institutions preserve and honour male-dominated (also Eurocentric and elite) canons of cultural expression is not questioned.

Moreover, revitalization's focus on the central city, designed by men and enshrining sexist assumptions about work, family, and leisure (Matrix 1984; Hayden 2002), ignores the spaces where many women's lives are focused – parks and playgrounds, schoolyards, suburban landscapes – and other social infrastructure where women's paid and unpaid work often occurs. While feminists cannot assume that social structures and values are somehow made literal and concrete by physical spaces (Boys 1989), I maintain that the choices made about where and how to redevelop reflect an agenda that reproduces gendered hierarchies of space. Brownill (2000, 123) notes that, in London's Docklands redevelopment, it was the "male, macho stuff in the docks that grabbed the attention," while women's concerns around public space and community were trivialized. Although I would not suggest that the masculinist valorization of particular sites and spaces means that women are automatically excluded or marginalized in these spaces, I do argue that a feminist perspective on revitalization must include an examination of the ways that gender ideologies influence notions of the highest and best use of property, and the ways that women's urban histories and experiences may be elided by the choices made about redevelopment.

Gendered Urban Lives

Embedded in such decision-making processes, and the policy outcomes themselves, are gendered assumptions about family, work, home, and lifestyle. The significance of gendered household and labour market trends, the complex relationships between reproduction, production and consumption, and women's experiences of urban processes such as gentrification, are key feminist concerns with respect to redevelopment (D. Rose 1989, 1996; Karsten 2003; Bondi 1999; Warde 1991). Geographer Ruth Fincher's (2004) research on high-rise developers in Melbourne, Australia, specifically unpacks the gendered assumptions that lie behind development decisions. She notes that the views of the male-dominated property development industry about women's housing choices at different stages of the life course have serious effects on the kinds of projects produced and the accompanying social infrastructure. For example, the belief that high-rise living is only appropriate for childless adults or empty nesters leads to a lack of infra-structure geared to social reproduction.

Similarly, there are gendered assumptions buried within the anti-sprawl, smart growth agenda that promotes intensification. The vision of a walk-able, transit-oriented city of small, efficient living spaces seems to offer women a way to ease the strain of multiple roles; however, as planner Sheri-lyn MacGregor (2002, 83) points out, no one asks who will "perform the extra work required to live sustainably in everyday life." As the challenge of living in an eco-friendly manner is passed on to households, it is women who will likely bear the burden of managing the day-to-day processes. If the social infrastructure necessary to make women's everyday lives less complex is not put into place, then the intensified eco-city may end up embodying a new set of gendered assumptions about city lives and city dwellers. Reurban-ization projects may reorganize or reproduce a gendered division of labour, producing qualitatively different experiences of the revitalized city for men and women. Therefore, feminist analyses of the types of redevelopment (e.g., residential intensification) and the kinds of lifestyles that are imagined in the entrepreneurial city must deconstruct the underlying notions of how work and family life are organized.

Intersecting Oppressions

All of these concerns are deeply intertwined with issues of class, race, sexu-ality, ability, and other forms of exclusion and privilege (Kobayashi and Peake 1994). Feminist research on the gentrification of inner-city neigh-bourhoods points out that the attraction of affluent professional women to central residential locations can result in the gentrification of working-class neighbourhoods or the conversion of live-work spaces into lofts and condo-miniums (D. Rose 1989; Bondi 1994). Accordingly, the ability of some women to participate in gentrification rests on the disadvantage and dis-placement of other women and other marginalized groups. Geographers Phil Hubbard (2004) and Marilyn Papayanis (2000) illustrate that crack-downs on prostitution, pornography, and other sex trades in the city are part of the revanchist agenda of cleansing and aestheticizing the city. Papay-anis notes that disorder and deviance are emblematized not only by home-less people and criminal activity but also by the visibility of sex trades and sex shops on the streets of New York City. Hubbard specifically suggests that the criminalization of prostitution in London reflects a masculinist urban agenda that favours more institutionalized and better-capitalized sex trades. These studies indicate that a feminist analysis of entrepreneurial urban restructuring is necessary to identify groups that are actively excluded or marginalized through this process and to understand how multiple systems of oppression operate together to structure the neoliberal urban agenda.

Selling Revitalization as Emancipation

Interestingly, gendered narratives are increasingly used to sell revitalization as good social policy. Toronto's *Official Plan*, while declining to specifically mention women at all, suggests that reurbanization will help to create a more accessible and equitable environment for the city's diverse population. More explicitly, the news media have picked up on several themes, particularly with respect to condominium development, that seem to support the notion that intensification and a return to the city are important sources of emancipation for women (Delap 2006; Southworth 1999). These sources have co-opted a watered-down feminist version of the notion that city life can be beneficial for women. In early feminist research on women and cities, sociologist Gerda Wekerle (1984) and others (i.e., D. Rose 1984) argued that "women's place is in the city" due to the service needs of mothers, particularly low-income single mothers who would have greater access to publicly funded infrastructures such as transit, affordable housing, and childcare. Social theorist Elizabeth Wilson (1991) challenged an implicit anti-urban stance within much feminist research by noting that urban environments permit a degree of autonomy, anonymity, and freedom from traditional gender roles that women are not likely to experience in suburbs or small towns. These themes have been recirculated in contemporary popular discourse around women and city life; however, they are emptied of any redistributive or equity concerns in favour of an individualized, consumption-oriented vision of freedom and gender equality. Feminists must ask: What fundamental equality issues are ignored or hidden by this theme?

One significant issue is that of safety in urban space. There is an implicit assumption that revitalization leads to safer streets for women. However, this claim is questionable when the desired eyes on the street are in highrise towers, and those towers are surrounded by concrete plazas with little foot traffic. Moreover, as geographer Alec Brownlow (2006) found in a study of crime statistics in Philadelphia, cities may downplay or hide violence against women in an effort to attract young, middle-class female gentrifiers to the central city. Similarly, narratives of revitalization-as-freedom ignore issues of workplace equality in the creative economy, which are of particular importance in a polarized labour market in which women increasingly work in precarious employment situations (Sassen 1998; Parker 2008). It seems that, in order to question whose vision of freedom is being promoted and what this vision lacks, there is an urgent need for critical scholarship that challenges the implicit association between revitalization and emancipation.

In selling revitalization, images of women and women's bodies are used in ways that seem to signal both women's place in the city and a mapping of the city (and its spaces of revitalization) onto the female body. Condominium advertisements are a key site for such imagery. Women's bodies and body parts are often used to symbolize the spaces of redevelopment. In Figure 2, the billboard's placement superimposes a woman's head onto two new condominium towers, while the symbols of the Fly Condominium brand (i.e., paper cranes) are imprinted upon her exposed neck. Her open mouth and poised fingertips suggest anticipation and curiosity. The city becomes both feminized and eroticized through these images. The use of women's bodies in this way raises significant questions about the place of women in revitalization projects, about the process of taking or claiming the city through revitalization, and about the pervasive gendered imaginings of the city that resonate through contemporary city building processes.

Constructing Gender and Gendered Identities

A concern with how a particular vision of urban life for women is becoming dominant raises a more complex set of questions around the ways in which gender itself, as a social construct and as an aspect of identity, is produced and reproduced by the co-evolving discourses and practices that constitute neoliberal urbanism. This requires a look at how the category "women" is actively produced and mobilized in ways that articulate with (or perhaps contradict) a neoliberal objective. Geographer Wendy Larner (2003, 511) notes that the notion of the neoliberal subject, constituted in a top-down manner as an entrepreneurial, self-reliant individual, needs to be complicated by "thinking about neoliberalism as involving processes that *produce* spaces, states and subjects in complex and multiple forms." In *Sex and the Revitalized City*, I draw upon the notion of governmentality to analyze the ways in which neoliberal rationality functions to mobilize particular (gendered) identities through specific governance strategies, one of which, I argue, is condominium ownership and governance.

FIGURE 2   *Fly.* Billboard for Fly Condominiums, Spadina Avenue, Toronto.

Toronto's Condominium Boom: The Sound of Privatization

Why have condominiums, as a particular *type* of high-density redevelopment project, come to form the foundation of Toronto's intensification strategy? Toronto's condominium boom articulates with an entrepreneurial revitalization plan for three central reasons: (1) condominiums satisfy housing demand through private development; (2) condominiums work to shift the scale of urban governance onto private communities and individuals; and (3) condominiums transform the tenure structure of the central city in favour of private home ownership. These different ways of understanding condominium development as a wave of privatization come together to illustrate how, at a structural level, condominium development reproduces a neoliberal city building strategy.

The Privatization of Residential Development

Condominium living in Toronto is not a new phenomenon. Since apartment ownership was made possible through the Ontario Condominium Act, 1967, condominiums have formed part of Toronto's highly diversified housing stock, serving as both owner-occupied and rental dwellings across the city. A condominium boom in the mid-1980s was brought to an abrupt halt when the high proportion of speculator-driven sales caused a crash in the market. Through the late 1980s and early 1990s, there was little condominium construction in Toronto as most new housing came in the form of low-rise, single-family homes located in the steadily sprawling suburbs. Since the late 1990s, however, new condominium construction and sales have climbed to record-breaking figures almost every year. At the end of 2006, ten years into this boom and beyond the point where many analysts had predicted a downturn in the market, the Greater Toronto Home Builders' Association (GTHBA) reported that new high-rise condominium sales in the GTA made up 44 percent of the housing market over the course of the year (GTHBA 2007); in 2007, 23,000 sales of new high-rise units were registered (Canada Mortgage and Housing Corporation 2008). The difference between this boom and the 1980s boom is that current growth is not primarily driven by investors hoping to sell quickly and make a profit; rather, the majority of condominium units are owner-occupied, and many are rented out as long-term investments. Interest rates at historic lows have shaped the high level of owner-occupation and lowered investor-driven sales in this current wave. While suburban development has not been halted in the GTA, rising land costs, combined with the availability of cheaper downtown housing in the form of condominiums, have slowed low-rise single-family home construction and reversed inner-city population decline (Bourne 2000b; Meligrana and Skaburskis 2005).

Clearly, the physical form of most condominium developments (high-rise towers or high-density townhouse or loft-style construction) fulfills the spatial goals of residential intensification. But the reliance on private-sector financing, building, and management of residential projects (almost all of which are in the form of condominiums) is representative of a major shift in urban housing strategy. The 2002 *Official Plan* is not the first planning document to value intensification and an increase in urban population. The 1994 plan, *The Liveable Metropolis*, and the 1983 plan, *The Official Plan for the Urban Structure* (Metropolitan Toronto Council 1983, 1994), also sought population growth in the core of the metropolitan region. However, previous rounds of intensification involved strong public-sector participation. Throughout the 1980s, for example, the public-sector model of residential development sought to encourage a mix of classes and land uses in the core, and numerous mixed-use social housing projects were funded (Wekerle 1988b, 1993). The federal and provincial governments, as well as the city's housing department, supported non-profit housing projects initiated and controlled by groups with particular and pressing housing needs, including single parents, seniors, women of colour, lesbians, and new immigrants. As neoliberal political regimes at the federal and provincial levels came to power in the mid-1990s, funding for social housing was withdrawn. This process started around 1990, with the federal Conservatives under Prime Minister Brian Mulroney, and was intensified by the provincial regime of Conservative premier Mike Harris in 1995. The city, faced with the downloading of fiscal responsibilities, was forced to scale back its own role in social housing (City of Toronto 2003).

Toronto's new *Official Plan* proclaims the city's intention to encourage a full range of housing opportunities through intensification and infill. This encouragement comes in the form of rezoning industrial lands for commercial and residential use, thereby opening up new areas for developers to colonize. It has not come in the form of new support for social, non-profit, co-op, or rental housing. This privatized housing strategy falls within a neoliberal governance model that reduces the role of the state and that courts private-sector leadership in policy making and urban development. Not surprisingly, then, the resulting forms of redevelopment, such as the condominium, reflect the interests and ideals of this particular set of stakeholders.

In particular, condominium development removes the need for the state to directly subsidize high-rise construction. The financial risks associated with high-rise, concrete construction are mitigated by the fact that lending institutions and private investors finance construction when 60 percent to 70 percent of the building's units are sold. Furthermore, once the building is occupied and the condominium is registered as a corporation, the developer is paid the full price of each unit by the homeowners (or their mortgage companies). The developer then repays her or his financiers and walks away from the project without being responsible for any long-term maintenance. In this scenario, the developer's investment is turned into profit within a few years, in contrast to the decades it may take to recoup the cost of land, construction, and ongoing maintenance for rental apartment buildings. Thus, the state does not need to provide financial incentives for developers to build high-density towers, as it would if those towers were non-profit, social, or even private rental housing. This allows the state to fulfill the city's housing needs without the massive expenditure required to build alternative forms of tenure; unfortunately, it also means that there is less public control over the form, location, style, and cost of the housing. Moreover, the reliance on private-sector financing and building limits the number of groups that will be seen as stakeholders in the process.

This process also allows the city to decrease its role in providing public spaces and public services to the new residents it so desires. The *Official Plan* notes that private developers are expected to include community services within their projects. Condominiums typically include some combination of amenities, including private security, private fitness facilities, social spaces, playgrounds, and private outdoor space. If the community needs of new urban residents are met through privatized development, the city has a decreased need to fund or expand the public realm or public services. Thus, private development of condominium communities is an effective way of managing the public and social infrastructure costs associated with residential intensification. While the city, through its planning approval process, has some input into the kinds of spaces and services that developers will include, there is limited input from the wider neighbourhood as to what constitutes a community service or community need. Community, therefore, is defined narrowly and exclusively by the boundaries of the condominium project. Moreover, the private and often highly secure nature of the facilities in such projects means they are not typically accessible to non-residents (Townshend 2006; Grant, Greene, and Maxwell 2004).

This reliance on the private sector for virtually all of the new housing built in Toronto over the past fifteen years has significant implications in terms of the potential for democratic participation in city building processes, the outcomes with respect to the location and target consumers for housing projects, and the amount and quality of public space and public services. There is very little analysis of or discussion about the impact of the city's withdrawal from housing development with regard to the decision-making processes. How do different stakeholders get a seat at the table, and how are various claims privileged, marginalized, or denied? When the goals of growth and competition go unquestioned, the agenda is stacked to favour those whose interests (development, profit) fit within this agenda. Other voices (community groups, advocates for low-income housing, residents concerned about schools and other social infrastructure) have less influence over the terms of the debate. Community working groups or advisory bodies may be set up when there are conflicts over rezoning or major redevelopment plans, but these are managed by private consultant firms. The lack of state input or funding to mitigate the effects of inequality in the housing sector means that such inequalities (across gender, class, ethnicity, and so on) will be reproduced or exacerbated (Wekerle 1997). As Fincher (2004) notes, condominiums and the convenience services they spawn are targeted primarily at young childless professionals, ignoring the needs of other city dwellers. Moreover, the lack of open, democratic participation in development decisions suggests that the assumptions of developers about housing needs (with assumptions about work and family embedded therein) will be manifest in the built environment (Fincher 2004; MacLaran 2003; Fainstein 2001).

Shifting the Scale of Urban Governance

Condominiums are clearly both profitable for developers and less financially painful for the city to approve and absorb than are other types of housing. But there are also key social and political reasons why condominium development may be so effectively positioned as a revitalization strategy in the context of neoliberal urbanization. These revolve around the fact that condominiums are private social and political entities that constitute somewhat independent communities within the municipal framework. Condominiums can be understood as one of an array of non-state governance arrangements that proliferate under neoliberal policy regimes (Swyngedouw 2005) and that function to control citizens without any direct involvement or responsibility of the state – a shift from government to governance. Not only does this allow the local state to reorganize the ways it will either control or take responsibility for its citizens, but it may also shift the scale at which city dwellers choose to engage as citizens or the sites at which they experience attachment and a sense of belonging (Townshend 2006; Lazerwitz and Ginsberg 1994; Mitrany 2005).

The common ownership and governance structure of condominiums makes them a unique form of housing. In Ontario, condominiums are mixed-tenure, limited liability properties, meaning that owners own only the interior spaces and structures of their particular apartment, loft, or townhouse. After most of the units in a development are occupied, a condominium corporation is formed to take over the management and maintenance of the community from the developer/builder. The corporation comprises all the owners and is run by an elected board of directors (also owners). The corporation owns the exterior spaces and structures, typically referred to as common elements. The board of directors is responsible for providing maintenance for the common elements; ensuring the provision of services like landscaping, lighting, security, and garbage disposal; collecting maintenance fees from owners; setting and enforcing the rules of the condominium corporation (on pets, noise, exterior decorating, etc.); and overseeing the operating budget of the corporation. Thus, condominiums have an element of common property ownership and their own private governance structure.

Research on so-called common-interest developments (CIDs) has looked at the conflicts that arise as a result of private governance, the potential for democratic participation within the community, the links that people feel to the condominium community and the wider neighbourhood, and the ways that privately governed communities may attempt to separate themselves from, or circumvent, the local state (Taggart 1995; Yip and Forrest 2002; McKenzie 2003; Chien-Yuan and Webster 2006; Strahilevitz 2006; Wekerle et al. 1980). For example, the common ownership structure means that the amenities are owned and maintained collectively by residents through monthly fees. Residents therefore have a vested interest in their own amenities and fewer requirements for open and accessible public space, public recreation or entertainment, or public provision of family programs (Townshend 2006; Foldvary 1992). The inclusion of private services within condominiums means that condominium owners have little incentive to support public funding for such spaces and services and more incentive to turn inwards towards their own, pre-paid amenities.

Many authors conceptualize condominiums as gated communities, which function not only to "systematically exclude those adjudged to be unsuitable and even threatening" (Flusty 2001, 659) but also to discipline residents in a way congruent with neoliberal ideals of consumerist citizenship, through both spatial and political arrangements (MacLeod 2002). Others have suggested that condominium communities provide opportunities for people to become involved in democratic forms of citizenship or to form new networks and new types of communities (McKenzie 2003; Wekerle et al. 1980). For women in particular, the integrated public/private spaces of a condominium project could foster connections that are beneficial to them in both their work and family lives (Mitrany 2005). In this way, the patriarchal separation of work and home has the potential to be subverted.

These social/political aspects of intensification have not received a great deal of public attention, although the news media occasionally run stories that draw attention to both the social challenges of intensified living and the ways that condominium communities form and interact. For example, residents may attempt to translate the common ownership structure into a common social structure by setting up activities and events within their condominium community (Cotroneo 2006). These examples of network and community formation allow the progressive rhetoric of local democracy to be used to legitimate the privatization of governance in some contexts (Bevir 2006).

However, the impacts of this privatized form of community in terms of the effects on broader engagements with the city require further examination. Does intensification through private redevelopment facilitate the formation of healthy urban communities, or are these communities so narrow and exclusive that the scale of local citizenship practices is reduced from the city or neighbourhood to the private condominium project? Furthermore, if condominiums are understood as embodying technologies of governance that translate or filter neoliberal rationality into everyday life, fostering the creation of autonomous, self-governing, rational subjects, we may be able to argue that the scale of urban governance is shifted increasingly onto the individual. What responsibilities does the local state evade in this scenario? Public safety, for example, is one particularly pressing feminist issue that may fall off the public agenda as private communities and the individuals within are expected to pay for and manage their own personal safety.

Shifting Tenure

The explosion of multi-family, high-density urban living spaces in the form of condominiums is quite a phenomenal shift in residential form for a city that has experienced major sprawl and the growth of massive edge cities since the postwar period (Harris 2004). But perhaps more significant than this, and much less remarked upon, is the shifting tenure structure of the city. Due, in large part, to the condominium boom, in 2001 the percentage of owner-occupied dwellings in the city of Toronto shifted higher than that of rented dwellings – 51 percent owner-occupied versus 49 percent rented (Statistics Canada 2003) – for the first time since the major postwar housing boom of the 1950s and 1960s (Choko and Harris 1990).[1] In 2006, this ratio increased to 54 percent owner-occupied, 46 percent rented (Statistics Canada 2008a). Over 75 percent of condominiums are owner-occupied (City of Toronto 2003), although the very small amount of new, purpose-built rental housing in recent years means that condominiums are expected to fulfill the city's rental needs as well (City of Toronto 2003). Over 20 percent of rental units in Toronto were condominiums in 2003 (Canada Mortgage and Housing Corporation 2004).

Condominiums are providing home ownership opportunities for a variety of housing consumers who may have had difficulty gaining access to home ownership in Toronto's expensive single-family dwelling market. Across Canada, the 2001 census data showed that female one-person households comprised the largest group of condominium owners, with 10.7 percent of these households owning a condominium, almost double the condominium ownership rate for Canadian households in general (5.8 percent) (Canada Mortgage and Housing Corporation 2001). In Toronto, single women are estimated to make up approximately 40 percent of new and re-sale condominium purchasers in the city (Cordileone 2002). Media reports also suggest that immigrant families, young people, and working-class families are gaining access to the ownership market through condominiums in and around the GTA (Laporte 2003a; Shim 2004).

In order to understand why the private ownership dimension of condominium development is significant, it is necessary to note the national and local culture of property. Canadian housing policy has always favoured private home ownership, supporting citizens' attempts to attain this tenure through a variety of financial incentives and entitlements (Hulchanski and Shapcott 2005; Wekerle 1997; Wekerle et al. 1980). More important, though, owner-occupation has been positioned as a social norm to the extent that the culture of home ownership is integral to the North American way of life (Choko and Harris 1990). This culture of property presumes that private home ownership constitutes the highest and best use of urban space. In the context of entrepreneurial governance strategies, this culture shapes the housing options in the city through the widespread assumption that the middle class will be drawn anywhere that home ownership opportunities are presented.[2]

Housing, while always viewed as a commodity in the capitalist economy, is increasingly seen as a vehicle for wealth accumulation under neoliberal economic regimes. Condominiums are well suited to rapid exchange on the housing market. Many are purchased as either shorter-term living spaces for their owners, who expect to make a profit, or as investment units to be rented out. Urban sociologist Jon Caulfield (2005) describes condominiums as a predominant feature of corporatized urban space, defined by geographer Edward Relph (1987, 188) as "a potential commodity to be exploited, managed or manipulated in whatever ways will ensure ... profitability." The massive number of condominium units opens a network for the increased (and more rapid) circulation of capital through the housing market. Lefebvre (2003) termed this the second circuit of capital, which increases the potential for capital accumulation both by large-scale global investors and individual homeowners. The significance of this tenure shift, and its articulation with neoliberalization, are discussed in greater detail in the next chapter.

A Feminist Approach to Researching City Life in Neoliberal Times

The frameworks for understanding condominium development presented in this chapter represent complex discursive and political formations that shape both a common-sense understanding of urban revitalization and its actual formation. Disrupting, unpacking, contextualizing, and reframing these narratives and practices are the goals of *Sex and the Revitalized City*. In order to tackle this task, I designed a multilayered project employing qualitative methods such as interviewing, visual analysis, and discourse analysis. Like most feminist scholarship, feminist urban research has often employed qualitative methods, such as in-depth interviewing, to understand the relationships between gender and urban environments (Bondi and Rose 2003). In part, the objective has been to understand women's affective experiences of urban places. As well, feminists often seek out the voices and stories of those who have typically been marginalized or silenced in accounts of the social, cultural, and political world of the city in order to correct the skewed understanding of the city and social relations that comes from androcentric, positivist urban social sciences (Booth, Darke, and Yeandle 1996; Garber and Turner 1995; Little, Peake, and Richardson 1988). Other feminist scholars have attempted to gain access to the perspectives of privileged groups and powerful actors in the urban context (McDowell 1998; England 2002). Feminists have also had to challenge the ethnocentricity and elitism of geography to include the perspectives of different groups of women across race, class, ethnicity, age, sexuality, and so on and to explicate how these intersect and interlock to structure women's and men's urban lives (McDowell 1993).

A central organizing principle for much feminist research is the notion of starting from women's everyday lives and experiences. Sociologist Dorothy

Smith's (1988) "sociology of the everyday" provides the methodological entry point for investigations that start with lives and experiences that have often been made invisible in mainstream social research. Wekerle (1999, 105) argues that, in critical urban research, "the interstitial spaces between the private and the public ... receive scant attention within the dominant economistic frame." These spaces, such as the home and the neighbour-hood, are often spaces where women's everyday lives articulate with struc-tural forces and changes in political economy. Therefore, starting with women's lives and experiences is a way of identifying and theorizing women's concerns within a broader context.

In this book, I attempt to connect these concerns to the issue of urban citizenship – how people speak to and enact everyday claims on the city and their sense of belonging and attachment to it (Isin 2000; Vaiou and Lyko-gianni 2006; Fenster 2005). It is difficult, however, to find a vocabulary for the everyday world of citizenship. Geographic work on citizenship employs qualitative research methodologies, such as interviews and content analysis, which have been somewhat marginal in citizenship studies. These contrast with the more normative aims (around notions of ideal citizenship and democratic practices) of the philosophical tradition in citizenship studies. Geographers seek to understand citizenship as it unfolds on the ground, in everyday life, in a variety of contexts – what could be termed actually existing citizenship (Desforges, Jones, and Woods 2005).

This is also an important starting point for feminist inquiries into the relationship between gender and citizenship in specific spatial contexts. Feminist studies of women's urban citizenship claims acknowledge the pro-liferation of rights claims based on lived experience or the right to inhabit (Wekerle 2000; Fenster 2005; Peters 1998; Naples and Desai 2002). This opens up new ways of understanding citizenship beyond formal actions and legal standings (Lefebvre 1996; Purcell 2003; Isin 2000). Studying enact-ments of citizenship, understood as an everyday process of engagement at various scales, allows us to connect the material realities of everyday life with political-economic structures. Citizenship is an effective concept for balancing structural analysis (i.e., how cities are shaped by economic and political restructuring) with human agency (i.e., how urban dwellers en-hance or defend their rights within a particular political-economic context).

Critiques from the Organic Café: Situating Myself

Feminist and postmodern scholars have struggled to demystify the mode of seeing everything from nowhere (Haraway 1991). We realize that neutrality is a fiction that disguises power, privilege, and politics. Every researcher has a subject position that affects her or his research at every stage from conception to final analysis. Self-reflexivity is the practice of being explicit about the shaping of the text by recognizing that we *"inscribe* rather than just *describe* reality" (Jones 1992, 25). By acknowledging the personal investments, value judgments, and biases that covertly inform all research, we can attempt to make certain that the invisibility of the author can no longer function as a mechanism of power that ensures the domination of certain accounts.

On a fairly regular basis throughout my work on this topic, participants and colleagues have asked me if I was indeed a condominium owner myself. During the course of this project, I went through the process of looking for a condominium, purchasing one, waiting through its construction, and finally moving into a condominium townhouse where I lived with my family for just over three years before selling the unit and returning to renting. I have therefore experienced a process similar to that experienced by the women condominium owners whom I interview here (except, of course, in returning to renting), and I am both a subject and critical observer of the processes and ideas put forth by the planners and developers with whom I spoke. More broadly speaking, I am a city dweller, a life-long Torontonian, and a woman; as such, I have attachments to the city and various neighbourhoods within it as well as my own set of everyday, gendered experiences that shape my relationship to the city. I also embody many salient privileges that mark me as belonging in this city and as having an unquestioned right to articulate claims for space – for comfort, for fun, for work, for whatever – within it. Furthermore, as a worker in the knowledge economy, I am, in many ways, one of the desired subjects of the revitalized city.

So what are my investments here? How do I problematize the spaces of redevelopment and new-build gentrification from my seat in the new organic café in a neighbourhood on the cusp of gentrification? There are no easy answers, no pat justifications or adequate apologias. As a critical feminist academic, my body and my everyday life contain and express the contradictions of these positions. It is pointless to deny the allure of the spectacle, the spaces of consumption, the shiny new living quarters, the theatre of difference and conflict that combine to make up everyday life in the postindustrial city. To do so would be to position myself as somehow outside of, or above, the very conditions and experiences that my participants describe. Instead, I acknowledge that I am very much inside these conditions (and contradictions) and that this works, in fact, as an entry point into my attempt to think critically about city building, everyday life, and identity formation in the context of revitalization. Like most feminist urban scholars, I seek to open up opportunities for claims to multiple, alternative urban ways of life, choice beyond consumerism, and space to challenge hegemonic gender identities. I also seek to renew collective projects for social justice.

Research Design

In order to make connections between revitalization agendas, condominium development, women's everyday urban lives, and gendered identities in the contemporary city, I attempted to design a project that would allow me to examine a variety of agents, subjects, and discourses. The primary methods are personal interviews, key informant interviews, and visual and discourse analysis. This approach gave me access to the voices and documents of city building agents, to women's own perspectives on condominium and city living, and to representations and visions of the revitalized city.

The central focus of *Sex and the Revitalized City* is based on interviews, conducted from July 2005 to May 2006, with twenty-one women condominium owners, recruited through a snowball process that began with acquaintances and contacts in the real estate industry. I ended the interview process when I felt that an appropriate level of data saturation had been reached (Berg 1998), although I was concerned with finding illustrative, rather than representative, cases. The participants themselves ranged in age from twenty-one to forty-six, and they were from a variety of ethnic backgrounds. I did not ask respondents to identify themselves based on race, ethnicity, sexuality, or other social locations; the background details that I collected simply included their educational history and current employment as well as recent tenure situations (see Appendix A). All had at least some postsecondary education. Two participants were full-time graduate students, and the remainder were employed full-time either as professionals in their chosen fields or as clerical and administrative workers. The majority (seventeen) lived alone, two were married, two had roommates, and only one had a child. Nineteen were first-time homeowners, and two had previously owned other condominiums. Their condominiums were located within the City of Toronto. Most lived in mid- to high-rise condominium towers; one owned a condominium townhouse.

In the interviews, I explored the meanings of condominium ownership and city living by asking respondents about the decision to buy a condominium, their experiences living there, their everyday routines, their decision to live in the city, and their intentions regarding how long they would like to reside in their condominiums and in the city (see Appendix B). The interviews lasted from thirty to seventy minutes, although on average they were around forty-five minutes long. Most of the interviews took place in public places such as coffee shops and diners; a small number occurred at the respondents' places of work or in their homes, in accordance with their preferences. I would characterize the interviews as semi-structured in that, although I had prepared an interview schedule, I was content to let the respondents explore tangents, gloss over certain questions, and ask me questions. And, at times, I changed the order of the questions to suit the natural flow of the conversation (Reinharz 1992; DeVault 1999). Nonetheless, all of the interviews covered the major themes, and, this being the case, I found it possible to read them in relation to one another.[3]

Overall, this group resembles the target market for many condominiums, a typical condominium consumer, according to the news media and condominium industry. However, this group is not designed to be representative, in a statistical sense, of all condominium owners who share these traits (themselves only one particular subset of all condominium owners). It is not my goal to base my interpretations upon the assertion that this group is a representative subset of a larger group; rather, it is to seek an illustrative sample and, thus, to analyze the narratives presented in relation to one another and in relation to the accounts of city building agents and representations of condominium and city living in order to seek out nuances, contradictions, and continuities. Moreover, I wanted to examine the complexity of individual experiences, an approach that is only permitted with a smaller cohort.

I have noted that I think that feminist analyses of urban revitalization and new-build gentrification are critical interventions into the story of the development of the neoliberal city. This perspective assumes, of course, that gender is a salient category of analysis. Feminist theory, however, also grapples with the intersections among gender, race, class, sexuality, and other dimensions of socially constructed difference. The analysis that I present in this book draws out the intersections between gender and class and complicates these observations with attention to age and relationship status. I am less able here to substantively articulate the ways that race and sexuality intersect with class and gender. This results, in part, from my methodological approach, which did not include asking participants to self-identify on the basis of race, ethnicity, or sexual orientation. The sample size is also insufficient to get a broad enough picture of all of these social differences.

Thus, I am reluctant to directly ascribe various aspects of their experiences to racism/race privilege or homophobia/heterosexual privilege. However, throughout the analysis, I do attempt to flag moments where the data suggest that these systems are explicitly working to shape the gendered and classed experiences of everyday life in the city.

It is also important to note that, in interviewing women who had specifically chosen to become condominium owners, I have collected narratives that are more likely to support the ideals of condominium living and to justify the choices of these condominium buyers than would have been the case had I also interviewed women who had made other housing choices. This process also filters out women who might be virulent critics of condominium living. However, this choice reflects an interest in disrupting the seamless narrative of condominium living as empowerment by examining some of the everyday meanings and experiences of the women who inhabit condominiums. So, while focusing on one (relatively privileged) group of women in the city has narrowed the range of potential responses to condominium development, it was also empirically necessary to gather and analyze the stories of such women in order to counter the sound-byte characterizations of condominium living as emancipatory. Nonetheless, I acknowledge that the story told here is necessarily partial and contingent on the methodological choices made.

For background information on the role of the city in facilitating or managing condominium development, I interviewed two City of Toronto planners, one in urban design and one a senior planner for the Waterfront Area. I asked for their perspectives on Toronto's reurbanization and residential intensification strategies, about condominium development in particular, about the social and economic impacts, and for their thoughts about future directions for growth in Toronto (see Appendix B). I also conducted seven interviews with representatives of condominium development firms active in Toronto. The representatives included one owner/president, three vice-presidents, one marketing specialist, and two market analysts. During these interviews, we spoke about their specific firms' developments and development decisions, about the condominium boom in Toronto, about consumers and the market, and about women in particular as potential buyers (see Appendix B).

While both the planner and developer interviews provided a great deal of contextual information, I was also interested in the ways that these individuals understood their roles in the city building process, the beliefs they held about city dwellers and condominium residents, and their perspectives on

city life in general. Therefore, I take their accounts not as objective representations of city planning and condominium development but, rather, as stories told about city building, identity, and city life.

All of the interviews (condominium owners, planners, developers) were
digitally recorded with the respondents' permission and transcribed by me
on an ongoing basis throughout the data collection process. The transcripts
were coded manually, using both a predetermined set of codes that was based
on the questions asked and codes derived from themes that arose in the
interviews themselves (Hay 2000; Jackson 2001; Charmaz 2004; Letherby
2003; Ramazanoglu and Holland 2002). I approached my analysis from the
point of view that all narratives are socially constructed and that they both
represent and produce the social world.

In analyzing the interviews as narratives, then, I looked to identify the
central themes that emerged; attempted to denaturalize that which was presented as normal, inevitable, and unquestioned; traced elements that were
related to gender ideologies and gender relations; questioned the moral
undertones; and investigated sites where power relations were sustained or
subverted. This involved the process of first decontextualizing the data
(breaking the transcripts up by themes) and then recontextualizing the material (by reading each theme across all of the interviews, including across
different groups of interview subjects). In this way, the narratives and my
analysis of them are interpreted and assigned meaning in relation to one
another (DeVault 1999; Reinharz 1992). My presentation of quotations from
respondents represents this process of recontextualization. While I have
been faithful to their exact words and speech habits, the quotes are positioned in relation to the words of other respondents. This analytic and representational strategy is a deliberate tactic designed to illustrate the
continuities and contradictions across multiple voices. In the following
chapters, the accounts of women condominium owners are presented after
other aspects of the analysis. This is also a deliberate strategy wherein historical data, the narratives of planners and developers, and examples of
public discourse form a complex story upon which the views of women condominium owners are layered. Through this method of textual representation, I hope to allow women condominium owners to speak back to this
story.

Urban geographers are increasingly interested in issues of representation
and interpretive strategies. My research indeed originated from my interest
in media reports and condominium advertising. The materials that I analyze
come from newspaper accounts collected from major local and national

newspapers and news magazines since 2003 (in total about 350) and examples of condominium advertising since 2003 (approximately four hundred ads). I also analyze state documents such as the City of Toronto *Official Plan* (2002) and its background documents, place marketing campaigns, and other relevant legislation such as the Ontario Greenbelt Act and the Ontario Places to Grow Act.

While these texts and images are produced by different actors with different interests, they are important to analyze as part of the process by which the story of revitalization and the process of condominium development are made to seem commonsensical. They construct a discursive field that produces what Foucault (1980) called regimes of truth. Thus, my analysis of these artefacts follows a Foucauldian strand of discourse analysis, wherein discourses are not simply reflections or (mis)representations of reality; rather, they have their own truth effects that construct the range of acceptable interpretations of a problem and its solutions: "Discourse is constituted by the difference between what one could say correctly at one period ... and what is actually said" (Foucault 1991, 63). Foucault (1991) argues that language, knowledge, and power are all interconnected through discourse and that the power to construct discourse lies not just with the elite or the powerful. Actors construct discourse, and discourse constructs actors (Modan 2007).

As I did with the interview transcripts, I coded the texts and images according to both pre-set codes and codes that arose from my analysis of the materials. Viewing the materials through a feminist lens, I was particularly interested in the ways in which the category of gender was embedded within representations of condominium living and city living. I was therefore concerned to note how various gendered identities and subject positions were being promoted or fostered in relation to the idea of the entrepreneurial or revitalized city. In addition, I looked at the discourses produced by these materials as articulating with dominant ideologies about urban growth, competition, enterprise, and culture. Thus, I was interested, in the Foucauldian sense, in investigating the conditions of existence of discourse and in relating it to the practical field in which it is deployed. For this reason, I take examples from my content analysis and read them relationally, with and against one another as well as the accounts of planners, developers, and women condominium owners.

I subscribe to the position that feminist research is a process, one that fluctuates between action, reflection, and practice. It represents a struggle to do ethical research, to destabilize the researcher's authority, and to

represent the multiple voices involved both faithfully and in ways that illuminate the concepts, critiques, and contexts in which the work is positioned. I assert that the interpretations and conclusions presented in this
book are not stable or absolute. There are many ways that the accounts
could be analyzed; there is also much missing that could not be included. I
urge readers to engage with the voices presented here from diverse perspectives and to resist a closed and static reading of my analysis.

Troubling Tenure
Condominium Ownership, Gender, and the Entrepreneurial Subject

*What has been termed the "ownership model" presumes
clarity and determinacy in the definition of what property
is, and tells us which relationships between people and
scarce resources are to be valued as such, and which are
not. There is a lot at stake here.*

– Nicholas Blomley, Unsettling the City

Securing particular property relations has been an integral part of North American urbanization since colonial times. Under entrepreneurial urban regimes, property relations are central to revitalization schemes, the re-shaping of governance, and the mobilization of neoliberal subjectivities. Property relations are sets of norms and practices that determine rights and obligations in relation to land or real estate; furthermore, they shape the ways that people relate to the state, the community, and other citizens. They may also structure affective experiences such as a sense of attachment to, and belonging in, the city. The ways that property relations mediate these social and political relations are highly significant in the context of wide-spread condominium development.

The increase in central city home ownership can be examined in relation to the economic and social rationales underlying gentrification (i.e., achiev-ing the highest and best use of property, the association of middle-class home ownership with responsible citizenship, etc.) and problematized as part of the neoliberalization and privatization of the city. However, these are not the only rationales shaping the rise of home ownership in Toronto, nor are they monolithic, top-down processes with predictable outcomes. There are other, relatively unexamined, co-evolving discourses that shape the nexus of condominium development and tenure. Specifically, I am concerned with investigating the interrelations between socially constructed gender ideologies and the particular culture of property that is produced within the structure of condominium ownership.

This entails an unpacking of both mainstream and critical understandings of tenure and home ownership. How does condominium tenure challenge common-sense notions about owner occupation? And how does it "trouble" the normative foundations of tenure relations? For example, common-sense assumptions about home ownership and private property are seemingly subverted by the common ownership of various spaces and the common governance structure in condominiums (Blomley 2004). This raises the critical question of whether the condominium ownership structure destabilizes or alters the normative link between owner occupation and democratic citizenship. But perhaps most important, it is critical to highlight the idea that condominium development is not solely a class-based process of urban change. There are critical gender dimensions to property relations that are being actively reworked in relation to the condominium boom. In this sense, interconnected ideas about gender, tenure, and citizenship play a significant constitutive role in this city building process. I argue that critical dimensions of home ownership – including notions of control, self-expression, improvement, progress, and freedom – are gendered and, moreover, are constitutive of gender ideologies and gender relations.

During Toronto's first wave of high-rise residential construction, condominiums and rental apartments were the subject of heated debates around their suitability as residential forms (Wekerle et al. 1980; Social Planning Council of Toronto 1973). Furthermore, the initial condominium construction boom was marked by high levels of speculative buying, which contributed to a crash in the market in the 1980s. Homebuyers looking for a stable investment came to view condominiums sceptically in this context. Given this pre-existing climate, the image of the condominium had to be rehabilitated in order for condominiums to overtake low-rise single-family housing as the preferred tenure form for new residential developments in and around the city in the mid-1990s. As one condominium developer suggested:

> It's an acceptable built form. It's not like it was in the '80s, where
> it had this sort of commodity component to it ... I think that
> condominium and high-rise living is something that is becoming

more mainstream, more so now than ever before, where you have
families that are actually looking at this as an acceptable form.
(Developer interview, 28 July 2005)

The mainstreaming of condominium living has been accomplished by
emphasizing the home ownership opportunity offered by condominium
tenure, and this has succeeded, in part, because of a growing anti-rent climate in Toronto. Although this rationale echoes the logic of the first wave,
where condominiums were set up as a moderately priced home ownership
opportunity in the context of strong social and political support for ownership, the current wave articulates with the neoliberalization of urban housing policy in particular and the neoliberalization of urban space and urban
life in general. While private property has always been central to the liberal
democratic and capitalist state, it is reinvigorated in the turn to entrepreneurial and competitive modes of urban governance, where, as Lefebvre
suggests, real estate supplants industrial production as the site for the
movement and accumulation of capital. It is not tenable to argue that home
ownership, or even condominium ownership, is *inherently* neoliberal; however, I argue that the particular qualities of condominium ownership en-
hance both the neoliberalization of urban space and the development of the
entrepreneurial citizen-subject. Condominium ownership functions as a
form of governance that translates neoliberal rationality into everyday life
by mobilizing certain subject positions and identities. Neoliberal governance, suggests Foucault (1997), fosters subjects constructed as independent,
rational, economic decision makers. This form of governance promotes the
rise of technologies and rationalities of self-governance or individual discipline. The purpose here is to interrogate how tenure relations may act as
disciplining technologies in the context of neoliberal urbanism. As Blomley
(2004, xvi) notes, "bodies, technologies, and things must be enrolled and
mobilized into organized and disciplined practices" around property.
Through the analytical tool of governmentality, condominium ownership
can perhaps be understood as a form of governance that constitutes and
transforms the subject by mobilizing the notion of the entrepreneurial subject. If so, what are the gendered dimensions, and how are gendered identities constituted in this context?

Building the Entrepreneurial City
As noted in Chapter 1, Canadian housing policy supports a free-market
system of allocation, dominated by the private home ownership market;

indeed, over two-thirds (68.4 percent) of Canadian households owned their homes in 2006 (Statistics Canada 2008a). As such, market housing is the primary focus of policy, while social housing and housing-related fiscal strategies form secondary housing policy arenas. Housing differs from other policy sites such as health care and education in Canada in that housing has not been considered a social right. It is seen as firmly within the domain of the private market rather than the purview of the welfare state (Carroll and Jones 2000). The federal government provides only residual support for social housing, restricts access to shelter assistance funding and programs, provides subsidies to the market housing industry, and produces an ideological apparatus that positions home ownership as the normative tenure form (Doling 1997; Fallis 1995). Over the past two decades, federal and provincial governments have scaled back their commitments to housing at such a rate that "Canada's housing system is now the most private-sector market-based of any Western nation, including the United States" (Hulchanski and Shapcott 2004, 6).[1] The clawing back and downloading of social housing funding from federal and provincial governments has placed enormous strain on municipalities, which struggle to provide adequate temporary and permanent shelter for residents.

The state's emphasis on private home ownership was clearly echoed by the condominium developers and city planners interviewed for this book. They were more than cognizant of the significance of home ownership to the success of the condominium in Toronto; in fact, home ownership was positioned as part of a broader narrative wherein condominiums are represented as beneficial to both their owners and the city at large. Furthermore, condominiums were also situated as part of a natural, inevitable progression to increased free market penetration of the urban housing system.

> Torontonians want to live in established neighbourhoods,
> and while there's a bit of a preference amongst middle-class
> Torontonians for house living, they realize that if perhaps they're
> not at a point where they can buy a house, or in terms of their
> family arrangement, or they can't afford a house in the sort of
> neighbourhood, that they might be able to afford a condominium
> ... We obviously value ownership in our culture. *(Developer
> interview, 16 June 2005)*

> So condos are a very good first-time buyer option. And that's the
> way you build equity ... But there also is the aspect that condos are

more acceptable now as a home, as a home ownership option or a
lifestyle option. *(Developer interview, 19 July 2005)*

The condominium is just the current economic model for high-
density housing construction ... The fact that there is housing
available to deal with the market is a good thing because the
combination of cheap interest rates and whatever has kind of
fuelled this boom, has resulted in a completely different rental
situation ... I haven't seen the statistics on it, but I know that the
high cost of rental, and the congestion and the difficulty of renting
at some point by the late nineties as the economy was heating up,
was actually forming a problem for the city ... Yes, it's an interesting
game in the planning world. I mean we can influence the market,
but ultimately the market tells us what we can build ... The market
has responded with the high-rise condominium as a form that's
different from, in particular, the old high-density neighbourhoods
in the suburbs where there were rental apartments. *(Planner
interview, 18 July 2005)*

Condominiums fit within the pre-existing local preference for home
ownership and are naturalized as a logical solution to a supply problem, an
affordability problem, and a policy problem for a city trying to combat
sprawl through intensification. Furthermore, in the comments from the city
planner, it is clear that the market controls the city building process with
little input from the municipality on the issue of tenure; tenure change is
seen as a by-product of a particular market process.[2] Moreover, the planner's comments invoke Toronto's on-again/off-again fixation with high-
rise, high-density planning in its periodic attempts to curb sprawl.
Characterizing the condominium boom as just the latest version of this
cycle seems to elide the potential significance of tenure change for the City
of Toronto.

Beyond the "logic" of a progression towards market housing, there is also
an underlying morality of property pitting ownership against renting that is
very effective, ideologically, at positioning condominiums as a desirable
housing option. This is based upon a deep-rooted linkage between property
ownership and citizenship, which dates back to early Western democracies
wherein the right to participate was predicated upon one's ownership of private property (Atkinson and Blandy 2007). Indeed, in Toronto the municipal franchise was restricted to property owners until the 1960s (Tindal and

Tindal 2004; Siemiatycki 2006). In contemporary times, moral judgments endure about the value of various tenure forms, such that different tenures are ascribed different power statuses in society. Blomley (2004, 88) notes that it is the tenurial status of the middle class that makes its members especially appealing as "vectors of urban renewal," surmising that middle-class renters would not be as warmly welcomed.

There is also evidence of a long tradition of imbuing homeowners with qualities that position them as desirable and effective citizens. In his exploration of the suburbanization of Canadian cities, geographer and housing scholar Richard Harris (2004) outlines some of these central beliefs. Owners are believed to be more invested in local life and inclined towards local issues. They are seen as stakeholders who will have an active interest in local politics but who will generally resist change. Because of their financial investment, and their ties to long-term mortgage debt, homeowners are argued to have an interest in political and economic stability and are thus seen as less likely to engage in disruptive political or labour actions. Generally, ownership is assumed to discourage radicalism and to create a more conservative society with a stake in the capitalist system and the status quo. Alternatively, renters are viewed as transient, disengaged, and less trustworthy than owners. This is heightened in the suburbs, where home ownership rates are higher than they are in the city.

In contrast, in the City of Toronto itself, gentrification (typically a process involving an influx of middle-class homeowners) has been conceptualized as a form of critical social practice that stands in opposition to conservative suburban home ownership. Caulfield's (1994) study of inner-city gentrifiers portrayed gentrification as a reaction against the homogeneity and conformity of suburbia and an anti-modernist valorization of traditional urban fabrics and mixed-use, diverse communities (for a critique, see Slater 2004b). Within this perspective, this community of middle-class urban homeowners is understood as essentially a progressive one that values difference, social diversity, and creativity. At times, this constituency can be mobilized in pursuit of a progressive political goal, for example in the formation of the group Citizens for Local Democracy in (unsuccessful) opposition to the Ontario government's 1997 plan to merge six Toronto municipalities into a mega-city (Boudreau 2000). An additional example is the mobilization of Annex and Forest Hill residents, galvanized by figures like Jane Jacobs and Marshall McLuhan, to stop the proposed Spadina Expressway in the 1960s (the project was cancelled in 1971) (Caulfield 1994). This oppositional form of citizenship is not one typically envisioned by the state as it tries to create a society of homeowners. However, it is an example of how a stable base of urban homeowners can and will enact its claim to local citizenship and work to protect its neighbourhoods and amenity spaces from redevelopment.

Condominium tenure reflects a critical shift in these moral and political conceptions of home ownership. In the case of condominium tenure, the morality of home ownership is less tied to the homeowner's connection to the local state as a democratic participant in society than it is to the home-owner's ability to actualize a form of entrepreneurial citizenship, wherein the homeowner is an economically (rather than politically) responsible cit-izen who is self-sufficient and rational. This ideal is promoted through a seemingly coherent narrative about the personal economic benefits of home ownership. Like other sets of discourse, this story creates its own truth ef-fects. In other words, the story that is told about the inherent good of home ownership is reflected back through individual narratives about the experi-ence of home ownership.

In the case of condominium development in Toronto, this narrative is propagated by condominium advertising and the news media, and it is also present in interviews with condominium developers.

> [Our] corporation has rental housing – today we have approxi-mately seven hundred rental housing units. So then we sort of segue into our low-rise and high-rise housing divisions, so low-rise, we'll rent you something, we'll sell you an entry-level town-home, we then move up from a town into a semi, then into a detached single. So our goal – another way to look at it is cradle to grave. *(Developer interview, 28 July 2005)*

These comments are clear about the presumably natural evolution of hous-ing consumption, from rental apartment to owner-occupied single-family housing. This naturalization of the hierarchy of tenure sets up ownership as the ultimate, and indeed only, goal for the housing consumer. Such a pro-gression is certainly a common-sense story in our culture, manifest in the popular notion of "moving up."

An important element of this goal is the personal financial security of building equity:

> Those underlying reasons are low interest rates. In other words, people feel that they're better off buying – you know, paying a

mortgage similar to what they would be paying in rent. Because
they're building equity. *(Developer interview, 16 June 2005)*

And so condos are a very good first-time buyer option. And that's
the way you build equity. So for a lot of buyers – like, I'm sure there
are lots of people, if you gave them a choice, they would say, "I
would rather live in a three-bedroom home, in the Annex, but I
can't afford it, so I'm going to have to buy at the Mosaic condominium project at Bloor and Spadina instead. And I'll build up
some equity over time, hopefully make some money on this unit,
and then my second step will be a townhouse or a detached home."
(Developer interview, 19 July 2005)

In this narrative, people make a rational economic decision to become
homeowners through the condominium market in order to move towards
the eventual goal of single-family home ownership. Building equity is presented as the logical choice given the broader economic conditions (i.e., low
interest rates).[3]

If you look at the economic picture, I mean we have had historical[ly] low interest rates. I mean, from a purchaser perspective,
you go, "Wow, how much longer are they gonna be at this low
level? And what it means for me is I can be throwing away eight
or nine hundred dollars on rent, and if I can dig deep and save my
Starbucks lattes, I can pay a thousand dollars a month and get into
home ownership, and I can build. And even if I sell something in
two or three years for what I bought it for, I've lived rent free." It's
another way of kind of looking at it. So you have that huge sort
of home ownership opportunity, and, you know, coupled with
programs, RRSP programs, others use minimum down payment
programs. *(Developer interview, 28 July 2005)*

In the "ownership through latte-denial" theory, saving for home ownership
requires self-discipline, linked again to the economic rationale that ownership will always lead to some form of profit or return on investment. Thus,
buying a condominium is seen as an inherently logical, rational decision
for the self-sufficient, entrepreneurial citizen. Moreover, the investment
quality of the condominium is tied to the ostensibly inherent moral good of
the home, drawing on underlying associations of the home as a place of

individual sovereignty, respite, stability, security, family, and responsibility (Atkinson and Blandy 2007). These associations seem to carry through whether someone buys the condominium as an investment to rent out or as her or his own home:

> Ultimately, our position is that we're creating homes. So a home
> is inherently a good investment for whoever buys it. Because
> ultimately, if you're buying as an investor, if you're buying as an
> end-user, essentially you're buying something where people are
> going to live. *(Developer interview, 21 June 2005)*

Similar assumptions about the desirability of achieving home ownership through the condominium market are expressed through the texts and images used in condominium advertising and in the news media. In some cases, condominiums are associated with freedom: this might include freedom from the control of a landlord, control over your own property, or freedom from the high maintenance of a freehold home.[4]

Advertisements also help convey developers' offers of financial incentives designed to help first-time buyers move into the ownership market, such as low down payment mortgages, cash back, paying the first year's property taxes, offering free upgrades or free furnishings, or waiving maintenance fees. In Figure 3, development firm Urbancorp offers consumers 0 percent interest for three years, while promoting the ostensibly low monthly cost of carrying the condominium. These offers provide attractive incentives for those trying to manage the additional financial responsibilities of home ownership; however, they effectively hide, or allow the consumer to deny, the reality that, once the incentives are over, there may be precipitous increases in costs, particularly if the developer has under-quoted the fees and property taxes to attract buyers. For vulnerable housing consumers, like many young or single women, these strategies may be very risky or detrimental to long-term financial stability.

Other advertisements specifically promote ownership as a superior form of tenure by contrasting it to renting. The slogan "Why rent when you can own" (with the question mark omitted) adorned advertisements for Domain Condominiums in 2005; the lack of a question mark suggests that this slogan functions more as a common-sense statement than as a genuine question. Pantages Condominiums advertised the development through the slogan "*un*rent and invest in yourself." Renting is positioned as an illogical choice, the opposite to home ownership. The notion of investing in oneself

FIGURE 3   *Zero interest.* Billboard for Connect Condominiums,
King Street West, Toronto.

invokes the entrepreneurial, self-sufficient urban citizen. In some cases,
condominiums are marketed explicitly to investors, emphasizing the capital
accumulation features of condominium ownership. Other developers offer
programs that allow buyers to put a small down payment on a condominium, rent another apartment from the developer until occupancy, and put

50 percent of that rent towards a greater down payment. Turning "rent into ownership" assumes the natural hierarchy of tenure and a progression along the natural course.

In a 2006 advertisement for Loggia Condominiums, the text assures prospective buyers that they will have "Real Neighbours": "At Loggia you don't need to worry that your neighbour is a renter or that a group of investors owns half your floor. Our homeowners are real people who know real value when they see it." Although the "neighbours" pictured in the advertisement are a diverse group across age, gender, and ethnicity, they have one thing in common: they are not renters. Embedded in these texts are deep-rooted assumptions about the intrinsic superiority of ownership and, indeed, of owners themselves. Renters and investors are not, by definition, neighbourly and are therefore undesirable in this type of community. This seems to draw upon an implicit assumption that owners have a desire for community and stability and that renters are the antithesis of such a formation. Moreover, these advertisements support the notion that the transition from renting to ownership is a natural evolutionary process.

The news media also report stories of "progress" from renting to owning through the condominium market:

Adam Zimmerman and Sharon Vokey's rented Ottawa condominium was small and prone to flooding. But when their landlord put it up for sale, the couple saw an opportunity to make the transition from renters to buyers. They were disappointed, however, when the quick, private deal they had hoped for evaporated and they came out on the losing end of a bidding war. The new owner offered to keep them on as tenants, but after that taste of near-home ownership, there was no going back. "We weren't about to pay his mortgage," Mr. Zimmerman said. In little more than a week, Mr. Zimmerman and Ms. Vokey struck a deal on a $155,000, two-bedroom condo in Ottawa's South Keys. Mr. Zimmerman and Ms. Vokey are among a growing number of young Canadians turning to condominiums for their first foray into residential real estate. (Leitch 2004, B8)

Although Adatia wasn't making a great deal of money when he bought, he didn't want to pay rent. If he lost his job, he reasoned he could always rent out his unit to cover his mortgage payments. Today, with the softening rental market, he figures a smarter option would be to sell. And if Adatia put his unit up for sale, he'd make a tidy profit. Today his Queen's Quay property would go for around $250,000 – about $100,000 more than what he paid for it. In retrospect, a wise investment decision for a then-22-year-old. (Prashad 2004, P1)

These stories, wherein renters decide to take a risk on ownership (despite the potential for floods or the possible inability to make mortgage payments) and are vindicated as wise investors, illustrate how these property narratives are positioned as commonsensical and taken-for-granted. Moreover, the condominium purchaser is portrayed as a smart businessperson, entrepreneurial and pioneering in her or his actions and intentions, and the moral of the story is that these kinds of choices will pay off. This discourse recalls the Thatcher government's strategy of privatizing council estates in the UK in the 1980s through the extension of home ownership to tenants, a process explicitly designed to promote a property-owning democracy with individuals positioned as private or personal capitalists (Forrest, Murie, and Williams 1990).

This particular version of the citizen-subject meshes well with the desired subject under neoliberal forms of governmentality (N. Rose 1996; Isin 1999; Dean 1999). The condominium purchaser seems to fulfill a vision of the self-sufficient and self-actualizing citizen through her or his financial discipline, autonomous decision making, and responsible shouldering of the duties of home ownership. Gentrification scholars Rowland Atkinson and Sarah Blandy (2007, 451) summarize this clearly: "The actions of homeowners may therefore be interpreted as those of sovereign consumers seeking both free and maximized exchanges, celebrating personal autonomy and upward trajectories of unimpeded equity growth." While it is true that responsibility and financial security have always been a part of the pro-ownership culture of property, the emphasis on profit making, risk taking, and entrepreneurialism in the world of condominium ownership is highly suggestive of the penetration of neoliberal rationales into the morality of home ownership.

A Growing Anti-Rent Culture

The notion that the condominium constitutes a wise investment that the disciplined housing consumer will actively choose is given additional support by an escalating stigma against rental tenure. This stigma is produced both through an ideological apparatus, including the media, and through legislation that supports the dominant morality of property. In Ontario, both provincial and municipal policies support owner occupation over rental tenure. Provincial legislation has worked to limit the rights of tenants to fair rent and eviction processes. The Ontario Tenant Protection Act, enacted by the right-wing government of Ontario premier Mike Harris in 1997, was said to be ironically named because it actually increased the powers of landlords to evict tenants and raise rents, for example, through the vacancy decontrol statute, wherein rent control was eliminated upon the turnover of a rent-controlled unit to a new tenant (Slater 2004a; Skaburskis and Mok 2000). The Residential Tenancies Act replaced the Tenant Protection Act in January 2007. The new legislation restores some tenant protections but notably continues to allow all buildings built after 1991 to remain exempt from rent control guidelines. This means that the majority of Toronto's rented condominium units will be rented at market rates. These policies help shape the markedly divergent housing worlds of owners and renters in Canada: on average, owners have twice the income of renters, and twice as many renters as owners live in inadequate housing (Hulchanski and Shapcott 2004).

Local support for gentrification efforts also reflects (and indeed reproduces) a negative attitude towards rental tenure and renters. Critical urban scholars note that city governments are actively encouraging gentrification in an effort to bring homeowners back downtown (Slater 2004a; Hackworth and Smith 2001). This involves intervening with strategies designed to limit rental options and to stigmatize areas with a high percentage of rented dwellings. In American cities, economist Michael Turk (2004) documents a precipitous decline in the construction of new rental housing and the correlated decline in affordable rental accommodation over the past three decades. Geographers Jason Hackworth and Neil Smith (2001) examine various stages of gentrification and note that, through earlier phases of gentrification, the state had some measures to restrict development in particular neighbourhoods. They maintain that, as both the institutions of the welfare state and the power of community opposition have declined, states have become more directly involved in encouraging gentrification. Cities increasingly depend upon the revenue generated by the gentrification of poor and marginal neighbourhoods and have thus partnered with capital to "facilitate a rapid expansion of the process" (Hackworth and Smith 2001, 470). Simultaneously, the act of pushing those most likely to oppose gentrification, like renters, further out of the city means that opposition has become fragmented and easy to ignore.

Popular narratives also marginalize rent-dominated areas by positioning them as blighted and unstable. In contrast, home ownership is viewed as the uncontested means to renew poor neighbourhoods, legitimating the implementation of home ownership initiatives or the conversion of rental stock to condominiums. In American cities, gentrification itself is becoming the standard measure of a city's success in responding to urban fiscal crises such as deindustrialization and disinvestments (Turk 2004).

In Toronto, the first high-rise rental apartment wave in the 1960s and 1970s was envisioned primarily as a source of housing for middle-class, childless young professionals. For example, St. James Town was advertised as an adult-only community and used the slogan "where there's more to living than just a place to live" to signal its recreational amenities and shopping facilities. Indeed, it lived up to this vision for a number of years, being described in the media as a "frolicking" community of twenty-something professionals (Darby 1969). A number of core areas continue to have well-maintained, expensive, and highly desirable rental buildings. Unfortunately, other developments, including St. James Town, fell into disrepair and have become deeply stigmatized as ghettoes for low-income, racialized urban dwellers. Negative media coverage of crime and other social problems in these areas has contributed to rental buildings receiving a bad reputation in Toronto; indeed, opposition to the development of new rental apartment buildings is often based on the tenure status of the buildings rather than on other issues, such as height or density (Choko and Harris 1990). In this context, there is very little political will to subsidize new construction of rental housing. However, there is growing political will to facilitate gentrification and private home ownership.

Geographer Tom Slater (2004a) examines the process of "municipally managed gentrification" in the Toronto neighbourhood of Parkdale, an area that had fallen into disregard due to the presence of group homes, recent immigrants, deinstitutionalized psychiatric survivors from the nearby Centre for Addiction and Mental Health, and the actions (or inactions) of slum landlords who run the many rooming houses and high-rise rental apartment buildings. In recent years, the city has expressed a desire to encourage social mix and to restore balanced housing opportunities (Slater 2004a). This is supported through city planning discourses that label the rent-dominated area as having an unhealthy demographic balance. The area is being rezoned to limit the division of homes into rooming houses. The idea is to encourage gentrifiers to buy the single-family homes in this neighbourhood, thus increasing the number of families and owner-occupiers. As in American cities, this new strategy of municipally managed gentrification contrasts with earlier attempts by the city to protect vulnerable housing populations from displacement.

There has been some debate in Ontario and in Toronto about how best to protect the city's rental housing stock, and measures include limitations on the conversion of rental buildings to condominiums as well as on the demolition and redevelopment of rental properties (see Hulchanski 2006). However, landlord associations have challenged these measures through the Ontario Municipal Board, arguing for their rights to convert their properties to their highest and best use in order to maximize their potential value (Federation of Rental-Housing Providers of Ontario 2005). The landlord associations argue that increasing the overall supply of housing in any tenure form will lead to lower housing prices, which will benefit all housing consumers, even those with low incomes.[5] This trickle-down economics-based theory of housing resonates with some of the interview responses from condominium developers, wherein developers explicitly positioned condominiums as affordable housing.

> I see the major problem that we're having in this market is that the low-rise industry, which is mostly single-family homes, has gone up exponentially. Specifically, I'm talking just the downtown core, which means that if a person wanted to buy a house and they're a starter family, for $500,000, you could get nothing in the city for $500,000. So the only other chance that they have is to get into the condominium side. And so that's what we're seeing, is a lot of people that are priced out of the housing market are moving into the condominium side. And that's why, in the past last quarter, you saw that there's a dip in low-rise sales, and there was an increase in multi-family sales, primarily for this reason ... because the single-family home had gotten so high that these people had started to move into the residential on the multi-family side. To make it more affordable for them to buy. *(Developer interview, 5 July 2005)*

> The advantages have a lot to do with providing affordable housing, en masse. Whether we can sort of specify what's a pro or what's a con, it's part of housing stock. It's housing stock in the city, especially when you're looking at intensifying urban centres so you want to have people live in dense urban centres, you need to house them. You need an alternate to single-family housing, and condominiums make sense. *(Developer interview, 21 June 2005)*

In Canada, affordable housing is defined by the Canada Mortgage and Housing Corporation (CMHC) as housing that does not cost more than 30 percent of income. CMHC notes, however, that housing providers and advocacy organizations tend to use a wider definition of affordable housing that often includes a whole set of housing options, including subsidized housing and non-profit housing. While condominiums are a reasonably priced home ownership option in Toronto, and they do contribute to the stock of rental housing, issues around affordable rental accommodation, alternative tenures, and social housing are falling off the agenda as condominiums are increasing in prominence in the city's housing market. If condominiums offer an abundant supply of ostensibly affordable housing,[6] then there may be little incentive to promote subsidized, rent-geared-to-income, or other tenures. Although Canadian housing scholar David Hulchanski (2006) has illustrated that increasing home ownership options does not cause a trickle-down effect that benefits rental housing consumers, condominiums continue to be pushed as an overall boon to Toronto's housing options.

This seems to articulate with a neoliberal philosophy of self-sufficiency and individual responsibility, combined with a rationality that cedes responsibility for affordable housing to the private market. Under neoliberal governance, the individual is increasingly held responsible for her or his own welfare in areas where the state once intervened to share the responsibility of social and economic well-being (Isin 1999). In the area of housing, the availability of condominiums, and their labelling as affordable, mean that the individual can now be expected to provide her or his own housing without state assistance.

Developers, advertisers, and news media both shape and draw upon common-sense narratives and the dominant culture of property to promote condominium ownership. Indeed, these agents actively shape this culture by positioning condominium ownership as beneficial to housing consumers and to a city facing a potential housing shortage over the next two decades. In the context of neoliberal urban revitalization agendas, these stories about condominium tenure function to secure a set of property relations – particularly the superiority of ownership over renting – that enables the continued legitimization of neoliberal policy prescriptions by not questioning either the definition of highest and best use as private ownership or the notion that homeowners are the most desirable citizens for the revitalized city. Although the support for home ownership in Toronto pre-dates neoliberalization, the massive numbers of condominiums that can be built

on relatively little land literally create fresh space for capital flows to circulate in pursuit of faster profits in the secondary real estate sector (Lefebvre
2003) – the sector that absorbs the flow of capital when the potential for
industrial production slows down. The discourses of powerful city building
agents normalize this process by facilitating, through a process that Foucault (1997) describes as both individual discipline and group regulation,
the filtering of neoliberal ideals pertaining to the ideals of home ownership.

Buying into the Neoliberal City?
How is the entrepreneurial urban citizen differentiated across sites such as
gender, race, ethnicity, age, and so on? Such differences have an impact on
the ways in which condominium ownership is enacted and experienced.
Moreover, dominant discourses will actively draw upon such differences to
literally and symbolically sell condominiums to housing consumers and to
the city. In particular, I am interested here in the ways in which gendered
narratives of freedom, empowerment, and autonomy through home ownership are mobilized to legitimate condominium development as progressive,
equitable, and emancipatory.

Women and Housing Policy in Canada
Gender ideologies and changing gender relations have always contributed
to the spatial structure of the city (Darke 1996; England 1991; Mackenzie
and Rose 1983), especially with respect to suburbanization in North America, but little has been said about how gender, as a social construct, is shaping (and is shaped by) issues of tenure change in the context of new-build
gentrification in postindustrial cities. More than two decades of quantita-
tive and qualitative research into women's position within the Canadian
housing market have produced a picture of entrenched, systemic disadvantage (Klodawsky and Mackenzie 1987; McClain and Doyle 1984; Novac
1990, 1995, 1996; Wekerle 1997). Although condominium ownership may
be altering this picture somewhat for professional women in urban centres,
there are still critical challenges facing women with respect to housing. In a
1984 article, Wekerle (146) observed: "Due to their low income, families
headed by women are more likely to live in central cities, to rent rather than
own, and to reside in public housing." Thirteen years later, Wekerle (1997)
detailed a strikingly similar picture in Canada, noting women's lower than
average home ownership rates due to low income, women's disproportion-
ate dependency on social assistance, the concentration of women in social
housing and the low-end rental market, and women's need for alternative

forms of tenure such as co-op and non-profit housing. In 2001, fewer than half of all female-headed households (both lone parent and single female) owned their homes, compared to over two-thirds of households in general (CMHC 2001). This reality has striking long-term economic consequences for women as the net worth of family units is drastically affected by home ownership status.[7]

State support for home ownership plays a significant role in shaping the picture of women's housing disadvantage. Woman-headed households are marginalized within mainstream housing policy as their lower incomes mean that these households can rarely afford to own their own homes. Additionally, women's housing needs, whether as heads of households or members of a two-adult household, have been subsumed into what is largely a heteronormative family policy, wherein women's housing needs were considered merely a corollary of the male breadwinner's needs. Women's concentration in low-end rental and other types of alternative tenure was viewed as a transitional phase in women's housing careers rather than as a genuine social and economic pattern that deserved policy consideration. Therefore, housing access has been tied to marital or parental relations for women, and policy has not considered their needs in a distinct manner (Chouinard 2006; Novac 1995).

Gender and Condominium Ownership

For some time, women, especially lone-parent professional women, have been a significant group of condominium purchasers, as geographer Damaris Rose (1984) noted in the context of Montreal. More recently, in major Canadian urban centres like Toronto, Vancouver, Montreal, and Calgary, where condominiums have become increasingly available over the past ten years, single women have emerged as a significant demographic in the ownership market, perhaps for the first time in Canadian housing history.

Condominium developers have not overlooked this socio-economic phenomenon, and they actively seek out this market for their projects. Their narratives reflect gender stereotypes as well as an awareness of demographic trends for a particular subset of relatively privileged young, urban professional women. Most condominium advertisements feature women, portrayed either as potential purchasers or as sexualized objects to promote a particular aspect of the development.[8] The news media have been especially fascinated with the rise of the young woman condominium buyer and, perhaps more than developers or their advertisements, have produced gendered narratives of independence and autonomy through home ownership.

These ideas about gender can be conceptualized as a constitutive element of the process of new-build gentrification. It is particularly important to analyze them because they remind urban scholars that, although ideas about gender and tenure may intersect with class, they are not reducible to class. As Fincher (2004, 329) argues with regard to the narratives of developers in Melbourne, "knowing these narratives is important, because they help to create (along with local economic and regulatory conditions) the forms of housing that are imagined and therefore are built."

Condominium developers draw on a variety of ideas about gender relations and women's urban lives in discussing women's interest in condominium ownership. These themes include women's changing family and labour market roles and women's "natural" propensity to consider the future in terms of their stability and security. Their characterizations positioned women as knowledgeable, rational, and logical. Developers based their comments on both anecdotal observations and the great deal of statistical information and consumer feedback that they typically gather through private research firms. Both of these types of knowledge shape their ideas about their condominium purchasers' identities and experiences and shape a fairly consistent narrative about the natural suitability of condominium ownership for young or single women.

> I think it's much more difficult being a woman today than it was, say, thirty years ago. 'Cause there's all these mixed issues of, you know, do you become a family individual? Do you become a professional? There's just so many different rifts. The reality is women are getting married, or generally people are getting married, at an older age. By the time someone is out of school, say twenty-five, work[s] for three years, four years, hitting close to thirty, they're ready to buy a place. *(Developer interview, 21 June 2005)*

In this description, condominiums seem to function as a way of resolving (within a largely heteronormative and middle-class range of options) the difficulties of being a woman in confusing times. Women can get married later but still become homeowners through a condominium purchase.

> I'm just sort of hypothesizing here. It would seem to me that young men would tend to rent, and buy when they were in some sort of long-term relationship. Whereas I think women will buy

without waiting for the relationship. *(Developer interview, 18 June 2005)*

It's now accepted that women are just making the decision and are financially independent enough to go ahead and buy housing, and not actually wait for marriage, or have to stay with their families, and not venture out on their own ... But it is interesting how single women do seem to be getting a leg up in terms of wealth and equity accumulation over men, and I think it might be, I think it might be something related to – sounds almost stereotypical – it's a bit biased – but I think women are a bit more – think more long term about where they're going and preparing for the future. And so they think about, "Okay, what am I doing now? Where am I going to be in ten years? I really should start thinking about equity and building a nest egg." And I think that might be one of the reasons why. They're just prone to thinking about the future more. *(Developer interview, 19 July 2005)*

Interestingly, these developers expressed the idea that women were more rational, thoughtful, economically savvy, and forward thinking than their male counterparts. While this might be, in part, a narrative targeted at a feminist researcher, it is also reproduced in and for other sources, such as the news media. The invocation of these subject positions suggests that there is a particular subset of gendered stereotypes that is purposefully mobilized to explain and promote women's condominium purchasing – the playful, immature, commitment-phobic, twenty-something male professional versus the logical, thirty-something, stability-seeking young female professional.

The news media have also enthusiastically picked up on the theme of condominium ownership as a form of empowerment for young or single women. In many cases, reporting on condominium-related issues is little more than editorial content designed to promote particular developments; often, developers actually write the articles that appear in the condominium sections of major newspapers. Thus, there is a built-in narrative bias. In this context, the media have noted that increasing numbers of women are choosing to own their homes and are outpacing men as homebuyers across Canada ("Toronto Condo Sales" 2006; Wong 2004; Cordileone 2002; Prashad 2004).[9] For women, buying a condominium is portrayed as an assertion of female independence, an eschewing of traditional patterns of marriage, and a claiming of economic power as members of the new professional middle class.

"I've noticed single women buy earlier in life," says Perala [a real estate agent]. Men tend to live at home longer and often don't buy until their thirties, she says, adding that most wait until they're in relationships to purchase property. Perala processes 20 to 35 mortgages per month and says about 5 per cent of her clients are young single men, compared to about 20 per cent who are single women. (Prashad 2004, B8)

Barry Lyon, a leading market analyst in Toronto for the downtown area, put it this way: "Tradition is biting the dust. They're not waiting for Mr. Right. They're in no rush to get married but they want to set up their homes. Women feel empowered now and they're breaking out of the old moulds." He said women are looking for security in a home. They want to put down roots and they want a safe environment to live in and see condos as a low-risk. And because condo living is an urban phenomenon, Lyon said, they naturally buy downtown. Typically in their 30s and 40s, Lyon said this group of buyers earn good salaries. Unlike most single men in the same age group, he said they tend to avoid shared living arrangements, preferring freedom and privacy ... "I tell you they've got a lot of money. Single women are free now and they can do what they want," said Linda Mitchell, Monarch's sales and marketing vice-president for high-rise construction. (Cordileone 2002, O1)

Cowan [a real estate agent] says that single men tend to pay under $200,000 for their condos and buy a one-bedroom unit, with one bathroom and one parking spot. After a few years, they'll often flip it and sell the unit for a profit. Perala [a real estate agent] adds no matter why men buy their first home, once they do, they're hooked. "Once they've tasted homeownership, they buy again," she says. Men either trade up and buy a larger home, or they'll buy another property for investment purposes, adds Perala. (Prashad 2004, B8)

Both developers' narratives and the stories reported by the news media construct a consistent image of the woman condominium purchaser as both autonomous and independent as well as economically rational and self-sufficient. Condominium ownership is thus seen as an expression of women's economic freedom and an assertion of their liberation from the traditional patriarchal confines of marriage and family. However, this is a temporally limited freedom as these narratives do not attempt to disrupt notions of the natural life course, wherein women will eventually marry and have children. These media and developer narratives express similar gender ideologies about women's desire for independence and stability in the home in contrast to young men's reticence about committing to home ownership at a young age. But these narratives also belie the notion that the condominium industry challenges traditional gender ideologies because they continue to emphasize women's need for financial security and personal safety, while noting that adventurous men will seek profits by flipping their condominiums. Women are seen as rational, long-term investors, while men are seen as risk-taking, profit-seeking capitalists.

For both women and men, however, freedom from renting and the potential for profits are significant factors in positioning the condominium buyer as an appropriate citizen of the revitalized city. Both are thus situated within the paradigm of capitalist accumulation. This illustrates the contingency and variability, but also the fundamental stability, of gendered constructs in a way that also illuminates the heterogeneity of neoliberal rationality, which is flexible enough to absorb seemingly contradictory ideas about gender relations in ways that still function to facilitate the rise of the entrepreneurial, propertied citizen. In analyzing the particular subject positions that arise or are mediated through urban revitalization projects, it is necessary to reject the inevitability of singular narratives and to acknowledge that the discursive and the material interlock to structure particular outcomes (Larner and LeHeron 2002). Thus, women's participation in the condominium market produces, and is produced by, multiple narratives with both social and economic dimensions. The constitution of particular identities as dominant is denaturalized by illustrating that identity formation, or the reshaping of forms of subjectivity, is not simply a response or effect of political economic shifts; rather, invoking specific identities and subjectivities is an integral part of the process of restructuring (Larner 1997). In this process, economic and cultural imperatives may be contradictory, such that gender stereotypes may be temporarily reversed or reworked in ways that facilitate the economic goals of creating an enterprise culture (Katz 2005; N. Rose 1996).[10]

This culture can only be attained through the enterprising activities and choices of autonomous individuals. Nikolas Rose (1996, 151) suggests that this enterprise culture accorded a vital political value to a certain image of the human being ... This image of an "enterprising self" was so potent because it was not an idiosyncratic obsession of the right ... It resonated with basic presuppositions concerning the contemporary human being ... The self is to be a subjective being, it is to aspire to autonomy, it is to strive for personal fulfillment ... it is to interpret its reality and destiny as a matter of individual responsibility, it is to find meaning in existence by shaping its life through acts of choice.

The governance of this self involves particular ways of acting upon the subject. Foucault (1982) sought to link these practices bearing on the self to forms of power by positing that power was not used to repress subjectivity but to create subjects who will govern themselves. In this context, narratives about home ownership through the condominium market function as a neoliberal morality tale about the wisdom of investing in home ownership at an early age. This morality tale can be seen as a normalizing (disciplinary and regulatory) rationality that obtains its power through the production of self-governing, enterprising selves.

Complicating this story about tenure and subjectivity is a feminist critique of gender inequality in liberal democracies. Feminists argued that the white, male property owner at the centre of notions of democracy acted as the basis for the exclusion of all other groups from the spaces and practices of democracy (Pateman 1989; Marston and Mitchell 2004). In this context, where participation was predicated upon property ownership, and property ownership was available only to white bourgeois men, women were inevitably excluded. Geographer Jane Darke (1996) suggests that urbanization during the Industrial Revolution may have intensified the rule of patriarchy because the city is inherently divided into pieces of private property. Not incidentally, in Anglo societies, women were also considered to be the property of men. In a somewhat ironic twist, the contemporary postindustrial city has become a place where private property ownership is positioned as a way of achieving gender equality.

Also ironic is the way that feminist-inflected discourses about women's autonomy, independence, and fulfillment in the city intersect with, or are co-opted into, neoliberal notions of autonomy and freedom to promote privatization and real estate investment. Neoliberal urbanism is well positioned to take advantage of, and commodify, these feminist themes as it strives to promote an entrepreneurial culture in the city and to mobilize enterprising urban citizens. Much as neoliberalism co-opts other progressive discourses,

such as ideas around civil society and radical democracy (see Bevir and
Rhodes 2006), and puts them to work in the service of goals such as privatization and commodification, it here uses feminist ideals to position condominium development as serving women's needs. The enterprising self is
produced through gendered notions of fulfillment, freedom, responsibility, and choice connected to private home ownership. To the contrary,
feminist critiques of women's exclusion and disadvantage in the housing
system and in the city as a whole do not, below the surface level, mesh with
neoliberal goals.

Everyday Meanings of Condominium Ownership

It is not sufficient to solely examine the role of women in gentrification;
rather, it is necessary to understand some of the many ways that gender, as
a social construct, works to shape the contemporary city. Ideas about gender
roles and gender relations, (somewhat) reworked and re-purposed, play a
constitutive role in the process of urban revitalization through condominium development. These narratives also produce the gender effects that they
narrate. Thus we can ask, how do these stories become hegemonic, and to
what extent do they shape the everyday experiences of tenure for women?
Geographer Liz Bondi (1991) argues that gentrification research tends to
view class as a social relation while treating gender as an a priori category.
Hence we must also consider how the creation of new home ownership opportunities, and the specific mobilization of gender ideologies to rationalize
this process, work to constitute gendered identities at a specific political-
economic moment.

This analysis raises a critical tension. On the one hand, the rise of condominium ownership for young or single women seems to fulfill in part the
(primarily liberal) feminist goal of encouraging women's independent control over assets and women's access to institutions (such as home ownership) that might mitigate the effects of lower lifetime earnings, lesser
pensions, and fewer investments or savings. On the other hand, this process
feeds into neoliberal agendas that open the city to capital accumulation
strategies and that define the project of women's emancipation in purely
capitalist economic terms. In the analysis that follows, this tension is made
explicit by positioning the respondents as women who have made reason-
able choices given the social and economic constraints that they face and, at
the same time, questioning the range of choices offered and how these are
shaped by neoliberal agendas. Specifically, I ask how the meanings of condominium ownership complicate the seamless narrative of empowerment

and challenge the common-sense linkage between home ownership and stable, responsible citizenship. The experiences described by women condominium owners point to connections between the affective experiences of home ownership through condominium development and broader changes in the ways that city dwellers relate to their communities and to the city at large. These changes are important markers of the social and political transformations wrought by entrepreneurial urban restructuring and urban revitalization plans.

Connecting Ownership and Empowerment

For women owners, condominiums provide a way to gain access to the social and economic advantages of home ownership from which single women, in particular, have long been excluded (Novac 1995; Wekerle 1997). Women expressed a clear preference for owning, which was framed primarily in economic terms as a form of financial freedom and autonomy.

> I thought of moving out, I thought I should really get, should buy a place here, just as an investment. I was thinking I could go in with my parents, or do something like that. Then I thought, "Why am I going to do that? Why don't I just live there? 'Cause I want to move out anyways. And then if anything happens, if I change my mind or want to move around, I can always sell it, and make money off it, and do it that way." ... I think that would be a wiser decision, for me to actually move in, and, you know, set up my goals, and do that. That place is a huge landmark, so even if I sell it in two years, I think I'll be fine, yeah. *(Jillian, age 30, lives alone)*

> I also knew, when you're a young woman spending a hell of a lot of money, my concern was, what if I need to sell? What if it's a bad market? But I also knew from having lived there that this was a desirable place for investors. It's close to the financial district, and also to King West. So there's a lot of people who are coming to the city for a year or two that would probably rent there. *(Ava, age 32, lives alone)*

Jillian and Ava clearly considered the investment aspect of the condominium purchase, rationalizing the risk by suggesting that there would be resale value in their properties. Jillian simultaneously connects this decision to her independence from her parents.

> I didn't buy it because I want to make money off of it. It's primarily
> my home, that's the number one reason. The investment side of it
> is important in the sense that it gives me more to bring to – like if
> I ever got into a relationship and wanted to bring that, that would
> be something that I could contribute. It's my own security blanket
> for future things. *(Amanda, age 29, lives alone)*

> I think it is stability, both long-term investment, and stability.
> Which I think are kind of the same thing, because, I mean, no
> matter what happens in my life, I always have my home. And even
> if I lose my job, and I end a relationship, and I end this and that
> and that, and everything else falls apart, I still have my home.
> *(Naomi, age 29, lives alone)*

Amanda and Naomi acknowledge the importance of financial investment in terms of long-term security. They also connect this to the desire for personal stability through home ownership. In these cases, stability is conflated with, or tied to, financial security.

As geographer Robin Dowling (1998) found in her study of homeowners in British Columbia, women often conceptualize the value of their homes in financial, not just social, terms, despite gendered stereotypes that would seem to suggest that women are more concerned with the home as the centre of family life. In my study, it seems that women condominium owners' narratives are shaped by, or reflect, the dominant culture of property that values and rewards home ownership as a wise financial decision and as an important step towards economic security or independence. Read against a shift towards neoliberal forms of urban governance, this suggests that the neoliberal emphasis on achieving personal economic security is translated into women's everyday lives through condominium ownership.

Few of these stories questioned the potential contradictions in defining freedom as life-long mortgage debt, which certainly reflects the dominant culture of property. Nonetheless, some of the women interviewed expressed concern over the difficulties of paying a mortgage, especially as single women. For example, Jillian told me:

> I didn't want to kind of live outside my budget, and live outside
> my means, and live for my mortgage. I didn't want to do that,
> because, you know, you have friends who buy beautiful condos,
> live by themselves, and they eat cereal. *(Jillian, age 30, single)*

In general, the parameters of empowerment are defined in economic terms. Freedom is achieved through the commodification of the home and the act of becoming a housing consumer. Viewed through a feminist lens that questions the ways in which women's freedom is constructed, the positive valuation of home ownership as independence, autonomy, and freedom suggests that women's independence is being recast as a function of their control over the private sphere of the home, at least financially. Although from a liberal feminist perspective this is a positive development, it is problematic to assume that women's emancipation can be found by women "buying into" one of the foundational structures of capitalist patriarchy, within a culture that still draws heavily upon sexist ideologies about women's roles, desires, and life courses.

There is a tension, however, between this interpretation and the possibility that home ownership at an early age, particularly within a culture that rewards home ownership and effectively punishes alternative tenures, may release women from one dimension of patriarchal control. Feminist housing scholars note that the relative poverty or comfort of senior women is often tied to their tenure status; there are serious concerns about women's ability to provide for themselves without the investment of home ownership (Wekerle 1997; Novac 1995). The desire for the benefits of home ownership on the part of those women who are able to attain it reflects a rational response to the knowledge that they cannot rely on a man, or the state, to take care of them. It may speak to an awareness of women's precarious economic status (especially single women), particularly in the realm of housing, and a willingness and ability to mitigate this vulnerability through the process of building equity and accumulating wealth for old age.

However, patriarchy does not operate solely at the scale of the household or the family, nor does financial independence completely break down normative gender roles and relations. Patriarchy interlocks here with neoliberal urbanism to structure a set of choices for women that defines freedom in economic terms as a process of wealth accumulation. I certainly cannot critique the individual choices of women condominium buyers to become homeowners when presented with the opportunity; however, the narratives point to the ways that women are drawn into the neoliberal revitalization project through normalizing tactics that discipline the self into acting as a rational consumer who assumes sole responsibility for her financial well-being. What is hidden in the interpretation of this move as freedom from patriarchal family relations is the ability of the state to step aside and evade responsibility for redistributing the wealth accumulated by the few who take this step. The flip side of the story of autonomy and individual responsibility for women condominium owners is the notion that those who cannot or do not behave in this way are to blame for their own misfortune (Isin 1998). This certainly does not articulate with a feminist vision of housing equality or the right to the city. The privileging of the wealth accumulation functions of home ownership, coupled with an ethic of individualism, elides the integral equity dimensions of feminist arguments.

"Moving Up" and the Hierarchy of Tenure

In a pro-ownership culture of property, the act of buying a condominium represents a transition that allows the buyer to move perceptibly up the hierarchy of tenure, which functions as a developmental, normative, and axiological scale. My respondents conceptualized the metamorphosis from renter to owner as a key moment in the attainment of adulthood, of financial responsibility, and of freedom.

> I don't think I'd ever go back to renting. It just feels so much better to invest in something that you're going to get your money out of later, and then some, and that you just have a lot more freedom with, that you can do a lot more to and a lot more with than you would bother investing in somewhere that you were renting. So, yeah, I'd say it's really important. I think, too, at my stage of life – or however you put it – I think it's kind of ridiculous to be renting, so it means a lot. *(Caitlin, age 31, lives alone)*

Caitlin clearly views home ownership as a necessary step in the life course; she also connects it to freedom and control over her own space. Like Maya and Colleen below, Caitlin explicitly contrasts owning and renting to make the point that ownership is a logical and financially responsible move.

> Well, sort of from a financial management point of view it makes more sense to put your money into equity in your own place. You're going to get something out of it. If you rent, it's not getting you – you're not building anything. *(Maya, age 30, lives alone)*

> I'm not really planning to make a lot of money, but I feel like I can't really lose. I mean with rent, I was getting – there was no chance of anything. Rent was a black hole, I threw my money away, I burnt my money. With my condo, depending on how long I stay,

and looking at the location where I am, it's never going to go
down. *(Colleen, age 28, lives alone)*

Colleen and Maya construct the move to owning as a freeing step by portraying renting as financially irresponsible. Below, Amanda and April explicitly connect the transition to ownership with freedom and fulfillment.

It's very freeing to go from renting to owning. *(Amanda, age 29,
lives alone)*

I feel good. Yeah. It's, I mean, you see a mortgage payment coming
out every week, since I pay mine weekly, but it's okay, because it's
mine. Whereas, like I say, when I lived in Japan or any other city
– Ottawa, Toronto, Vancouver, Victoria – you know, every month
you'd write that cheque or you'd pay your rent and you'd just be
like, "Ugh! Ouch! Making somebody else rich." It's more fulfilling,
yeah. *(April, age 37, lives alone)*

Renting is understood as irrational, ridiculous, and perhaps even painful.
Ownership, on the other hand, is a step towards freedom or fulfillment of
some kind. The transition to ownership, moreover, is viewed as a necessary
stage in the life course that marks a move towards adulthood.

I didn't want to ask my parents to co-sign. I wanted to do it on my
own. If I couldn't do it on my own, then I wasn't ready. So I went to
the bank, and to be honest anyone can get a mortgage these days
... And it's easy and it's great, for young people and young women
especially. And I think you need confidence in yourself to actually
say, "This is what I want to do." Yes, it's scary, but if you're at that
age where you feel you can move forward with your life, like I did,
it's a major challenge, but I think you can do it. Nothing to hold
you back, really. *(Jillian, age 30, lives alone)*

I felt really, really independent. And there's a lot of responsibility
that goes with it, and it's just, I don't know, I felt more adult, I
guess. *(Alicia, age 30, lives alone)*

Jillian and Alicia invoke independence, confidence, responsibility, and adulthood. Jillian constructs her move from her parents' home to condominium

ownership as a challenge that she overcame, one that other young women should be able to take on.[11] Condominium ownership here serves as a formative developmental experience. Sandra and Colleen, in the comments below, note the importance of taking this step as individuals rather than relying on others. Condominium ownership is, for these women, a self-actualizing moment:

> It's also, like sometimes I have a bit of a love-hate relationship with my condo, because it means I can't just take off and live in New Zealand for a year or something like that. But it's kind of a little bit of a step towards adulthood. You feel more like a responsible human being when you have your own place and stuff like that, so. Not that there aren't plenty of responsible renters, but you know it was just sort of a ... You know when I first bought it, when I first took possession, I came here by myself, the first day, and the entire place was empty. And I just, I sat down on the floor, and I was like, "Holy crap." But it was just, like an overwhelming feeling, but also a really fantastic feeling of knowing, "I have my own place, this place is mine." So from that perspective it's pretty cool. And just not relying on other people. *(Sandra, age 28, lives alone)*

> I'm proud of it. I'm proud that I have something that's my own, that I can say that I've done it all by myself, I didn't get help from anybody. I like to be able to make it on my own. And renting – not only was it a waste of money, but I just felt like I wasn't going anywhere. I still felt very much like I was still – you know, I had temporary furniture, nothing matched, it was the yard sale put-togethers, I felt very much like a student, and not very much like a grown-up. *(Colleen, age 28, lives alone)*

Naomi literally merged condominium ownership with adulthood when she bought her first condominium on her eighteenth birthday. Her self-described "obsession" with owning her own home superseded other formative events in young adulthood, like buying a car or going to university:

> I mean, I bought my first condo when I was eighteen, and I was – I literally had to wait, I had to get them to wait four days until my birthday came, so that I could sign the legal papers. If you're under eighteen, it's not legal. So I've always wanted to own my own

> home. I was single when I bought the first place, and I was just
> like, my mom was like, "You don't need to buy a place, you're only
> eighteen, you're gonna go to university, you're gonna have all this
> stuff going on." I'm like, "Nope, wanna buy a house." So I saved up
> for years, and it was such a focus. I was just obsessed. *(Naomi, age
> 29, lives alone)*

All of these comments are striking in their almost seamless reflection of
a historical (and still prevailing) morality of property wherein private property ownership, and its exchange, are seen as essential to the development of
the self as a free actor (Blomley 2004).[12] The importance of private property
in neoliberal economic agendas suggests that the link between private property ownership and the actualization of individual will is still highly pertin-
ent. However, this link was developed in a time when women had few
property-related rights in the West. So how can we conceptualize the formation of gendered subjects in relation to home ownership? My respondents' narratives suggest that, in terms of the gendered dimensions of this
hierarchy of tenure, the transition to condominium ownership is a medium
through which women can "grow up" outside of a heterosexual partnership.
In becoming fulfilled through property ownership, do young, single, independent women substitute condominium ownership for marriage?

This shift can only be read as subversive within a liberal perspective that
sees women's empowerment occurring within existing social, political, and
economic structures. Freedom through property ownership articulates with
neoliberal rationality in the linking of personal fulfillment with the taking of
individual responsibility for financial stability (Isin 1999). Atkinson and
Blandy (2007, 451) connect neoliberalism directly to home ownership,
arguing:

> Its [i.e., neoliberalism's] triumph as an ideology has been to dominate the
> understanding of home as a means of exchange and economic self-interest
> while connecting with deep social needs for predictability and security, to
> say nothing of the escape from the servitude and economic "irrationality" of
> renting.

In experiencing or expressing a sense of freedom, fulfillment, and independence through the transition to condominium ownership, women condominium owners are inducted into an entrepreneurial regime that is based
on an ideal autonomous, enterprising, rational citizen-subject. Situating

this experience within a patriarchal context that has limited women's rights and autonomy with respect to private property, however, suggests that we should not deny the potential benefits that some women may accrue from condominium ownership, including a measure of independence and fulfillment in daily life. Nonetheless, the particular contours of this independence and fulfillment are determined and policed by a neoliberal rationality that regulates and sustains the normativity within these ideals across differences such as gender. Moreover, it works to stratify women across class and, likely, race, ethnicity, and ability as well, in that these ideals are attainable only for those who have the financial means to buy property in the first place.

Ownership "Lite"
One of the normative dimensions of home ownership can be seen in the connection between home ownership and social and political responsibility. How are the responsibilities of ownership understood and experienced by women condominium owners? Ownership involves rites of property, or acts and rituals that mark one as a homeowner (Milner 1993). These are tied to a morality of property that views ownership as a natural improvement over other tenure structures and that assumes that owners themselves will continue to enact both physical and moral improvements on the landscape (Blomley 2004). However, the common ownership structure of condominiums and the payment of maintenance fees eliminate many of the (public) acts of improvement that typically mark one as a homeowner. The women interviewed here interpreted this as freedom from the responsibility of physical maintenance.

> I really like the mentality that you can close your door and you don't have to worry about anything else outside, like mowing my lawn, or washing my car in my driveway – I have no urge to do that. (Nadia, age 25, lives alone)

> I think mostly for me it's about not having to do any maintenance. Sort of having the freedom to do what you want to do. (Hope, age 29, married)

> I like to travel a lot, and having the condo the way it is, I can easily leave it for a week, two weeks, three weeks at a time and not worry about needing to maintain it or anything besides watering plants, but that's a huge, a freeing thing. (Amanda, age 29, lives alone)

Nadia, Hope, and Amanda connect freedom from maintenance to the freedom to pursue other lifestyle choices.

> It was definitely appealing that I wouldn't have to shovel my own
> walk, mow my grass, or do gardening, or, you know, take care of a
> roof, all that stuff that's just a lot to deal with when you're a new
> homeowner and first moving back into the city. So I thought this
> was a good step for me. But the next step for me might be getting
> a townhouse. So you get more of a feeling of being in a house, a
> little bit more responsibility with maintenance, but not as much
> as a full [house]. *(Maya, age 30, lives alone)*

> I'm not interested in landscaping or gardening or any of those
> things, so the fact that I don't have to worry about that at all,
> and the fact that I don't have a roof that could start leaking or a
> basement that could flood, I'm not at a point where I really would
> see the benefits of having any of those things, so I don't have to
> worry about them. *(Lynn, age 28, lives alone)*

Maya and Lynn suggest that their desire for minimum maintenance is connected to this particular stage in their life courses and their housing careers in that they feel unable to deal with major physical maintenance problems.

> I don't think I could possibly handle a house on my own. I mean,
> my toilet has broken and I've fixed that. One of my windows broke
> and I fixed that. That type of thing I could totally handle. But if my
> roof started falling apart or something like that I'd be like, "Aaaah,
> oh my god!" Not to be a big sissy girl, but you know what I mean.
> It definitely is good to know that some of those major problems
> are taken care of. *(Sandra, age 28, lives alone)*

Sandra's comment about being "a big sissy girl" indicates that she is aware of gendered stereotypes around women's lack of skill with some household maintenance tasks and that she does not want to place herself in this category. Nonetheless, she assumes that she would panic if a major problem arose. For single women like Sandra, the condominium corporation steps in as a surrogate husband or father to take on those maintenance functions.

April and Molly make note of the cost of maintenance and suggest that it is preferable to pay for it through condominium fees.

Maintenance in my building, no problem. I'll pay for it. I'd rather
pay for it. You pay for it either way, so ... *(April, age 37, lives
alone)*

It's a little more stress-free. And it's, I think it's one of the reasons
we were attracted to it as a condo. Just, when we had friends who
we would see, you know, buy resale homes, and it's first of all just
renovation work to do. But also in terms of maintenance, it wasn't
something we were really ready to take on then. But definitely ...
having others do the maintenance work was a bonus, and we
have appreciated it. *(Molly, age 33, married, one child)*

Condominium ownership seems to produce, or perhaps presume, a desire for a "close-your-door-and-forget-it" relationship to property. Within
the common ownership and governance structure, monthly fees cover regular maintenance, amenities, and often some utilities; decisions about common physical improvements are made and paid for collectively. For the
women in *Sex and the Revitalized City*, especially the single women, this
aspect of condominium ownership took away some of the fear of shouldering the responsibilities of first-time home ownership. These worries
could be based in the stereotypical division along gender lines of domestic
tasks into ostensibly feminine duties such as cleaning and organizing, and
masculine tasks like repairs and property maintenance. They are also connected to cost as the difficulties of paying a mortgage, taxes, bills, and other
fees often mean that there is not much room in the budget for unexpected
repair costs.

These issues are typically framed, though, as lifestyle choices. Condominium developers and the news media also endorse condominiums as a
good choice for first-time female homeowners because of the decreased
maintenance and "worry-free" lifestyle.

People increasingly have a desire to live in an apartment rather
than a house because of convenience factors. There's a kind of a
lifestyle image associated with an apartment rather than – they're
not as much of an encumbrance, I suppose, on one's lifestyle as a
house is. You're not the person responsible for the maintenance.
Houses, you know, typically house building is a family-making
machine, whereas condos I think are viewed as kind of an
alternative. *(Developer interview, 16 June 2005)*

> Well, people just want to go home and relax. Not have to worry
> about cutting the grass. Everything is done, and everything's
> secure. *(Developer interview, 28 June 2005)*

What is not mentioned in these accounts is that, while condominium ownership reduces individual responsibility for structural maintenance, the domestic tasks typically assigned to women inside the home are not perceptibly reduced.[13] Thus, the lifestyle component of condominium maintenance, while sold as part of the package of gendered emancipation, does not really disrupt gendered household roles. For single women condominium owners, the common maintenance structure simply functions as a surrogate patriarch with respect to the gendered division of labour.

Some women condominium owners found their condominium fees undemocratic.

> I find the condo fees unfair, because it always goes up, even though
> you are no longer using the facilities. You're almost not home, but
> every year it goes higher and higher, based on how they calculate
> it. You may be conserving energy, you're never there, but some
> people use a lot of energy, leave the a/c on all day long, and you feel
> the cost, the monthly fees. *(Jaime, age 33, lives with roommate)*

Jaime points to something that Wekerle et al. (1980) found thirty years ago – that one of the major dimensions of dissatisfaction with condominium ownership is the lack of control that owners have over their maintenance payments. While the monthly fees are sold as a way of helping new homeowners to predict their monthly budgets, they can in fact rise precipitously and may not, as Jaime notes, seem to reflect an individual household's pattern of consumption. The escalating monthly fees can potentially cause hardship for owners whose budgets are stretched. This is a concern in the case of young or single women condominium owners, who may not be able to absorb rising costs. This issue points to yet another way that the story of condominium ownership as emancipation is indeed contradictory and not as seamless as proposed.

Another dimension of dissatisfaction arose with respect to limited opportunities for engaging in gardening or other outdoor work.

> I've always preferred, I've always liked the idea of having a house,
> and I would have much preferred a house because I could garden.

It would be my own space and I could do whatever I want with it.
(Stephanie, age 35, lives alone)

Because I've lived in a house before, when I was renting prior to
this, and I actually really liked maintaining the garden, and the
lawn – kind of outside, backyard idea. So the maintenance, no,
never scared me away. That's definitely not why I bought a condo.
(Caitlin, age 31, lives alone)

Stephanie and Caitlin missed being able to perform some of the public acts
of home ownership – improving their properties through the maintenance
of the landscape. Stephanie explicitly connects this to the issue of control,
one of the issues identified by Wekerle et al. (1980), who suggest that the
restrictions imposed by the common ownership structure can at times be
onerous.

Condominium tenure, it seems, attenuates women's experiences around
the physical enactments of property ownership. Moreover, many (although
not all) respondents here quite forcefully rejected any desire to engage in the
types of acts that are typically associated with the social, moral, and physical improvements ostensibly brought by private property ownership. As
Blomley (2004, 89) notes,

Programs of renewal often seek to encourage home ownership, given its
supposed effects on economic self-reliance, entrepreneurship, and community pride. Gentrification, on this account, is to be encouraged, because
it means the replacement of a marginal anticommunity (nonproperty owning, transitory, and problematized) by an active, responsible, and improving
population of homeowners.

Ironically, condominium tenure *assumes* a population of homeowners that
actively seeks to avoid the responsibility of such improvements. Thus, new-
build gentrification through condominium development may not bring
about the expected self-reliance, entrepreneurship, and community pride,
at least not in the same ways as traditional gentrification is thought to do so.

At its extreme, the "ownership 'lite'" position manifests itself in the increasing popularity of the hotel-condominium complex or spa-condominium.
These are high-end projects that incorporate hotel services such as room
service, housekeeping, concierge, spas, restaurants, and gyms. The following

excerpt from a *Toronto Star* article entitled "When Home Is a Hotel" elaborates on some of the ideals of the new ownership "lite":

> "A very international kind of person is attracted to this concept," says Baker [a real estate agent]. "It's a well-travelled group, obviously a wealthy group, who can picture using the services of a doorman and going downstairs to get a manicure or to the hairdresser. It is like hotel living." In the case of the Ritz, residents can access services at Ritz-Carlton hotels around the world. "For example, if you wanted to have flowers delivered to your brother in New York or arrange for theatre tickets in Paris, your concierge would arrange for that. You get worldwide hotel amenities at your fingertips. That's an advantage to living atop the Ritz." Buyers who don't want to live above a big hotel but want those kind of services might appreciate more intimate boutique projects like 550 Wellington, which will offer 350 condominiums and 100 hotel rooms. "There are currently a lot of condo developments in that neighbourhood (King St. W.) and the hotel aspect differentiates this project from others in the area," explains 550 Wellington developer Peter Freed. "It's geared to an upwardly mobile buyer who works hard, plays hard – and the services available carry a lot of weight in the purchase decision." (Hanes 2006)

The cosmopolitan identity imagined in this vision of city living is far removed from the traditional notion of the stable, improving, community-oriented homeowner of the liberal democracy.

For women, hotel-condominium projects seem to offer a new level of freedom, allowing them to take advantage of domestic services. These developments capture the intersection of class and gender; it is significant that the most exclusive condominiums offer freedom not just from traditionally masculinized maintenance tasks but also from feminized domestic duties. These spaces are certainly targeted at the elite condominium purchaser, and, as such, the elements of class distinction are extremely important. However, the notion that this type of condominium ownership provides gendered emancipation from the drudgery of housework and other responsibilities illustrates the ways that gender stereotypes intersect with class in order to sell this form of home ownership.

Common-sense links between home ownership and stable, responsible citizenship are complicated in the case of condominium ownership, illustrating that neoliberal visions of city life may represent a more strictly privatized ideal of home ownership than do traditional liberal views. The desired subject of this tenure form is one who seeks a lifestyle that is relatively unencumbered by the responsibilities of home ownership. In making this suggestion I am not, however, attempting to position the normative association of home ownership with stability, improvements, and responsibility as preferable to the apparent shift towards a less responsible citizenry; indeed, both of these ideals have highly problematic implications in terms of, inter alia, the development of various forms of communities and their potential to encourage or allow alternative lifestyles to find a place in the city. I do wish to highlight the fact that, in selling condominiums as a part of a low-maintenance, unencumbered lifestyle, developers and the media expose a crack in the discourse positioning home ownership as superior to renting and as desirable for the city as a whole. The comments of women condominium owners also illustrate this tension by highlighting the freedom that comes with the lack of maintenance. This seems to suggest that the type of connection to home and community presumed by the traditional liberal notion of home ownership is less applicable to condominium living. The nexus of condominium tenure and gender emphasizes this to an even greater extent in that freedom from maintenance is seen as a particular gendered benefit of condominium living. In this scenario, women's supposed emancipation from their domestic role, or from the need for a male partner to take on this role, is connected to a privatization and commodification of the practices of home ownership.

Condominium Ownership in the Life Course

The stability dimension of home ownership is further challenged by the relatively short time spans through which many people own or occupy their condominium units. Fincher (2004) found that, in the case of high-rise development in Melbourne, developers understood their consumers to be either young, childless professionals who would eventually move to a larger, single-family residence or empty-nesters returning to the city and desiring a smaller, lower-maintenance living space. She argues that these assumptions are deeply tied to gendered notions about the normal life course. In Toronto, women condominium owners had a similar perspective on the way the condominium functions in their life courses and their housing careers.

> I don't feel like I want to put a whole lot of money or energy into
> doing really substantial things in here. Like, I'll do small things like
> picture hanging and stuff like that, but, you know, in terms of

major overhauls, I don't think I would do that because I think ultimately I probably will want to get a house ... I think it's probably true for me and true for a lot of people because a condo's a "starter home." It's not something that you anticipate living in for a really long period of time. So I guess from that perspective the commitment to it is probably less than it would be if you buy a house. *(Sandra, age 28, lives alone)*

The label of "starter home" signals a clear association between life course and housing career. For Sandra, this translates into a lesser commitment and lowered expectations regarding improvements. Again, the association of home ownership with stability and improvements is disrupted, this time with respect to length of residence.

If I meet Mr. Right, and get married and it's time to have children, a one-bedroom condo – isn't ideal. Not going to work. Then it's time to go to a house. Plus then I have someone to do the shovelling and the lawn-mowing! So as long as I'm single, I see myself right here. *(Colleen, age 28, lives alone)*

Ideally I want to be in a house again one day soon, because, you know, I like the gardening. I would hope when I do eventually get married and have kids that it – maybe to start here, but to move again within the neighbourhood, to a house. *(Caitlin, age 31, lives alone)*

Maybe in the next two to five years, if I do move, it'll be a move up. It'll probably be a condo or a loft or something like that. I've always been interested in loft living. That's like the big city thing, kind of the New York thing. So that's something that I'm considering. A house? You know, not downtown, 'cause that's atrocious. If I live in a house it'll be back in the suburbs. So, you know, maybe that's when I'll be married, or ready to give up city living. But I think a house is further down. I think I would probably rather move up into a larger condo, or a loft within the city. *(Jillian, age 30, lives alone)*

I would say it's probably a medium-term option. I'm probably going to live in a condo until I can afford to buy a nice house that's

fairly close to downtown. Or even technically in downtown, like
somewhere not too far from here. Just so that I can have a yard.
But probably not within the next ten years or so. I probably will
continue to grow my business, and just be comfy in my condo.
(Naomi, age 29, lives alone)

These four women are not in a hurry to move out of their condominiums,
but they all see themselves in a house in the future. For Caitlin and Colleen,
this potential move is connected to marriage or partnership and children.
Colleen, in a humorous vein, even invokes the need to have a man to take
care of certain domestic tasks that come with freehold home ownership. In
contrast, Hope and Nadia, below, suggest that there might be long-term
benefits to condominium ownership, even in the context of marriage and
children, because of the lower maintenance responsibilities.

If I have children I might have to move out, to a house. Although I
may want to stay in a condo, because then I might have more time
with them, so it's kind of a trade off. *(Hope, age 30, married)*

Either a larger condo, or maybe like a condo townhouse. Definitely
something where, either I'm married, or I don't maintain anything.
I really hope my husband likes to do all that stuff and has all the
time to do it, because I really do prefer the whole condominium
lifestyle. You never have to worry about that kind of stuff. *(Nadia,
age 25, lives alone)*

Nadia, like Colleen, also considers marriage a possible substitute for the
condominium lifestyle.

Although most of the women whom I interviewed did not express a desire to move to the suburbs, most saw the condominium as a less attractive
or feasible option for raising a family than a single-family dwelling. This may
reflect dominant ideologies about the unsuitability of apartment living for
families, a major concern during the first wave of debates on high-rise living
in Toronto. It may also simply reflect how these ideologies are literally built
into the form of the condominium, indicating that, in fact, it is very difficult
to sustain family life when dealing with a lack of social infrastructure, very
small living spaces, or few child-friendly common spaces.

Two other women's responses suggest that, for a slightly older group of
women, the condominium might represent a permanent lifestyle choice.

April and Leigh (ages 37 and 46, respectively) do not have children, nor do they express any desire to get married. They anticipate no significant life-course events that would alter their decision to own a condominium.

> [A condo is] the only option ... I call it a "lock-and-walk." Especially when I go travelling, I can just lock it behind me. I get a friend to stay to look after the cats, but it's fine. *(Leigh, age 46, lives alone)*

> No, I don't think so. No. I mean houses are nice and whatnot. But, I mean, the only time I would consider that is if I finally decided that I wanted to drive, which is just not an option. *(April, age 37, lives alone)*

April and Leigh's experiences also support the notion that there are age, life-course, and family-related dimensions in women's choices around condominium tenure.

Women make a diversity of choices with respect to their expected length of tenure and have a variety of expectations around the condominium as a home. This diversity suggests that planners should not make assumptions about the kinds of urban citizens that will be produced by the process of increasing home ownership in the city. Furthermore, there seems to be a contradiction between the city's ostensible desire for a stable, politically engaged base of homeowners and the desire for the individualistic, entrepreneurial, profit-seeking neoliberal citizen. The propensity of condominium tenure to encourage the expression or performance of enterprising subjects illustrates that the normative links between home ownership and democracy may become destabilized in the revitalized, redeveloped city.

Conclusion

The story presented in this chapter is about the interplay between socially constructed gender ideologies and the particular culture of property that is produced within the structure of condominium ownership. Neoliberal rationality, with its ideals of freedom, autonomy, self-sufficiency, consumption, and privatization, is filtered through condominium tenure into the everyday meanings and experiences of urban life for women condominium owners. Simultaneously, gendered ideologies are deployed to help facilitate the construction of the condominium owner as an entrepreneurial citizen and a self-actualized subject. Moreover, gender constitutes, and is constituted by, various dimensions of condominium ownership in Toronto. Many analyses of home ownership pay little attention either to the ways in which the homeowner is a differentiated subject or to the notion that multiple discourses intertwine to constitute the ideology and experience of home ownership in the neoliberal city. In examining various constituent sources of discourse about condominium ownership, I argue that gender plays a significant role in creating the social, cultural, political, and economic landscapes of new-build gentrification.

Condominium ownership may function as a way of drawing young, middle-class women into the social, economic, political, and moral structure of private property ownership ahead of marriage or long-term partnership. However, the traditional liberal vision of the stable, community-oriented, property-improving homeowner is subverted in favour of the neoliberal ideals of fast profit making, privatization, commodification, and the pursuit of personal autonomy. Women's actual narratives and the experiences they represent serve to complicate some of the common-sense assumptions about home ownership, citizenship, freedom, and life course, while illustrating how neoliberal ideals filter through condominium ownership into everyday experiences and shape the meanings of home ownership.

Examining the gender ideologies and gendered experiences of condominium ownership alters the story of neoliberal urban revitalization by illustrating the multiple discourses that work to constitute city building processes and to construct appropriate identities for the citizens of the revitalized city. Gender ideologies are intertwined with ideas about class, property and land use, and the moralities of property in general. The notions of highest and best use, the hierarchy of tenure, and capital accumulation, for example, are all inflected with ideas about gendered emancipation and fulfillment in order to sell condominium development as a revitalization project.

Finally, the ideologies and practices of condominium ownership function as a form of governmentality, based on a neoliberal rationality, that seeks to promote or elicit an entrepreneurial, autonomous, consumer citizen. In contributing to the rising "regime of the self" (N. Rose 1996), condominium ownership taps into an increasingly dominant ethic of individual responsibility, wherein the free subject chooses to govern her- or himself according to the ideals of autonomy, self-sufficiency, and self-improvement. Condominium ownership works as a normalizing process that both disciplines and regulates (Foucault 1997). In drawing out some of the gendered manifestations of this regime of the self, I suggest that the subject positions produced through neoliberal governmentality are flexible enough to accommodate seemingly contradictory positions (i.e., the self-actualized property-owning woman is simultaneously dependent on the condominium for help with household maintenance). At the same time, this conflicted position still absolves the state of any responsibility to shelter or support the citizen.

The production of this subject suggests that economic engagements are becoming more dominant as dimensions of city life and citizenship. Although I cannot make sweeping claims about how urban citizenship is defined and enacted, even for women condominium dwellers, urban living, in the context of condominium ownership, is increasingly defined as essentially a wealth-accumulation strategy. The short-term intentions of many respondents also suggest that the city is courting a highly mobile, transient population of city dwellers who may not make long-term commitments to the city or seek out ways to participate in civic life. It is perhaps ironic that many of the ostensible qualities that make renters undesirable are the very same qualities that are fostered through condominium ownership.

3

Under Construction
The Place of Community in the Neoliberal City

Condominium environments are distinguished by common property ownership and a shared, ostensibly democratic, governance structure. These features have the potential, it seems, to allow condominium living to subvert the neoliberal ideals of autonomy, individual responsibility, and privatization. Indeed, mainstream representations have linked the concept of community to condominiums in ways that seem to suggest a resurgence of interest in the social ties and affective engagements of city dwellers (Greer 2006; Cotroneo 2006). At the same time, though, condominiums have been criticized as gated communities that exclude various social groups, militarize urban space, and commodify the home (Atkinson 2006; Raco 2007; Blandy and Lister 2005; Raposo 2006; Low 2001; Keil 2007). These contradictory characterizations raise critical questions about the ways that the governance structure, common spaces, and particular public/private distinctions within condominium developments function in the context of the shift towards neoliberal, entrepreneurial forms of governance.

To what extent, and in what ways, can condominiums be understood as communities, gated or otherwise? Furthermore, in the process of building the revitalized city, how is the notion of community mobilized? These are the central concerns of this chapter, framed specifically around the gendered dimensions of condominiums as communities and the notion that, in part, gender works to shape city building through a set of ideas about community. I am interested not only in how women define, enact, and ascribe meaning to the social interactions and shared responsibilities of condominium living but also in how the ways in which community is defined and experienced in this context shape a sense of belonging, engagement, and attachment to the city at large. In other words, how do the twin imperatives of neoliberal redevelopment and capital accumulation filter through the notion of community to shape everyday relationships to the city?

This discussion is informed by a critique of neoliberal urban agendas, which is concerned with the securitization of urban space and the shift towards new regimes of governance outside the state (Blakely and Snyder 1997; Low 2003; Lang and Danielson 1997; Townshend 2006; McKenzie 2003; Osborne and Rose 1999; Isin 1999; Swyngedouw 2005). In characterizing condominiums as urban gated communities, however, this framework does not address the possibility of beneficial social networks, support, interdependence, and democratic involvement with governance structures (Wellman 1979; Hipp and Perrin 2006; Forrest, LaGrange, and Ngai-Ming 2002; Purdy 2003). For example, feminist literature addressing women's claims to a right to the city, expressed through practices such as housing activism, local community activism, and the creation of mutual support systems within neighbourhoods and housing projects, suggests that there are benefits to high-density living for marginalized groups that may be ignored within a critique of neoliberal urban development (Vaiòu and Lykogianni 2006; Kristenson 1997; Lind 1997; Secor 2003; Wells 2005; Kruzynski 2005; Wekerle and Peake 1996; Wekerle 2004). During earlier waves of high-rise construction in Toronto and other North American cities, scholars were concerned with understanding how these new living arrangements facilitated or inhibited the development of social networks, interdependence, and support systems among residents (Conway 1977; Abu-Lughod 1960; Gans 1962; Keller 1968; Wekerle 1976; Wellman 1979). Concerns around safety and security in high-density urban environments also developed in this context (O. Newman 1972). At the current moment, however, there is relatively little public debate about high-rise or high-density living based on social concerns. The power of the anti-sprawl discourse has effectively silenced debate about the social effects of condominiums as high-density forms. Because of this silence, we need to ask how people experience these living arrangements today. Condominiums, I argue, create new geographies of inclusion and exclusion that help to define who is thought of as a community member or a fellow citizen. At the same time, the reshaping of public and private space through condominium development creates new constraints and new opportunities for citizenship and community engagement, particularly for groups such as women.

Deploying Community as a Neoliberal City Building Tool

Appeals to the notion of community help shape the rationale of condominium development. "Community" is a term that is typically used in a common-sense way to denote either a particular social group, or a particular
quality of relationship. It usually signifies a more direct set of relationships
than those within the broader society or between people and the state. Cultural and political theorist Raymond Williams (1976), in his brief genealogy
of the term, notes that it seems never to be used unfavourably, unlike various other terms for social organization. It is this strong positive connotation
that makes "community" a preferred word for city building agents to use in
describing their developments. It is also a red flag for critical scholars who
seek to denaturalize common-sense words and to understand the conditions
of their strategic deployment at particular political-economic moments.

Communities are not necessarily territorial, but common usage often
implies a spatial definition. Concern for the loss of community typically
stems from concern for human spatial arrangements, such as the village
versus the industrial city (Toennies 1963; Durkheim 1964). Urban sociologists Georg Simmel (1971) and Louis Wirth (1938) countered these
perspectives by theorizing that urban environments offered more opportunities for contact and for the development of larger, more heterogeneous
social networks. Communities may be sites for the enactment of everyday
citizenship claims – the right to belong, to participate in local life, to make
decisions, to claim an identity, and so on (Vromen 2003). Communities can
also be mobilized to make group claims on the city, such as to stop particular developments or to request resources (Caulfield 1994; Boudreau 2000;
Wekerle and Peake 1996). Communities are also defined, in part, by exclusions (Young 1990). Keeping these tensions around the concept of community in mind, I consider how the spaces, scales, and normative ideals of
urban community are imagined, enacted, experienced, and inscribed in the
city through condominium development, and I assess the potential consequences of this process for gendered urban citizenship claims.

The notion of community is regularly invoked by planners and developers to describe both condominium projects and the neighbourhoods in
which they are situated. In order to unpack and denaturalize the implicit
assumptions that underlie this consumer- and policy-friendly terminology,
I examine both the discursive and physical construction of condominium
communities as interlinked processes. There are central questions here.
How is the notion of community used to mask or soften the capitalist logic

of accumulation? How does the logic of highest and best use become encoded in the ideal of community? How does an implicit hierarchy of community posit gentrification as necessary for the creation of community?

Community Builders?

The accounts of city planners addressed various social and economic challenges in and around the creation of new communities in the context of condominium development. The planners were concerned, in part, with the specific elements that they deemed constitutive of community. These included open space, social infrastructure, and hard services such as water and transit. They also addressed the demographics of condominium communities as well as some of the difficulties in attracting and keeping a stable population in areas with a lot of new condominiums. Of particular interest here are the ways that condominium developments are viewed as necessary for the process of neighbourhood revitalization. The connection posited here between revitalization and the creation of community points to a troubling conflation of gentrification and community. In other words, the economic logic of putting land to its highest and best use is tied into the idealized – and problematic – notion of creating communities.

One planner described the negotiation process with developers and neighbourhood groups over the constitution of a community on Sheppard Avenue in North York.

> We did a visioning exercise with the landowners and the surrounding rentier groups over a fourteen-month period. We came up with a plan that went significantly beyond, for example in terms of park dedication, giving it beyond what the 5 percent planning act would have given us, and we were able to do that because we worked with the landowners and the Parks Department and found out what happens if you transfer the density to get a bigger park. It's not like the density went off the table for the developer, so the developer wasn't losing things, and we found a way that we were able to balance less development blocks in a more intense and urban form to allow us to get a bigger park. At the same time the developer gave us a large piece of not just the land, through that subdivision process, but also a chunk of money, so we'll be building a community centre in the first phase of it. *(Planner interview, 18 July 2005)*

This narrative describes the tension between the city's interests in providing a community centre and park, and the developer's desire for higher densities on the site. The community centre and park are seen as elements that help to create a community in an area of new residential development. The planner goes on to note the importance of providing social infrastructure in areas of new development in the context of "mistakes" made in the Harbourfront area:

> So we've learned from Harbourfront where we, you know that first mistake where we basically, at the edge of the universe down there on the Waterfront, we put that whole neighbourhood, in particular ... social housing, at the foot of Bathurst Street with no grocery store, no community centre, no school, whatever there was. There was – it's not just the buildings, it's the community, and the community is the shared spaces but also the institutions that communities need, in particular schools and the recreation centres, the markets, the little parks. *(Planner interview, 18 July 2005)*

He also noted that planners struggle to secure funding from the city for amenities and services in areas with a sudden increase in residential development:

> We have a serious challenge to continue to provide amenities and services for all of the people. You know a lot of people have moved into the North York Centre, and we haven't built that many new parks and recreation centres for them. So we are lagging behind, and it's largely because, not because we don't have plans for them or we don't know what we want, but that we don't have the money. *(Planner interview, 18 July 2005)*

In addition to the difficulties of providing public services, a planner for the Central Waterfront area acknowledged that private retail and commercial establishments were lacking or difficult to sustain in condominium-dominated areas with a mobile population:

> A lot of the areas down there – it's a transient population. I mean, we're building six-hundred-square-foot units. People are not going to live in a six-hundred-square-foot unit for more than a couple of years. They're a starter home, and then they pick up and they leave. So there is a lot of movement in that area, which is somewhat

problematic because it's hard to keep people there. There is a lot of movement. And in addition to that, even with some of the commercial establishments, there's a lot of movement, they don't stay there for very long. They're there for six months and then they fold, which kind of boggles the mind sometimes because you're thinking, "You have twenty thousand people living down there, they gotta shop somewhere, they gotta eat somewhere." And the biggest complaint we get from people who move down there is, "Well, there's no grocery store down here." No, there's not. I mean, there is going to be, I mean Loblaws is locating in the former Daily Bread Food Bank building, so that's great, that was fantastic news. But again it is taking longer for those services to come on stream. *(Planner interview, 22 July 2005)*

This planner also pointed to another challenge faced by the Waterfront area – that of keeping a stable population:

In essence you could be in a condo and stay there and not have to deal with anyone else around you, as opposed to living on a street in a house where you do know who your neighbours are, and you are an active part of that street. You're much more insulated living in a condo ... The other thing we're also finding is what they call now the "hotel suites." These smaller units are being targeted to people who are retired, who now live in Muskoka full-time, but they also want, they also come down to the city for their cultural attractions. And instead of staying in a hotel overnight, they stay in a unit that they've purchased. So during the week it's empty, but on the weekend, they're here. *(Planner interview, 22 July 2005)*

These challenges imply a fundamental contradiction in planners' attempts to construct community through the provision of an integrated, mixed-use built realm, not to mention a contradiction in the term "resident." Planners work with a notion of community defined by an established, institution-based, stable neighbourhood. Condominium development may undermine this understanding of community, particularly in the downtown core where insulated, transient, or part-time residents may not support, desire, or utilize the open spaces, commercial establishments, and social services that planners would like to provide.

This problem recalls some of the concerns raised in the early wave of high-rise battles, when critics argued that high-rise development would have a negative effect on the surrounding community, in part, because of the ostensibly transient nature of high-rise residents (Wekerle 1976; Wekerle and Hall 1972). Current critics of such developments point more towards the insulated nature of new-build gentrification projects as living spaces that facilitate disconnection from the existing community or neighbourhood spaces (Atkinson 2006). In my analysis, it appears that planners deploy the concept of community to idealize the kinds of developments that are produced through a market-driven process of residential intensification in Toronto, even as they openly acknowledge the contradictions between their ideals and the realities on the ground.

Despite some of the challenges and contradictions that they struggled with, the planners viewed condominium development as an important part of Toronto's reurbanization and revitalization agenda.

> I think that the city has been significantly improved by the last
> eight years of condo development, and that as well as providing
> way more options for people to live, different kinds of units in
> different kinds of neighbourhoods, without roommates and the
> pressures of sharing, um, it just also has given [a] whole new life
> to areas of the city. *(Planner interview, 18 July 2005)*

In this account, condominiums give "new life" by bringing community into different neighbourhoods, which here include former industrial districts and disreputable areas. This view implicitly posits a direct connection between new-build gentrification (bringing people into the core) and the creation of community (defined in a particular way as a stable, established, mixed-use neighbourhood). While planners do seek to integrate these groups into the city through the provision of institutions and services, the nature of condominium living – securitized, privatized, insular, transient – may subvert attempts to connect condominium dwellers to the broader neighbourhood in substantial, formal ways. This problem is elided through the assumption that gentrification leads directly to the creation of community. This slippage suggests that current planning ideals draw on a neoliberal rationality that conflates social goals, such as the creation of community, with redevelopment and economic growth. In this case, the notion of community is mapped onto the logic of highest and best use through redeveloping vacant or abandoned areas. A normative link is thus established between the notion of community and the incoming new middle class.

The news media also posit similar connections, publishing frequent stories wherein condominium development rehabilitates deindustrialized areas of the city by creating real communities:

> Since moving into the Liberty Village area south of King St. W. five years ago, Ken Gangbar has seen the pace of urban renewal in the neighbourhood accelerate. Condominium and townhouse projects have risen on both sides of the King St. corridor west of Strachan Ave., bringing more people into the area. With the growing number of residents have come more stores, restaurants and other commercial development. The area's gradual revitalization and readily available space in old factories and warehouses near King and Dufferin Sts. are attracting new businesses to the neighbourhood. "This area is becoming more and more popular," says Gangbar, 37, who lives in a loft apartment beside his ceramics studio near Mowat Ave. and Liberty St. Gangbar sees Liberty Village well on its way to joining the list of downtown neighbourhoods that have become destination points, such as the Distillery District, Queen St. W. and the entertainment district. "It's becoming one of those desirable pockets you see around the city. More and more it's becoming part of that list of places that are interesting to go to," Gangbar says. (Lighthall 2004, P1)

In this story, condominium development is positioned as the hero in a tale of progress towards the ultimate goal of revitalizing neighbourhoods, which involves the creation of new living spaces, consumption spaces, and tourist sites. This integrated urban realm is integrated only insofar as it attracts or contains desirable people and places. If community is thus created through revitalization, then previous inhabitants, renters, homeless populations, and other less desirable groups are defined relationally as somehow non-community or, perhaps, pre-community. This attitude reflects the same assumptions made in the 1940s and 1950s about the inability of poor and racialized people to form proper communities, an assumption that led to slum clearance, urban renewal, and public housing estates (Purdy 2003; Slater 2004a). Now, however, there is less focus on creating improved communities for the poor and more focus on replacing those lesser communities with gentrified ones.

One example of this logic comes through in a quote from the Waterfront planner (above), conveying his excitement that the Daily Bread Food Bank has moved from its downtown location at Queen's Quay to the western peripheral area of Etobicoke, making room for a large, higher-end grocery store that will serve the waterfront condominium residents. In a similar set of circumstances, the Goodwill "Buy the Pound" Store left its downtown headquarters and moved to the eastern peripheral area of Scarborough to make room for a condominium development at Jarvis Street and Richmond Street. In these cases, the institutions that served previous communities are seemingly less valued or desired in the revitalized vision of community in Toronto.

Do condominium developers reproduce this rationality? Developers use the term "community" repeatedly, especially in relation to multiple-building developments. This is perhaps because it sounds warmer and more positive than "massive redevelopment project," but it also seems to signal a set of assumptions about the connections between shared spaces and the development of community sentiments, on the one hand, and between condominium buildings and their surrounding neighbourhoods, on the other. The term "community" also invokes the idea of mutual moral obligations and positive group interactions. I suggest that there is an implicit assumption, again, that redevelopment improves upon previous community formations, or that it automatically confers the status of community on particular spaces and groups.

Developers portray themselves as community builders in much the same way as do city planners, providing the spaces and opportunities for communities to develop.[1] However, they tend to view the lack of existing social infrastructure as an opportunity rather than as a potential problem. For one of the architects and founders of a smaller development corporation, notions of community distinguished his firm's approach to design, location, and planning:

> Both in terms of urban planning, residential design planning,
> community understandings, social-cultural understandings, all
> those aspects need to come together to form an understanding
> of what your product is going to be. Unfortunately, a lot of the
> development that's been happening in the city is void of its context,
> so it becomes – when they look at the site they see what kind of
> density can be achieved on the site, and what's the most cost-
> effective way of doing it. And away the developer goes. It becomes

> imperative to look at how buildings impact urban form, how they
> impact urban culture, how they impact social culture. Those things
> need to be regarded. And it's the buildings that we build that begin
> to inform those and adjust those. Architecture and built form
> ultimately is a response to those socio-cultural factors. *(Developer
> interview, 21 June 2005)*

This developer explicitly links the built form of condominiums to the kinds
of communities in which they are situated, seeing good developments as
those that reflect (and perhaps shape?) the socio-cultural context of the
neighbourhood. The notion of community, however, reflects specific ideals
of revitalization:

> For us community and neighbourhood are very important. We like
> to go in areas that have a flair to them or have a richness to them.
> Our project at King and Bathurst was very much about that. It was
> recognizing – that little pocket we see as being sort of a real down-
> town neighbourhood. And we just like, we felt it had – it was close
> enough to parks, it was close enough to the cultural scene, in a
> sense. It was close enough to work areas, connections. Like, it just
> seemed right for us. *(Developer interview, 21 June 2005)*

Here the developer characterizes community according to the presence of
certain open spaces and socio-cultural attributes, which presumably will be
attractive to the people his firm targets as potential consumers. The particular area was chosen because it was seen as a "*real* downtown neighbourhood" (my emphasis). A real neighbourhood or community, then, is defined
by its selling points, raising the question of what areas would not be seen as
real neighbourhoods: presumably areas without such pleasant amenities.
Community, conflated with particular neighbourhood attributes, is important, it seems, as a marketing ploy. Rather than being important in their own
right, the existing community and neighbourhood features are instrumentalized as features of the condominium development. This is echoed in a
realtor's comments to the *Toronto Star* about a condominium development
in the well-established neighbourhood of Little Italy:

> Europa offers a new condominium in a traditional Toronto neighbourhood.
> "Most people want something that's brand new, but in a traditional, estab-
> lished and well-rooted neighbourhood," says Nestor Repetski of Winick

Realty Corp., who is marketing the Little Italy project ... "This is one of the oldest neighbourhoods in the city," Repetski says. "It goes back 80 to 100 years and is beautiful with its gated homes and canopied trees." Repetski says sales have been going well and the building is more than half sold. "We're getting a very large group of single people buying there and over 50 per cent of the buyers are single women," Repetski says, pointing out that they like the newness of the place, as well as its location. (Hanes 2005, P9)

Apparently, women can combine the best of two worlds in this case: the newness of a condominium and an old, established neighbourhood (where, presumably, they could not afford resale homes, given Toronto's high-priced housing market). While this sound-bite does not provide many details regarding why single women constitute over 50 percent of the buyers, it suggests that condominiums located in traditional neighbourhoods are more attractive than are those in recently developed neighbourhoods. Perhaps there is an assumption that women are less attracted to projects in brownfield areas or less established neighbourhoods, or that women naturally desire community, defined according to the attributes of an established neighbourhood.

In these accounts, a dichotomous set of assumptions about community is at play: first, that new communities can be created by simply combining certain key ingredients (open space, coffee shops, grocery stores) with a large residential population and, second, that communities are pre-existing entities into which condominiums can be inserted and off of which they can feed. Each of these assumptions contains internal contradictions. The first ignores the fact that the necessary ingredients – services and amenities – do not magically appear in new developments and may actually be sorely lacking for long periods of time. The second assumes that young, single, and transient condominium owners will form community ties within the surrounding neighbourhood and not simply use it as a temporary "consumption niche" (Vaiou and Lykogianni 2006; Forrest 2004). In either scenario, the notion of community is emptied of the ideals of social interdependence, mutual support, and shared interests. Instead, it is used to elide the problems associated with these simplistic assumptions about community and to legitimize the logic of the highest and best use of property.

Creating Community within the Condominium

For developers, creating community is not just about the strategic placement of condominium developments within so-called real neighbourhoods;

it is also about portraying themselves as actively creating internal communities through the provision of shared spaces and areas for social interaction. Developer visions about the uses of such spaces help shape for residents the everyday experience of community within condominiums.

One developer is very articulate about his understanding of community and how to facilitate its development:

> I think the ideas that drive our projects, where we look at notions of community, we look at notions – you know, a lot of developers call their projects communities, but a community isn't a physical entity, you know ... The building begins it. The building acts as the – provides the opportunities for communities to form. Communities are socio-cultural phenomenons [sic], they're gatherings of people who have common interests, there's something common about their desires. We try to facilitate that through, you know, [one project] for example has a large courtyard space. It has amenities and spaces that relate to it, so it creates opportunities. We have a yoga studio where there'll be instructors available. It's about a – the cliché is called lifestyle, people sell lifestyle – but we really sort of try to take that and incorporate it into the different levels of the project. *(Developer interview, 21 June 2005)*

In this narrative, the formation of community is facilitated by bringing together people with common interests and desires, and by the provision of shared spaces within which people can pursue such interests. There is nothing unique about this, but his final comments – about yoga and lifestyle – illustrate the extent to which community (defined by shared interests and activities) is managed, facilitated, and predetermined by the developer.[2] Moreover, the interests that are catered to – lifestyle features – are designed to reflect the tastes and values of a fairly narrow set of citizens: the new middle class of young, creative urban professionals.

> You must always have a party room, or multi-purpose room, because people – because we design the suites to make them affordable, they get somewhat smaller in size, so we look at the common areas of the community as an extension of that home ... People are very health-conscious today, for the most part. Even if they aren't, they think they want to be. So we put in as a standard, in every single condominium there will be an exercise facility for

them, something like that. If you want to get into pools, or the
bowling alleys, or tennis courts, theatres, this, that, and you name
it – we would look a little closer as to who we think that buyer
might be, and we would cater that project. As an example, a couple
of months ago we opened up a project downtown, and we went
after what would be a younger demographic ... We looked at the
amenity space. Basically cut it in half – one side is all to do with
your physical well-being, whether it's yoga, or aerobics, or anything to do from that perspective, that would rival or better any
kind of a club that they could belong to. And then the other side
is the party side – integrated with theatre, and socializing, dining
and whatnot ... We thought that two-thirds of those buyers are
probably going to be single, and the other third are going to be
younger couples. *(Developer interview, 2 August 2005)*

This account makes explicit the ways that developers design the shared
spaces based on age, lifestyle, and class assumptions about the potential
buyers. This is not surprising, but it is important to problematize in the
context of thinking about community. In many ways, the shared interests
and characteristics of the community are pre-selected based on market research. The fact that condominium developers construct common spaces
to reflect the desires of certain demographic groups also indicates that
community is deliberately and narrowly constructed. In both of the above
examples, the spaces provided to facilitate community sentiment or socializing are already targeted at a predetermined community: young, middle-
class professionals. This may function to pre-emptively exclude potential
community members who do not see their interests reflected in the shared
spaces.

The common denominator, for the most part, is that all these
people that are buying these condos, most of these people who
are buying these condos are people that don't have kids. There is
certainly a segment of that marketplace – but the driving factors
are people without children that want to live somewhere in the
urban core. *(Developer interview, 28 July 2005)*

So we're going for first-time home buyers, we're going for the
move-down market, people called the baby boomers, who've
perhaps had their kids move out of their homes, moving to those

sorts of homes. We're going for unconventional family types, so
for instance at [a project near Church Street] we targeted our
marketing, not exclusively, but in large part, to the gay community,
because the project's obviously right near the Village there. And,
so everything. Generally people who I think want to live in proximity to cultural and that sort of, that downtown – transit, shopping, museums, whatever. They want to be where the action is.
(Developer interview, 16 June 2005)

In each development, the target consumer is fairly specific, and the common spaces are designed to suit the expected needs and desires of this
group. This is also reflected in condominium advertisements, many of which
include renderings of swimming pools, party rooms, fitness centres, and
outdoor patios.

The process of pre-selecting a community has consequences beyond the
immediate context of the condominium. Drawing a very specific group of
residents into particular city areas will help to shape the surrounding neighbourhood and community in their image; it also suggests that private city
building agents have a central role in shaping the image of the desired urban
citizen and urban community. The pre-selection of communities raises important issues around indirect or exclusionary displacement that are not
often addressed in the context of new-build gentrification, in part because
they are difficult to quantify (Slater 2006; Davidson and Lees 2005; Atkinson 2000; Newman and Wyly 2006; Marcuse 1985). These very specific
notions of community may be implicated in displacement processes. Insidi-
ously, the feel-good language of community may work to further soften
these hard edges of gentrification.

The common spaces and amenities within condominiums are also set up
as quasi-public extensions of the individual's privately owned unit. This is
meant to augment very small individual units in which there is little space
to have a party or to exercise. At the same time, it shifts, or stretches, the
boundaries of public and private space in ways that may create opportunities for people to subvert the exclusive and isolated nature of the private
home, which is typical of the North American culture of property. However, these spaces may also act as substitutes for neighbourhood places or
public spaces outside of the condominium development. Thus, the boundary of private space has been extended beyond the private home but not
beyond the walls of the condominium. Indeed, these shared spaces may
result in fewer community engagements outside of the development (Lang

FIGURE 4   Children's playground. Play areas in a townhouse condominium
complex, Bloor Street West, Toronto.

and Danielson 1997; Blakely and Snyder 1997; Blandy and Lister 2005; Raco
2007). For example, private swimming pools and terraces are often referred
to in advertisements as "private oases," perhaps in implicit contrast to the
"public chaos" of public places and facilities. In Figure 4, a children's play
area within a townhouse condominium complex is walled off on two sides
by tall fencing, disconnecting it from the live/work lofts on the other side,
where some families with children live. The playground is set deep within
the condominium complex (itself set back from the major thoroughfare)
and is not visible from the nearest streets, effectively privatizing the space.

　　Despite some examples of spaces geared to families with children, the
following excerpt from a newspaper article on the reporter's search for a
condominium suitable for families with children illustrates that many of the
community spaces included in condominiums reflect a very narrow conception of community, one that often implicitly excludes families with children:

The condominium market in major urban centres is a clear example of this family-averse attitude. Some argue that population density is a good thing. These urbanists decry the "suburban sprawl" with its big lawns, big cars and big shopping malls. However, people who want children need a home large enough to raise them in a healthy and practical way. Condominium builders don't actually state that they are antithetical to families, but the promotion and construction of their developments display this disregard for children. The developers extol the virtues of the location: right in the heart of the city, close to boutiques, cafes and nightclubs. They wax eloquent about the adult-oriented amenities: gym, sauna, billiard room, tennis or squash courts. And they blazon on billboards the affordable "starting from" price, which is always for the "bachelor" suite. Hardly ever do you see child-friendly features: parks, playgrounds and large living spaces. (Timmons 2005, A11)

While the tone of the above report suggests more concern with supporting traditional family forms and suburban lifestyles than with promoting social justice and inclusivity in the city, the reporter does identify the problematic limitations of condominium developments. His experience suggests that condominiums are geared to an age-segregated, adult-only lifestyle that identifies urban living with a particular demographic rather than catering to a diversity of ages and lifestyles or providing affordable urban housing for a variety of household types.

In contrast, other media reports indicate that condominiums are not inherently inimical to family living (Greer 2006). In some condominium developments, the residents create for themselves a family-friendly atmosphere, using the common spaces for networking and for children's social activities. One reporter describes the development of a parent network in a high-rise downtown condominium, in spite of the challenges faced by families looking for suitable condominiums:

The parent network began in August, 2002, and has become a lifeline for new parents, drawing on experienced moms and dads and long-time residents to source schools, day care and neighbourhood drop-in programs ... The Skypark terrace, the size of a football field, gives [children] a place to run around and play with a ball ... A few parents plan to move when the kids get older, yearning for a backyard patch of grass, but none want to commute. All say that the proximity of schools is paramount. Just how many families live in condos in the GTA is unknown, as many condos are leased and renters aren't tracked ... Most condos aren't designed with kids in mind. Developers say there's no demand for family-style condos, partly because most families couldn't afford larger units in downtown condos, which are selling for an average of $300 per square foot. Most condos are still seen as starter homes for young, single buyers, or twilight homes for downsizing empty nesters, says Mimi Ng, a specialist in condominiums with N. Barry Lyon Consultants Ltd. She says many condo advertisements have an urban, hip feel, pushing a carefree lifestyle that doesn't include kids ... Toronto Councillor Olivia Chow, the city's [former] children and youth advocate, recalls a planning report several years ago that urged developers to build more family-style condos. But nothing much has changed, she says. She stresses it's not only the interior space that matters. Condos are part of the larger community, and people need a well-planned neighbourhood to be able to enjoy a high quality of life. She says families in Toronto need affordable housing, and condos are affordable. (Laporte 2003a, P1)

These reports express concern that condominiums are designed and marketed in ways that deliberately deter families with children from purchasing or renting. The second article notes the development constraints that shape these practices, in particular, the belief that young families cannot afford larger units. This logic may be self-reinforcing, resulting in few suitable units being built and, therefore, little demand for condominiums from families. These concerns echo the debates that flared during Toronto's first high-rise boom, where battles over the legality and morality of adultonly high-rise developments centred around the ways that families would be excluded from these new communities and neighbourhoods, and on the potentially negative consequences for the nuclear family living in apartments (Social Planning Council of Toronto 1973; Worthington 1973).

It is clear from the above example, however, that people can appropriate the shared spaces of the condominiums for uses that suit the needs of the actually existing community, regardless of the developer's intentions for those spaces. The terrace becomes the site for children's play. The article also described parents' successful efforts to have the condominium board pay for a sandbox and a Halloween party. In this way, condominiums have the potential to become spaces of representation (spaces that reflect the everyday uses and appropriations of space by ordinary people) rather than the representations of space (controlled, planned, pre-defined spaces) imagined by developers (Lefebvre 1991b). This particular example also seems

FIGURE 5   Dead space. Common area between condominium towers,
Liberty Village, Toronto.

to support feminist research, which intersects here with Lefebvre's theories,
on women's work to claim space and services within residential communities, suggesting that everyday concerns (places for children to play, places
to talk with other parents) serve as the sites and stakes for struggles to claim
a right to the city (Gilroy and Woods 1994; Dowling and Pratt 1993; Hayden
2002; Klodawsky and Specter 1988; Wekerle 1993). Unfortunately, many of
the shared spaces built into and around condominiums are little more than
what Lefebvre would have called representations of space – planned spaces
that lack the vitality of everyday life and reflect a top-down approach to the
development of a public realm. In Figure 5, the common area between two
condominium towers is quiet, dark, and uninviting.

Nonetheless, the proliferation of narrowly envisioned spaces targeted at
very specific demographic groups suggests that planning policy should consider the ways that the types of amenities provided in condominiums can
work in tandem with advertising to exclude potential buyers who do not see
their interests or needs reflected in a particular project.[3] The developers
interviewed here articulated clear ideas about whom the potential residents

would be and about what they would desire in terms of common spaces and activities. The underlying logic of community that developers seem to draw upon is based on several key ideas: first, that community exists in given neighbourhoods and can be used to market condominium projects to specific consumers; second, that community is created by bringing together the provision of shared spaces, such as yoga studios, fitness rooms, and spa facilities, with a targeted demographic whose values are reflected in these spaces; and third, that community in condominiums is an extension of the private home. What these conceptions ignore or elide is the problematic predetermination of what that community will look like, what its members will share, and where it will exist. By predetermining the contours of community in this way, developers may end up excluding various groups, pushing people out at different stages of the life course, or creating obstacles to other types of community formations in their developments. Moreover, the sharing of such spaces does not automatically suggest that residents will generate social contacts with people who live in close proximity or that this will be a democratic, equitable, or fair community (the amount of conflict generated by shared spaces is evidence to this effect). Nor does it guarantee that there will be social, political, or economic engagements with the surrounding neighbourhood, despite the careful selection of communities for condominium developments. As Susan Bickford (2000) suggests, privately developed market housing projects, in the context of neoliberal urban agendas, are not "utopian social experiments," nor are they aimed at redressing social inequalities in the ways that, for example, women-led co-op developments were in the 1980s in Canada. We can critique developers' deployment of community as a strategy designed to articulate with the profit-centred motives of real estate redevelopment rather than as a strategy designed to provide opportunities for grassroots organizing or for diverse community groups to claim spaces in the city. The general lack of debate about these effects of condominium development suggests that the notion of community has successfully meshed with the goals of rapid capital accumulation, maximizing the exchange value of urban space in ways that, in the city at large, are accepted uncritically.

Community and Everyday Life

The preceding analysis does not, however, fully capture the complexities of how these policies play out in everyday life for particular groups of city dwellers. In examining the actual ways that women socialize, network, and experience community sentiments, four central concerns emerge. First, the shared spaces of condominiums may represent a shift in the boundaries of public and private space. How does this facilitate community and social life within the development, or reduce anonymity and privacy? Second, in new condominiums in particular, the kind of community that is constructed is largely based upon shared traits and (assumed) shared interests within a predetermined demographic group. How does this influence women's definitions and experiences of community? Third, the common governance structure is a potential site of engagement with the condominium community. Do women use these structures to pursue their claims? Fourth, connections to the surrounding neighbourhood are constitutive, in part, of urban citizenship. Is the neighbourhood simply a consumption niche, or is it a place to which women feel connected as condominium dwellers?

Common Space, Common Demographic

For Molly, Ava, and Jillian, the shared spaces of the condominium, such as the rooftop gardens, playgrounds, and hallways, helped in developing community sentiment and interpersonal relationships.

> Molly: Sometimes there might be some issues, but there's the plus side of having a closer-knit community and knowing your neighbours.
>
> Interviewer: Do you find that there's a community feeling in this project?
>
> Molly: Yeah, definitely. With the neighbours around here. I mean not, you know, not necessarily everybody, but from the get-go there has been sort of that neighbourly feeling. Especially in the summer. Yeah.
>
> Interviewer: So making use of the little playground out there?
>
> Molly: Exactly, exactly. Yeah, it's been great to be able to meet people like that.
> *(Molly, age 33, married, one child)*

> Now that I've lived there long enough, I know people in the building. So when you see people in the hallway, you say, "Why don't we go do something?" Like on Sunday night we'll go to the patio and have a barbeque ... On the whole it's easy for me to see people, just going out in the hall. *(Ava, age 32, lives alone)*

Jillian expresses excitement about the social opportunities afforded by living in a building where the common spaces are designed to bring her and other young people into social contact.

> They [developers] also wanted to have an area where people could get together, and kind of entertain, and meet other people and socialize. So those were the big things for the facility, the rooftop garden, the barbeque area, and I think the way that they created it was very much like a common area, so you feel like you're at home and you get to meet new people ... And I guess the people who live in the building, I guess people my age, you know, that sort of age group. 'Cause you just get a sense and feel of the community, you know ... The other thing that you didn't ask, which I thought you might, is just with me being single, this is an amazing opportunity to meet the man of your dreams or whatever. Just meeting new people, our entire building is open to that. That's the kind of environment. I actually have a girlfriend, well, she went to school with me, she bought at [this project], she's single as well, and one of the first things she said, she said, "What kind of people are buying here?" And I told her the demographics are young, just like us, up and coming. She says, "A lot of hot single guys?" I said, "You never know. I hope there is!" That's another exciting part, meeting new people, female and male. *(Jillian, age 30, lives alone)*

In these examples, the shared spaces redefine the boundaries of public and private space. These comments echo findings that there is great value, especially for women, in housing that provides spaces for interaction and socializing (Wekerle 1988a; Andrew et al. 1994; Hayden 2002). For mothers with young children, like Molly, this is an advantage of condominium living. Molly could watch the playground from her kitchen window, which made it easy for her to find opportunities to socialize with neighbours and to entertain her child. For Ava, the hallways are like the neighbourhood streets, where she runs into friends and makes plans for further socializing in other shared spaces (like the barbeque area). Jillian sees the shared space as a place to potentially meet a romantic partner and make new friends (recalling Wekerle's [1976] early research on singles in high-rise complexes). The common amenities create opportunities for socializing, opportunities that may counter the private aspects of private home ownership. The possibility and conditions of these social interactions are, however, already shaped to some extent through the presence of a similarly defined age and class group that shares a similar lifestyle, especially within new condominiums where the original target demographic group is still resident. In particular, the common spaces have functions (or are appropriated to uses) specific to certain stages in the life course.

In older condominiums, length of residence and the presence of pets were important factors in this regard:

> I mean, the people who work there, we all know the security guards, and we know the maintenance guys, at least I do, I don't wanna talk for other people, but you always know who the people are on your floor, you know the people in your wing – you don't know them, you just know that they're who they are. People chat in the elevator, and the dogs – it's a pet friendly building so the dogs – that's what I find really brings people together. People chat to each other about their dogs all the time ... That was one thing that actually really surprised me was, like I thought, moving into a building, people are just in their homes. But I guess because lots of people own, rather than rent, there's people who have been there for a long time. *(Samantha, age 33, lives alone)*

> Mine has more sense of community, but most of the people in my building are like long-term residents, who've been there for ages, and just older people, not as many younger people. And a lot of the people in my building, they own pets, so they kind of know each other by their pets. They talk, so they know each other in the building. *(Jaime, age 33, lives with roommate)*

Samantha and Jaime note that long-term residents and people with pets help to create a sense of community in their buildings. Their detached descriptions, however, suggest some sense of being outside of this community, perhaps because they are younger, do not own pets, and have been living in their buildings for shorter time periods. This suggests that shared traits are as important as shared spaces for fostering a sense of belonging in the condominium community.

In contrast to this mild detachment, Naomi, Leigh, and Colleen effusively describe the deep social and professional networks in their condominiums:

Actually [another resident] and I work together – we didn't before
– we met in this building. And there was another girl who lived in
the building who also had her own business, and the three of us,
over the past year or so, have gotten so much business out of each
other, and have started this little, like, network, business network,
between the three of us. And it's just been crazy how much business we've got through each other ... And no matter what you say,
it's always like, "I know somebody who does that or who can do
that" ... Like, there's a painter who's painted all of my friends'
places, there's like all kinds of handy men and different random
helping people who can further your business, and further everything. It's really pretty cool. There's people who can get you cheap
flights, all kinds of stuff. All we need is our own garden to grow
our own food and then we'd never have to leave! *(Naomi, age 29,
lives alone)*

Naomi is enthusiastic about the support she receives from neighbours, and
she suggests that there is a great deal of neighbourliness among the residents, who share or trade their skills and knowledge with one another. In
some ways, the condominium operates as a marketplace for her. The presence of helpful neighbours (and handy men) also suggests that condominium living can successfully replace a patriarchal figure in the home.

One of the guys in the building started a website ... It instigated us
forming a sports team ... and the sports team evolved into a little
social club ... There's this whole network going on. We do team
sports. We did the "Amazing Race Toronto" together, we do condo
crawls. It's always a laugh because I'm twice as old as the youngest,
and ten years older than the oldest. So I'm one of the oldest in the
building. Not one of the – but it's just a very, very young building.
But because I travel and I backpack a lot, I tend to go with younger
people anyways ... But yeah, so it's a great community, and I met
a girl three doors down, she's moved out now, but she ended up
being in the same line [of] work as me. She worked from home –
I got her involved in projects, she's flourishing business-wise, I'm
flourishing business-wise, and [another woman resident] works
with me sometimes, in some of my work. Yeah, so it's good. It's a
great place to – it's a safe place to network. *(Leigh, age 46, lives
alone)*

Leigh feels that, even though she is older than many of her neighbours in the building, her desire to participate in social activities and to network professionally makes her a part of the community. Community, in this case, is defined by shared interests rather than social identities.

> We have kind of an informal community starting. Between one of the concierges and some of the residents they've decided that they wanted to have more of a community than just a place to live. So they hold these little informal potlucks and things, where everyone brings something and sits down and chats, and you actually get to talk to your neighbours instead of just passing them in the halls. There's a lot of young professionals in there, and everyone has different shifts. You can go a week without running into anyone in the hallway. Like half the time you don't even see anyone. So it's just every month or two, they have a little dinner where we all go and get to know each other. *(Colleen, age 28, lives alone)*

Colleen notes that it is necessary to actively set aside time and space to develop community and neighbourly relationships because the young professionals in her building are very busy. Her comments suggest a difference between the way that residents define community and the way that developers define it: a community is not "just a place a live," it has to be actively created in daily life. Interestingly, in this case the concierges were instrumental in starting the social gatherings, suggesting that staff might sometimes do the work of keeping community going. It also indicates that, in some condominiums, the boundaries of community are not limited to residents but may include people who work in the building as well.

These participants articulate the ways in which condominium living can support personal, economic, and social objectives. Naomi, Leigh, and Colleen seem to define community as a semi-organized group or network that engages in shared activities or whose members support each other in some way. For these women, this was a very positive aspect of condominium living. Naomi expressed satisfaction that her personal business had benefited, Leigh found an active social life, and Colleen felt that monthly potlucks took away some of the anonymity or disconnectedness that resulted from living closely with strangers. These experiences can be interpreted as indicating an empowering facet of condominium life for women: the condominium provides a safe and convenient environment in which to develop relationships. This may be one way that women city dwellers can experience the benefits of community and neighbourliness without the perceived risk of interacting with strangers in public spaces.

This finding seems to resonate with the claims of feminist housing scholars such as Dolores Hayden (1980, 2002), who have often argued that communal living arrangements can be highly beneficial to women, especially when contrasted with the isolating features of single-family, low-density housing. Somewhat amusingly, Toronto's moral panic over high-rise housing in the 1970s was fuelled, in part, by the belief that apartments were *too* conducive to women's social lives and, apparently, led to an unnatural "passivity" in men. The *Toronto Star* reported:

> The Social Planning Council warns against the perils of high-rise living and how it can affect a family in a negative way. They warn that apartment living makes the adult male passive because he is not responsible for the upkeep of the building where his family resides. They warn that children who live in apartments have less social contact with others in their age group. They warn that women dominate the apartment landscape and are seen and heard while men seem quieter, less mobile or absent. (Worthington 1973)

The idea that women are "seen and heard" in this type of environment is echoed in more recent (though less panicked) scholarship. Housing scholar Michal Mitrany (2005), examining high-density condominium neighbourhoods in Haifa, found that women benefited from increased social interactions in such neighbourhoods, although, over time, factors such as frequent moving, indifference, and new immigrants constrained social interactions. In my study, the tight networks and active social lives that some women experienced indicate that the communal aspects of condominium living may in fact help women to negotiate the tension between the need or desire for security and privacy, on the one hand, and the desire for public life and sociability in the city, on the other.

However, not all of the women respondents valued socializing and deep levels of interaction, suggesting that there may be different definitions of empowerment, or satisfaction, for women who live in condominiums. Some women resisted engagement with their condominium communities. April and Chloe expressed reservation towards the idea that condominiums should function as communal living spaces:

> Toronto's supposed to be this aloof city where nobody talks to each other, and I just moved into Sesame Street. I'm not kidding.

It's shocking. And almost to the point where it's annoying ... I like being anonymous. I really, really do. Especially being a single woman, I don't like people knowing my business because, you know, you don't know what creep lives next door. *(April, age 37, lives alone)*

I like to have my own space. I don't want to be bothered by people that much. It works out. It's pretty much all professionals. There's not that many kids, and I personally don't really like to see kids running around all the time, so it works well for me ... I take the stairs to avoid small talk. *(Chloe, age 23, lives with partner)*

Sandra, below, expresses a tension between wanting a "community feeling" that mimics a traditional single-family neighbourhood and enjoying the privacy and independence of high-rise living:

So without wanting all the responsibilities of a house, I still wanted it to feel a little bit like a community ... We actually had a barbeque where it was like all the owners, kind of a seasonal barbeque kind of thing, where everybody could get together and meet each other, which is, I guess, something that tends to happen at street parties. So I think it's kind of nice to have that sort of feel in a building ... But at the same time I kind of like the fact that it's not like everybody on your street knows exactly what you're doing all the time ... For me it's a lot about independence. *(Sandra, age 28, lives alone)*

In resisting the social network of the condominium and seeking out increased privacy, these women challenge some of the gendered stereotypes that are used to position condominium living as empowering for women in that they refuse to engage in collective activities and social bonding and prefer to maintain their independence. According to Wilson's (1991) history of the links between urban development and gender ideologies, this type of attitude in women has been seen as threatening to the social order and has led to attempts to control women in urban space. While condominium development does not expressly function as gendered social control for women who are "dominating the landscape," the negative reactions of some women to the presumptions about community suggest that city builders and urban scholars cannot assume that people welcome community in predictable ways.

Conflict and Control

Being part of a condominium community can also generate conflicts that are related to the reworking of public and private space. Shared governance seems to be a particularly thorny process, and the news media frequently address this issue in condominium advice columns.

> Even if you do your homework, there's no guarantee you'll avoid problems. Condos, high-rises in particular, come with their own unique set of lifestyle issues. In a high-rise, you can have people above, beside and below you. The source of a noise can be one or several floors away. You should never knock on someone's door or send a nasty note. Contact your security desk or property manager. They are paid to handle complaints and should do so discreetly, without identifying you. Whether your neighbours own or rent, they can't just do as they please. If they play the stereo too loudly, allow their children to ride their bikes in the corridors or let Fido yap away, the board has a duty and a right to step in. (Laporte 2003b, P1)

These instructions on how to handle conflicts also point to the challenges of operationalizing community. Property managers or the board of directors mediate neighbourly relations. In this way, conflicts are funnelled through neutral parties and adjudicated according to the condominium's rules of conduct (Yiu, Wong, and Yau 2006). While this may be important for maintaining civility in close, dense living quarters, it is also a way for residents to distance themselves from the dirty work of community, the day-to-day struggles to make communities function despite differences. Wekerle et al. (1980) found that this bureaucratization of governance could limit residents' sense of control and engagement. This stands in contrast to research on women's co-ops, where shared governance is part of what makes such developments successful (Wekerle 1988b).

The women whom I interviewed described some of the conflicts that they experienced or anticipated. These were often related to their lack of complete ownership and control over the property:

> One thing that bugs me is that the public spaces that we share are protected by private security ... [This is] reflected by the decisions of the board, not necessarily your opinion. There's also, like, a lot of the apartments are rented out, and sometimes there's nobody there for months at a time. And the other problems that we have are we have a fire alarm malfunction, so it goes off in the middle

of the night ... You have more control over your domain, but your building is shared. *(Ava, age 32, lives alone)*

Condo living itself, I guess you can kind of hear people walking in and out. But I guess that happens anyway ... I guess maybe when you have to share these common areas with other people, and some of them won't be as responsible. Like the common areas are kind of marked up. I'm already anticipating the free weights – up in our workout area – I'm already anticipating somebody's going to walk off with those. Stuff like that. Because you're living with all these people, and you have to share all that stuff with them. It's not quite like your own space. *(Maya, age 30, lives alone)*

You don't have, I think, as much of a sense of personal ownership as you would if it's your own house completely. You know there's – we own the house, we don't own the outside walls. Right? You know, so there's that. There's still a little bit more rules, right? And you have to work a little bit more with others. So sometimes that's good, but, you know, it would be nice, it doesn't feel always like that small step of owning your own place. *(Molly, age 33, married, one child)*

These women felt common ownership and shared governance to be limitations on their freedoms as owners. As noted in Chapter 2, there is a strong normative link between ownership and freedom, and it shaped the desires of these women to become condominium owners. Molly comments that it is sometimes good to work with others, but she seems to understand common-interest living as a step below freehold ownership in the hierarchy of tenure. In this view, having to share and work is viewed as a negative or lesser way of living. Additionally, the presence of a framework of legal relations and obligations among residents of common-interest communities may work to inhibit social relations or confine them to the realm of legalities (Blandy and Lister 2005). Social interactions are based upon conflict rather than upon shared interests. This raises the question of how women respond to the opportunity to participate in governance and how this relates to a sense of community within their condominiums.

Women had widely divergent responses to questions about their desire or willingness to participate in formal governance structures. They also had differing reasons for choosing to engage or disengage with these processes.

I really would like to participate in that. In the past, like in a rental building, I don't think I would. I just feel like I'm not really a part of the decision, I don't own anything there, I'm just using stuff. But for sure, once I own it, you know I hear a lot of this stuff from my friends, about the things they decide on, and I definitely want to have a say in that, you know. *(Jillian, age 30, lives alone)*

Jillian contrasts her sense of ownership of the condominium with her lack of involvement in a rental building. Getting involved in decisions may be a way of staking a more substantial claim on the property and of avoiding the potential alienation that can come from being just one resident in a large high-rise building.

Sandra and Leigh were the only women to whom I spoke who were, or had been, members of the boards of directors in their condominiums.

I am a terrible joiner, to the point where I just don't even know when to say no. I just thought it would be really interesting. And I wanted to know more about the condo, more about what was going on. There didn't seem to be any communication at all from the previous board to the condo owners. Like you only heard about them when it was time to do the budget. So I just thought, both for my personal understanding, and also for the opportunity to communicate better with other condo owners, so I thought that would be good. And I think actually, not just because of my joining, 'cause of some of the other people that are on as well, I think a lot of that is actually improving. *(Sandra, age 28, lives alone)*

Interviewer: Why did you get involved with the condo board?

Leigh: To protect the value of my asset. And we were – the first year of a condo the developer gets to appoint an arm's-length property manager. It was never arm's-length. It was absolutely corrupt from the get-go. And I fought with the board because my instincts were telling me that the woman that was our property manager was in cahoots with the developer. Therefore, she was not doing a service to us, she was doing a service for him. Making sure that the work wasn't getting done, telling people that their warranties were up when they

> weren't, just doing all sorts of stuff. And it took me
> months and months of battling ... And that's how we
> ended up getting the new security and the new prop-
> erty manager. So as far as – I think my job's done. I
> think I've done as much as I can for this building. I've
> protected my asset, which is what I set out to do. And
> anything else is just peripheral stuff that's not gonna,
> you know, significantly impact on anything.
> *(Leigh, age 46, lives alone)*

In these comments from Sandra and Leigh, we hear diverging rationales for their participation. Sandra connects her reasons for involvement to a desire for community, a wish to empower herself with knowledge about the condominium, and a need for improved communication. She feels that she has had some success in this regard. This appears closely aligned with feminist understandings of how and why women participate in housing – as part of an interest in shaping and promoting cooperation and community (Wekerle 1988a, 1988b; Smailes 1994). Leigh, on the other hand, is concerned with the investment quality of her unit and her building. Leigh's case is a strong example of how the governance structure of condominiums can be appropriated by residents to take control over decisions that affect not only the building's daily life but also its overall infrastructure. For Leigh, being on the board was less about shaping community than it was about protecting her interests as a homeowner, reflecting again the economic aspects of empowerment for women through condominium ownership.

These differing responses suggest that it is inadequate to make gendered or essentialist assumptions about how and why women will participate in condominium governance. Furthermore, many women have little or no desire to "empower" themselves in this way:

> It's funny you ask, because I just got a notice of the upcoming
> condo meeting at the end of the month, and I've been to those
> before, and I kind of find them to be, you know, complaint-fests,
> you know. People are there, they've got a face to complain to and,
> you know, I'm gonna get the notes to it, in a week anyways, and I
> don't have any complaints. So I was considering going, but the
> majority of this building, I'd say from what I know of the building,
> are, I'd say at least 65, 70 percent, are considerably older than me,
> and I've heard them in the hallways, in the elevators, in the bus,

and it's a lot of complaining, so I don't think I really want to
participate in that. It doesn't interest me. It's on a Friday night,
come on ... This is where I live. I don't need to be responsible for it
beyond kind of my four walls. *(Caitlin, age 31, lives alone)*

For Caitlin, attending condominium meetings is a burden and a potentially
tedious "complaint fest." She distances herself from other residents based on
age, and this, in part, shapes her unwillingness to engage with them as community members through the medium of governance. Her comment that
the meeting is on a Friday night points to the possibility that, for younger
women with active social lives, lifestyle factors might deter them from participation. However, her final words are particularly telling with regard to
where she draws the boundaries of community.

Chloe's comments are somewhat similar to Caitlin's in that she does not
feel the need to participate because she is not particularly attached to the
community, due to her intent to move soon:

I've never considered it. I wouldn't mind if I did, but it's not somewhere I'm planning on being for very, very long, so I'm not willing
to put that much effort into it. *(Chloe, age 23, lives with partner)*

This suggests that investing time and energy in governance is related to the
condominium owner's long-term goals. For Molly and Lynn, condominium
participation seems burdensome in terms of the politics involved as well as
in terms of the time commitment:

No. I have a non-profit background, and so I've probably considered it at some point, but in terms of just politics, I don't need
to get involved in that. *(Molly, age 33, married, one child)*

Anything's possible. If they start making rules that I disagree with
or worry about, then for sure. But I'm very busy. I have my day job
and I also run my own business, so for the most part I figure as
long as I'm not unhappy with the way things are running, I'll just
keep my distance from that whole thing. *(Lynn, age 28, lives alone)*

For these women, the prospect of participating in condominium governance
seems anything but empowering. It is conceived of as a burden or as simply

unnecessary. Moreover, for women like Chloe, who do not see themselves staying in their condominiums for more than a few years, it is simply not worth the effort. Factors such as length of tenure, age, and lifestyle are important to consider when assessing the democratic potential of condominium living.

Condominium governance structures can be examined as part of a contemporary transformation in the art of government. Geographer Erik Swyngedouw's (2005) evaluation of such new governmental arrangements suggests that they are "Janus-faced" in that they exhibit the potential for empowerment but are positioned within a neoliberal economic order that celebrates the so-called virtues of self-managed risk, prudence, and self-responsibility. Rather than giving voice to the marginalized, these arrangements depend upon the ability to exercise entitlements and institutional power and indicate a shift in the direction of greater individual responsibility.

The neoliberal analysis can be read against feminist work that sees local governance structures as fruitful sites for women to learn about, and engage in, democratic politics. Political scientist Carol Pateman's (1970) study of the ways that work-based democratic structures educate women in the workings of formal political organizations suggests that, under certain conditions, women could feel empowered to take a strong role in decision-making processes. Like the neoliberal analysis, feminist work acknowledges the power relations that function to empower some groups over others as well as the types of institutional power that shape such engagements.

How do these frameworks articulate with the everyday experience of condominium governance for women condominium owners? My analysis of the narratives here is, first, that the governance structure can potentially be a site where women can take control over decisions that affect their daily lives and the overall conditions of the buildings in which they live. However, this requires that women actively choose to engage in governance. If, as this research indicates, many women opt out, the empowering function of shared governance is not operationalized in everyday life. Although these women did not say that they felt disempowered or silenced by institutional power arrangements or elites that held control in their condominiums, the fact that participation was seen as onerous and burdensome suggests that there is little that actively encourages them to take on the responsibilities associated with participation. This raises questions about representation. To what extent are women's concerns voiced when women feel it is not worthwhile to participate? This feeling may be facilitated by the fact that condominiums

are not sites of long-term residence for many young women or by a culture
of property wherein people do not want to be held responsible for decisions
"beyond [their] four walls."

Conclusion

At the outset of this chapter, I sought to understand where condominium
living articulates with and departs from two broad perspectives: one that
views condominiums as exclusive, gated communities and one that posits
condominiums as sites for democratic engagement and social connectedness. Bringing a feminist perspective to bear on these seemingly dichotomous positions complicates matters by raising questions about how
condominiums, as communities, are shaped through gendered ideologies
and experienced in gendered ways.

While community, as a concept, is deployed largely in aid of neoliberal
city building imperatives, the everyday experience of community in the
context of condominium living is more complex than a straightforward
argument about privatization and commodification suggests. This observation should not, however, be read as an uncritical endorsement of high-
density urban new-build gentrification projects. In fact, the ways in which
these spaces and governance arrangements can be said to work for some
members of a relatively privileged group of young, professional women
simultaneously highlight the ways in which these spaces and arrangements
exclude, both directly and indirectly, other city dwellers in a variety of problematic ways.

Can condominiums be understood as gated communities? Condominiums are developed and marketed as exclusive communities with amenities
and advantages for residents only. The term "community" functions as a
warm and positive key word that justifies and legitimates gentrification.
This works through a slippage within the notion of community, wherein the
simple placement of a high concentration of people in a residential form is
conflated with the ideal of community. Labelling new-build gentrification as
creating or revitalizing communities helps to evict (as Tom Slater [2006]
argues) the problematic aspects of gentrification from public debate.

Within the condominium, the shared spaces and common governance
structure provide opportunities for women to engage in social and professional networking and to become involved with the democratic decision-
making process in the condominium. On the face of it, these features
suggest that condominiums might work for women in the same ways as, for

example, women-led housing co-operatives. By subverting the isolation and privatism of the privately owned, single-family home, condominium living offers women a chance to form their own connections and support systems and to become engaged and empowered through governance. The condominium was, for many women, a site of social connections and, for a smaller number, a site of political engagement. However, condominiums stop far short, I think, of the feminist model wherein housing functions as one of the many sites and stakes of women's struggles for urban citizenship. The women for whom condominiums do function as sites of engagement represent a relatively privileged few who have the means to buy a place in these communities. Even these few may also choose to emphatically disengage from any notion of community, preferring privacy, anonymity, and a lack of responsibility for governance. These findings complicate the idea that condominiums, by the mere fact that they have shared spaces and governance, will facilitate public participation and social connectedness. They also suggest that there is nothing inherently empowering or emancipatory about condominium living for women; while some women find ways to turn the representations of community constructed by planners and developers into actual spaces of representation for themselves, simplistic or essentialist assumptions about women and community do not hold.

In reading this chapter against the previous chapter's analysis of condominium ownership, a tension emerges between the ostensible community orientation of the condominium dweller and the self-reliant, individualistic citizen produced through narratives of home ownership. Is the neoliberal rationality that, I argued, promotes the development of the entrepreneurial citizen through condominium ownership undermined through other aspects of condominium living, such as shared space and common governance? The creation of relatively private and insulated communities such as condominiums can be understood as part of the overall reorganization of governance under neoliberal regimes, wherein the proliferation of new governance arrangements represents a shift towards an ethic of increasingly localized or individualized self-governance and reduced state responsibility for citizens' well-being. The private construction of community spaces (the quasi-public shared spaces of the condominium) is one way that condominiums reduce the social burden of the local state and place increased responsibility in the hands of property owners. The city negotiates the provision of community space with private developers in a process that ultimately creates common spaces accessible primarily to condominium dwellers.

Condominium owners are then responsible for maintaining their own community spaces. In this process, the ethic of self-reliance and individual responsibility is not subverted.

Perhaps the clearest example of the ways in which condominiums can function as gated, privatized, and depoliticized communities is in the provision of private security. In the next chapter, I explore how ideologies of gendered fear and vulnerability intersect with processes of capital accumulation to legitimize securitization of the city and to expand the frontiers of gentrification.

4 Securing Relations of Threat
The Intersection of Gender, Fear, and Capital

Urban revitalization policies are discursively linked, in part, to urban fears and relations of threat. Irruptions of violence and moments of anxiety may threaten visions of the spectacular and safe city that are central to the urban renaissance so desired by cities competing for a place in the global urban hierarchy (Hall and Hubbard 1998; N. Smith 2002; Raco 2003; Peck 2005). At the same time, however, many scholars have argued that a systemic culture of fear is integral to the success of neoliberal urban agendas, particularly where notions of danger are used to legitimate revanchist gentrification and redevelopment efforts (Davis 1999; Marcuse 2004; Mitchell 2005; Bauman 2000; Graham 2004). In Toronto, these tensions have been inscribed in the city, in part, through the creation of tens of thousands of securitized residential condominium spaces within the central city. These spaces are produced partially through gendered ideologies about cities, bodies, safety, and danger that (re)emerge or are (re)invigorated in the context of Toronto's revitalization hopes and fears. The dynamic tension between freedom and fear, profit and risk, highlights the gendered constitution of the neoliberal makeover of the city.

The relationship between gentrification, the politics of fear, and neoliberal urban redevelopment programs has garnered a great deal of attention in recent critical urban literature (Helms, Atkinson, and MacLeod 2007; N. Smith 1996, 2002; Atkinson and Blandy 2007; Atkinson and Helms 2007; Lees 2003). In conceptualizing contemporary gentrification as part of a revanchist strategy to reclaim the city for white, middle-class, and elite groups, scholars like Neil Smith (1996) point to the cultivation of relations of threat among competing groups of urban dwellers and the spatialization of these relations through redevelopment projects. Although new-build gentrification projects are celebrated and marketed as symbols of the spectacular, cosmopolitan, and entrepreneurial renaissance of the postindustrial city (Davidson and Lees 2005), they also represent the pervasive undercurrent of urban insecurity, which is to be managed through gating, policing, and technological interventions (Bauman 2000). This paradox is arguably central to the politics of urban revitalization, which draws on ideals of the city as a place of freedom, pleasure, and adventure. Part of what makes it a place of excitement constitutes the other half of this paradox, that is, the notion of the city as a place of danger and anxiety. In a similar vein, the imagery and discourse of revitalization present the city as feminized and empowering for women but also as a source of ever-present threat (Wilson 1991; Pain 1997). This apparent contradiction is integral to the circular logic of revanchist urbanism, wherein fear of the other justifies displacement and redevelopment, and the need for redevelopment (highest and best use) legitimizes the violence of displacement and marginalization (Blomley 2004).

Geographer Mike Raco (2007, 309) writes that "a new politics of risk and risk-avoidance has emerged around imaginations and perceptions of 'personal safety' and 'security' ... Developers are now encouraged to create defensible spaces within city centres in order to make them more selective and secure." Diverse theorists point to the heightened anxieties about everything from immigration to terrorism to environmental catastrophes, all of which are used to justify increasingly militarized city building and governance practices throughout the West (Davis 1991, 1999; Bauman 2000; Baudrillard 2003; Virilio 2005). In connecting this to gentrification, many scholars critique the violence underlying processes of displacement and eviction (N. Smith 1996, 2002; Slater 2004a, 2006; Atkinson 2000; Gibson 2004; Newman and Wyly 2006).

Although Toronto's image has never been primarily defined by a "scary city" rhetoric, and the city itself is experienced by many as a safe, clean, and friendly place to live and visit (Yutangco 2009), in recent years an increasingly panicked discourse has arisen around public violence. This panic reached new heights, and had a particularly racialized character, in the summer of 2005, which the media dubbed "the summer of the gun." Over a particularly violent two-week period in this season, there were twenty shootings. By the end of 2005, fifty-two out of seventy-eight homicides in Toronto involved firearms, including the highly sensationalized Boxing Day death of a fifteen-year-old white girl caught in the crossfire of a shootout among black youth in the downtown's central shopping hub (Yutangco 2009). While much of this violence is perceived to be concentrated in poorer neighbourhoods and social housing projects at the periphery of the city, the increased calls for, and use of, police CCTV in busy downtown areas suggest that these anxieties are not so neatly contained (Doolittle 2008). Moreover, the masculinized features of ostensibly gang-related violence do not mean that women in Toronto feel immune to danger. Local feminist literature documents a long history of women's struggles to create safe streets, parks, and public buildings across the city (Whitzman 1992, 2002; Andrew 1995; Kern 2005). While critics of neoliberal urbanism have identified poor, racialized, and other marginalized groups as the targets of revanchist urban tactics and gentrification practices (MacLeod 2002; Flusty 2001; Kipfer and Keil 2002), the gendered dimensions of "scary cities" have less often been addressed in this context. While Hubbard (2004) critiques the ways that revanchist urbanism reinvigorates masculine, phallic power in relation to the criminalization of certain sex trades in the UK, he points out that gender has been largely sidelined in theory and research around policies and practices of neoliberal urbanism (see also Papayanis 2000; Koskela 2002).

Revanchist urban politics also interpolate with men's fears and threats to middle-class, white masculinity. Neil Smith's (1996) explication of the urban pioneer and the frontier-taming dimensions of gentrification illustrates one of the ways in which we can begin to understand the role of masculinity in urban revitalization. In addition, attempts by some cities to "clean up" sex trade zones and other displays of sexuality often disproportionately affect gay and lesbian neighbourhoods, suggesting another way in which revanchist practices speak to threats to masculine heteronormativity (Papayanis 2000; Delany 1999; Kipfer and Keil 2002). While I did not interview male condominium owners for *Sex and the Revitalized City*, I am sure that many would articulate concerns around residential security. I found it useful, though, to focus on women in order to tease out the ways in which urban revitalization policies in general, and condominium developments in particular, have tried to position women's emancipation as one of the specific windfalls of these processes.

There is a particular need, I suggest, for scholarship that makes connections between theories of the revanchist city and the rich interdisciplinary feminist literature on women's fear of violence in urban settings (Day 2001; Gordon and Riger 1989; Kern 2005; Koskela 1999; Koskela and Pain 2000; Mehta and Bondi 1999; Valentine 1989, 1992). The literature on neoliberal urbanism primarily positions fear and relations of threat as both produced by, and productive of, capitalist processes that might incidentally draw on racism, sexism, homophobia, and other prejudices to provide the particular contours of insecurity and anxiety (Kipfer and Keil 2002; MacLeod 2002; N. Smith 1996; Davis 1999). Feminist theory positions fear less abstractly as resulting from gendered socialization processes, experiences of harassment and violence, and the shape of the built environment (Valentine 1989; Pain 1991; Starkweather 2007). Moreover, fear affects women differently across social class, race, ethnicity, sexuality, ability, age, and citizenship status. Feminists also understand fear as a central dimension of women's subordination. Geographer Hille Koskela (1999, 112) emphasizes the centrality of space to women's fear, noting that "space and social characteristics are mutually modifying, interacting dimensions that deeply affect the nature and shape of women's fear. Fear of crime is constantly modifying women's spatial realities ... [However,] space is not just a medium for interaction but is also *produced by* this interaction" (my emphasis). Thus, the sexual objectification of women in public space, through harassment and sexist imagery (Rosewarne 2005), not only produces fear but is also part of the social production of (patriarchal) urban space (Lefebvre 1991b). This notion is a potential linkage point for bringing a feminist perspective to neoliberal urbanism – a perspective through which we can view the spaces of revitalization, and the wider neoliberal city, as produced by multiple, co-evolving sets of discourses and practices.

Condominium security articulates with concerns about community and citizenship in several ways. Security represents the literal gates through which interactions with, and connections to, the surrounding neighbourhood are mediated and negotiated. The security perimeter marks the boundaries of bordering communities. It also helps to define public and private space in the sense of determining who has access to different urban spaces and, for condominium dwellers, in terms of what counts as home or personal space and what counts as shared, communal, or public space. The issue of security illustrates the ways in which this particular model of city building is predicated on gendered ideas about safety and fear in urban space. It also functions to shape contemporary gendered norms about everyday life in the city, teaching women who is considered part of their community and who is not as well as which spaces they should feel comfortable in and which they should not. Security features may define and reflect, both materially and symbolically, societal ideals about who is considered deserving and in need of protection in the revitalized city, thus marking out a complex class/race/gender geography. Security is also significant in condominium marketing, where it is used to position condominium living as a form of empowerment for women in the city. My main argument is that the gendered dimensions of the tension between freedom and fear are vital to the success of new-build gentrification. Through the commodification of fear and safety, of women's freedom and women's sexuality, neoliberal processes of privatization, securitization, and capital accumulation are able to circulate with increased speed through expanding markets. Moreover, women's everyday lives and urban identities are shaped by this tension, drawing middle-class and professional women into the project of the revanchist, entrepreneurial city.

Constructing "Peace of Mind"

What are the gendered rationales that shape condominium security? Condominium developers raised the topic of security in the context of discussions about the attractive features of their condominium developments and about women as condominium purchasers. They uniformly noted that security had become one of the most common features of condominium projects, including services such as twenty-four-hour concierge service, security guards, key card entry, video surveillance, and, in one case, hand-print door locks.

> To a certain degree, twenty-four-hour concierge has almost become a default. It's actually more the exception not to see it included in projects. *(Developer interview, 19 July 2005)*

Developers also suggested that these features are key factors in women's decisions around condominium ownership:

> Actually a lot of our projects do have a lot of females ... The majority is, it's the security. I can show you a list of our security ... Basically this would be standard for all of our buildings. From the twenty-four-hour concierge, [the] concierge always has access ... This would be for all of our suites and buildings. *(Developer interview, 28 June 2005)*

This representative was insistent about the importance of safety features for women buyers. She gave me a brochure for one of her firm's developments, which listed twelve so-called "peace-of-mind" features, including uniformed twenty-four-hour concierge/security, card access, entry-phone system, security cameras, coded suite intrusion alarms, and gated underground parking.

Another developer detailed a project's innovative security features and explicitly acknowledged that these features are designed to "target" first-time women buyers:

> The interesting thing about the building is that we had a lot of
> security features in there. Which women really liked. There's one
> thing they call a bio-metric hand reader, so we were the first to
> incorporate this, where you actually have to program your hand in
> there, to get access into the building. So that was a unique feature
> that really targeted the first-time woman buyer that was there. And
> they like the security of the facilities that are in there, they don't
> want to pay a lot of maintenance fees and so on, so those are the
> kinds of things that were attracting the young women to buy in
> there. *(Developer interview, 5 July 2005)*

While this developer is certainly drawing on his firm's market research to assert that "women really liked" the security features, developers also tap into common-sense or stereotypical notions about young women and fear in urban settings. In targeting the first-time woman buyer as a demographic through the incorporation of security features, developers assume that this woman is insecure as a city dweller and with regard to living alone. She requires the reassurance of "peace-of-mind" features to quell misgivings about living in a high-density project in a downtown area.

One of the developers interviewed was also a condominium owner. She drew upon her personal experiences to explain women's desire for security services:

> I mean, personally speaking ... my particular street is very quiet,
> and so after office hours it gets a bit quiet, and there are a couple
> of clubs in the area that kind of get rowdy at times, and so I've been
> always so glad – even though it drives me crazy, my maintenance
> fees are so high – ... but I'm always very glad that there's a concierge
> there. Because whenever I'm walking into my building at night, I'm
> always thinking, "Okay, if worse comes to worst I can just run to
> my building, and there'll be somebody behind the desk who will
> threaten away." But I do think that, for women, they probably

would find the concierge aspect very important. But there is the cost consideration. *(Developer interview, 19 July 2005)*

Like Fincher (2004), I found that developers draw on traditional ideas about women's fearfulness in urban space, about what causes fear (rowdiness, deserted streets), and about women's need for protection in these spaces. In many ways, this resonates with more general feminist studies of women's fear of violence in urban spaces, which have often concluded that there are many features of urban built and social environments that trigger fearfulness in women (Koskela and Pain 2000; Valentine 1989; Pain 1997; Duncan 1996; Burgess 1998). However, the extent to which security is considered a selling point for condominiums is striking, especially when one considers the high cost of incorporating and maintaining these features within the project.[1] Although gendered safety concerns are not the only rationale for incorporating these features, gendered expectations about fear are part of this city building process, encoding and enshrining those expectations into the built environment. The previous chapter's discussion of the ways that developers understand community also suggests a tension or contradiction here: if condominiums are placed in carefully selected neighbourhoods with the expectation that the condominium automatically either creates community or becomes part of a pre-existing community, then why is it assumed that condominium dwellers need or desire so much protection and insulation from that community? I return to this point and attempt to answer the question as I consider women condominium owners' responses regarding security.

The Logic of Security?

In discussions with women condominium owners, most of the participants expressed the feeling that security was important to their choice of a condominium and in their daily lives:

> As a single woman living on her own, I think the security is a big issue. Especially living [in] downtown Toronto, you always hear stories of crazy things that happen, so that is definitely a big thing. *(Rachel, age 22, lives alone)*

> The concierge is actually a really big thing. I don't think I'd feel as comfortable living right [in] downtown Toronto. I mean, I love the location, but there's just a fair number of homeless people and not that far away there's drug dealers and prostitutes and stuff like

that. You know I feel completely comfortable in this building. I've
never felt uncomfortable here once. And I think the concierge,
knowing that they're there, that's part of that. The pass-codes,
things like that, there's card entry. And video cameras, like
surveillance cameras in the underground parking garage. So all
that stuff contributes to making it feel comfortable living here.
(Sandra, age 28, lives alone)

I liked that it was a low rise. That there was – not so much a sense
of accountability – but just in really big buildings you feel like no
one really knows anyone, you don't know if the people who are in
there belong there or not. Part of it was a security thing. They do
have twenty-four-hour security, in the lobby. *(Colleen, age 28,
lives alone)*

These comments illustrate that personal safety is still an important issue
for women living in the central city, one for which they are willing to take
individual responsibility by paying (through their monthly condominium
fees) for security personnel and technology. The security features help
women to manage, mitigate, and negotiate urban insecurities. To some extent, the responses here might reflect gendered socialization processes and
reflect a dominant cultural script that assumes that women *should* feel fear
in urban public spaces (Valentine 1989; Mehta and Bondi 1999; Day 2001).

   In contrast, some participants were nonchalant about the presence of
safety features.

It's funny you ask, because, in all honesty, other than the key to get
in the front door, I had no idea we had a security camera that you
can access on Channel 59, and I can see the front and back of the
door. But no, like with regards to this place, I don't know, I've never
felt, or so far I've never felt, unsafe – in the parking garage, in the
front or back entrance, in the hallways, nothing. It's just a very nice
area, nice tenants. I've never felt insecure. I wasn't looking
specifically for security features. *(Caitlin, age 31, lives alone)*

Not really. I mean there's a concierge, a twenty-four-hour concierge, which is not so much a security thing for me but more like,
anything I need I can always like, like, you know, if a package gets

delivered – it's more for business than it is for security. *(Naomi, age 29, lives alone)*

I feel very, very safe here. I feel like I can – I mean, I leave my balcony open all the time. I always leave my door open – I shouldn't, but it's a perfectly safe building. *(Leigh, age 46, lives alone)*

We have a concierge, a twenty-four-hour concierge. And there's usually one person at the desk, and at least one person just sort of wandering the building patrolling. It seems pretty good. Obviously no security is foolproof, but it's pretty close. All safety is kind of an illusion, but it's a better illusion. *(Lynn, age 28, lives alone)*

These comments suggest that developers may overstate the need for security and that women, even first-time women buyers, can feel comfortable and safe in urban high-rise buildings. As Lynn points out, the feeling of safety is a social construction, a collective illusion. By acknowledging the experiences of women who are not particularly concerned with safety in the condominium, we can ask what other logics are at work that seem to require that this illusion be perpetuated and positioned as an inherent need.

It is here that neoliberal agendas articulate most clearly with gender ideologies in the process of city building. The logic of capitalist urban development, wherein capital seeks out ways to prime marginal spaces for reinvestment (N. Smith 1979; Harvey 1985), can draw upon the ideology of gendered fear and use the provision of safety as a way to smooth the path, and speed the spread, of new-build gentrification. Areas of the city that would otherwise be deemed too risky for investment (because they are assumed to be undesirable to key segments of the target market) are opened up for redevelopment when security features attenuate the ostensible risk. Women's gendered vulnerabilities rationalize this process as developers get to claim that they are concerned for women's safety. Again, this logic seems to belie the positive notion of community used to market condominium development.

Transforming "Dodgy" Neighbourhoods

Women's gendered vulnerabilities are also used to legitimate the more widespread militarization of space (Davis 1991) that occurs when private developments police their surroundings and set up exclusionary boundaries (see also Gibson [2004] for a discussion of securitizing the city in the context of revitalization). The women whom I interviewed seemed very aware that their condominium developments were part of a broader gentrification process that was transforming "dodgy" (in Lynn's words) downtown neighbourhoods into ostensibly safer places by making them into consumption niches or tourist sites:

> When I first moved in, people would come out at three o'clock in the morning, drunk, and start fights, and I actually saw this one guy getting his head kicked in ... I guess the fact that they're building a condo across the street is actually a deterrent to that. *(Sandra, age 28, lives alone)*

> The condo in the Distillery, while it was a really hot neighbourhood at the time, by the time I sold it, it was like, you know, big hype around it. When I first moved in there, even the pizza guys wouldn't come to my place. They were like, "What? Mill Street? There's no houses on Mill Street." Cabs would drop me off at the corner of Parliament and Mill, they wouldn't go down that street. They were worried that I would have somebody there to mug them. I was like, "Okay, great. So you're gonna make, like, a single woman walk down the street in this nasty deserted warehouse neighbourhood. That's great." It was completely deserted. But after five years, it doubled in price. *(Naomi, age 29, lives alone)*

Naomi's experience with her first condominium illustrates how rapidly developments such as condominiums can transform "nasty" neighbourhoods into highly desirable locales. As a young single woman, however, she had to negotiate a deserted warehouse area in order to realize the benefits (and profits) of redevelopment.

> I'm right on the edge between a fairly nice part of town and a kind of dodgy part of town, so – it's interesting to watch, too, how everything just keeps getting upgraded and gentrified just by nature of the fact that you're downtown, so everyone wants to be there. They're building some [condos] just one building over from our building, so ... I think, if anything, not that it's necessarily a good thing, but I think that the gentrification of the downtown

area is gonna keep going, until the downtown is going to become
almost as much of a safe little neighbourhood as some of the older,
richer neighbourhoods are. *(Lynn, age 28, lives alone)*

Lynn recognizes and names condominium development as gentrification,
and she is aware of the ways that gentrification spreads from one neighbourhood to the next. She links gentrification to urban safety by making the assumption that gentrification brings safety (or the perception of safety) to
formerly "dodgy" places.

It's sort of run-down, needs improvements. Unfortunately, everybody knows it's high drug traffic, high prostitution, so that, you
know, I'd like to see it cleaned up, not in a necessarily – you have
to just hide all the negative elements – but just to, you know –
obviously, I think most people, especially families – you know,
some of that just to make it a little bit, feel safer, and, you know,
beautify it somewhat. *(Molly, age 33, married, one child)*

Molly notes the issue of the perception of safety, suggesting that improving
and beautifying the area would create a sense of safety. She does not express
hostility towards the "negative elements," like drug traffic and prostitution,
and does not even suggest that these things should be eliminated from the
area. For Molly, it seems that more subtle changes to the physical environment would make a difference in her perception of safety and of the area as
welcoming for families. April, on the other hand, is more critical of the "unfortunate" elements in her neighbourhood:

I walk down Queen a lot, and I'm like, "Wow, it's a whole different
world." There's crackheads, there's drunks and bums, and it's very
unfortunate, but at the same time I'm like, "Whoa, boy, do I have
to be careful." I make sure I'm holding on to my purse. And it's not
that I feel like they're going to do something to me, but they're
going to grab my purse or whatever. So that's one great thing about
Richmond [Street], it's just a straight through and, yeah – I didn't
realize it until after, and I was like, "Oh, this was a much better
choice." And also because Adelaide [Street] as well is a one way,
going the other way, I have this surrounding my entire building.
(April, age 37, lives alone)

April enjoys the fact that her condominium has a defensive position in that it is bordered by one-way streets with lots of vehicle traffic and little foot traffic. This is one very subtle way that new developments create effective borders between their residents and the marginalized groups that occupy surrounding neighbourhoods, echoing earlier research in crime prevention through environmental design (O. Newman 1972).

Despite general appreciation for the various security measures offered by condominiums, all of the women interviewed expressed a lot of comfort with the urban environment and an overall sense of safety, belonging, and confidence that cannot be attributed to private security features. The willingness of some women to move to less established neighbourhoods or poorer areas of the city can be read as resistance to the broad socialization of women into fear of urban space (Pain 1991; Koskela 1997). Condominiums in marginal neighbourhoods may also be more competitively priced, attracting young, first-time women buyers who perhaps cannot afford projects in more established areas of the city. Simultaneously, however, putting extensive security features into these condominiums works to sell women on marginal neighbourhoods with few services and bad reputations. Gendered ideologies about safety and fear, then, are connected to cycles of uneven development through the ways in which they work to facilitate capital accumulation in ever more city spaces by opening up new segments of the housing market (i.e., young women buyers) and new spaces of the city.

Living on the Edge

Having a sense that one lives in a "nasty" or "dodgy" neighbourhood with "drunks," "bums," drug traffic, and prostitution may explain why some women were enthusiastic about the social networks and community ties that they had developed *within* their condominiums. Interestingly, though, some women condominium owners expressed an affinity for the "borderline" nature of the neighbourhoods into which they moved.

> It's pretty borderline, because it kind of borders – you know, if you
> go a little bit east of here it's kind of seedy, and if you go north of
> here it's kind of seedy, but if you go south or west – it's like financial
> district, St. Lawrence Market, very sort of posh. So it's a little like
> me. A little – you know, I could sort of be a little trashy, or I could
> be a little posh, depending on the day, or how I feel. So I like it. I
> like it. Like if it was all – if the building didn't border on a some-
> what seedy neighbourhood, it would probably be a very expensive

building too. So I have no problem being like, "Okay, I'm a block away from Moss Park or whatever it is," where there's a lot of, a lot of – I don't know, just seediness, I guess. I like the neighbourhood. It's close to everything too. *(Naomi, age 29, lives alone)*

It's a perfectly safe neighbourhood. Any neighbourhood is safe if you have the attitude that you look after yourself, you know? I don't feel compromised in any way, you know? We're supposedly living near crack alley. Well, when you've slept on floors in places like New Delhi and travelled the way I've travelled, really this is, this is the Hilton – you know? ... And I think the twenty-four-hour security did appeal to me. But if it was taken away it wouldn't be a big deal. But I know it won't be taken away because many people bought because they were attracted by that. *(Leigh, age 46, lives alone)*

Naomi and Leigh live in the same building just east of the downtown core, in an area that has long had a negative reputation due to the presence of men's shelters, prostitution, drug-related activity, and nearby social housing and immigrant neighbourhoods. Their comfort and confidence here challenge certain gendered stereotypes that suggest that women are naturally or inherently fearful in such places (Kern 2005). Wilson (1991) suggests that women have often found excitement and freedom in the ostensibly dangerous spaces of the city. It is important, though, to situate this experience in relation to broader social and cultural processes. For example, Neil Smith (1996) problematizes the trope of the urban pioneer, part of the intrepid first wave of middle-class gentrifiers who brave liminal urban zones to tame these places and reclaim them from the disorderly and deviant urban poor. There is a certain aesthetic tied to being on the edge of a dangerous or unknown frontier that groups who are often precursors to gentrification, like artists, might express (Bain 2003; Ley 1996). The women whom I interviewed did not typically express openly revanchist attitudes or hostility towards the people with whom they shared a neighbourhood, but they are undoubtedly caught up in the larger revitalization project that seeks to cleanse and remake space in the image of the middle class.

Naomi's description of her feelings about her neighbourhood also alerts us to the issue of identity formation through these processes. She conceptualizes the east-west axis of her neighbourhood as reflecting her personae and her personal style: "A little trashy or ... a little posh." Anti-racist legal scholar Sherene Razack (1998, 2002) suggests that white, bourgeois identities are *made* through boundary crossings into spaces marked as "other." Razack theorizes that the ability to transgress into less respectable spaces, and return unscathed, is one way that this subject comes to know her- or himself as white, middle class, and dominant. In this case, choosing to live in a borderline neighbourhood (or representing oneself as having an affinity for the neighbourhood) is perhaps one way that these women come to know or understand themselves as authentically urban. By asserting a right to inhabit these places, women condominium owners subvert the notion that urban space is circumscribed by danger and fear, but they also participate in an identity-making process that positions them as dominant, normal, ideal, desirable urban citizens in contrast to marginalized and minoritized groups.

Given these relationships between security, safety, and the production of revitalized urban spaces, it is critical to question the extent to which women condominium dwellers, particularly those who live in borderline neighbourhoods, will engage in public and/or political life, attempting to become members of the community outside of the condominium. Hope and Ava both note that their areas do not have a lot of services, and this creates a sense of isolation (which Hope values as privacy):

> It hasn't got a whole bunch of shops along there, so it doesn't get a lot of foot traffic. It feels like your space when you get home, you're not sort of sharing it with everybody. *(Hope, age 29, married)*

> I actually don't like the immediate neighbourhood, it's not very neighbour-like. Like, we don't have cafés or groceries, or dry cleaners or whatever, although that's starting to change. It's a bit of a tourist trap. *(Ava, age 32, lives alone)*

Hope enjoys the secluded nature of her residential area, while Ava is irritated by the fact that her neighbourhood is geared to tourists rather than to the needs of local residents. In both cases, however, their comments suggest a lack of connection or attachment to the immediate neighbourhood.

In talking about their neighbourhoods, my respondents often addressed the social and economic polarization that they witnessed around their condominiums and discussed the ways that this affected their perceptions of personal safety (Kern 2005). Below, Rose and Stephanie note the visibility of "sketchy characters" and homelessness near their condominiums, while

Sandra expresses a tension between feeling "fairly safe" and limiting her own mobility at night.

> I look over the city that's really nice, but I also overlook Yonge Street, and I see "Seductions" [a lingerie and sex shop]. It's a bit seedy. It's a kind of seedy area, with lots of sketchy characters around. Bay Street is usually nice, but Yonge is a little bit more sketchy. *(Rose, age 22, lives with roommate)*

> I mean, it's an improvement from where I was. Because Queen and Church is still – condos are going up, but it's still a bit of a no man's land. Homelessness is probably more evident. On the walk to work, in front of the Metropolitan United Church, there's a whole bunch of homeless people. Which are obviously realities of the city. But you know, I don't see it every day anymore when I walk to work. *(Stephanie, age 35, lives alone)*

> I generally feel fairly safe in my neighbourhood. There's always lots of people around. I wouldn't go walking around at, like, one o'clock in the morning in my neighbourhood by myself, but then I'm not sure there are too many places in Toronto where I would. That is the trade-off of living in a big city versus someplace else. *(Sandra, age 28, lives alone)*

Like many other women interviewed here, Samantha had somewhat ambivalent feelings about her neighbourhood and its inhabitants in terms of safety, and this affected her enjoyment of the public or open spaces in her neighbourhood. But like Naomi and others who enjoyed the borderline nature of their neighbourhoods, Samantha asserts that the marginalized groups who inhabit the streets "bring the neighbourhood alive."

> Where I lived before, I could walk for hours, I was close to the Mount Pleasant Cemetery, it was very safe. And here, there's Trinity-Bellwoods, there's the lake and the park, but to get to either place you have to go through the city streets or whatever type of environment. You know, there's the homeless people, a lot of, not a lot, but there are homeless people here, and people from the mental health – the CAMH [Centre for Addiction and Mental

Health] – so, but I like that – it brings the neighbourhood alive. But for a woman, walking by herself, it's like, I don't want to deal with this, you know? So that's something – sometimes you just wanna take a walk and not have to worry about what I'm going to run into. But you get used to that. *(Samantha, age 33, lives alone)*

Colleen discusses neighbourhood "character" in much the same way:

One of my first days coming home from work, I was working a four-to-midnight, came home at midnight, and there was a man peeing in the corner of the Wellesley subway station. And to myself I said, "Is this where I've moved? Was this a good idea?" And then there's the people who sit over at the bank, drinking out of their paper bags. I was like, "I don't know if I feel safe here." But then I also realized that it's the same people every day. You leave them alone, they leave you alone. I adjusted to it fast ... You get to know it and appreciate it and laugh it off ... I thought, "Character. My neighbourhood has character." And I've just chosen to look at it that way. No one is scary, there's not a lot of crime here, just character ... It's a source of amusement. I feel safe, I walk out any time that I want to. *(Colleen, age 28, lives alone)*

Samantha and Colleen describe the process of becoming accustomed to seeing homelessness, mental health issues, public drinking, and urination. They also seem to develop a sense that these people are part of the neighbourhoods' "character" and appeal, although it is not clear whether this affection for "character" actually extends to the "characters" themselves. In a paradoxical manner, the very elements that make these women feel less safe are those that they value as dimensions of authentic urban life, suggesting that perceived dangers and out-of-place bodies are also desirable commodities (Modan 2007). Again, I highlight here the identity-making processes at work, wherein (relatively privileged) women can position themselves as authentic or rightful urban dwellers because of their acceptance of the danger, disorder, and deviance associated with living in particular city neighbourhoods.

In terms of community or neighbourhood connections, women's engagements are likely to be affected by their perceptions of safety and fear in those neighbourhoods (Mehta and Bondi 1999). It is important, then, as condominium developments continue to locate in disinvested, marginal, or brownfield areas, to consider the potential effects on new residents' sense of attachment to, and engagement with, that community. As the earlier analysis of planners', developers', and media constructions of community suggest, there may be an assumption that such areas do not have communities, or are not real neighbourhoods, until gentrifiers move in in numbers. But if revitalization is assumed to create communities, then the experiences of women condominium dwellers may expose a flaw in this logic. Simply building new residential spaces does not necessarily create a sense of community, particularly as it pertains to community within the wider neighbourhood.

Securing the Self

In examining the experience and meaning of living within securitized and sometimes isolated urban developments, I ask: Does this type of urban living inhibit opportunities for intersubjectivity or relationships across difference (Young 1990)? Bickford (2000, 358) argues that "the possibility of achieving a genuine public realm inhabited by multiple 'we's' is blocked through these [city building] practices ... [T]hey produce the illusion of safety for some at the expense of actual danger and discomfort for others." In a similar vein, Atkinson and Blandy (2007) raise the idea of defensive home ownership, suggesting that social anxieties are reflected in the built environment and that the processes that confer protection and security are based, in part, on ownership and affluence. Women's experiences of urban living vis-à-vis condominium security suggest that these gates do mediate understandings of who is inside and who is outside the community, of who needs protection and who represents danger. At the same time, though, most of the women did not articulate a highly defensive posture or a sense that the others outside the gates deserved punishment or did not belong in the city. Therefore, I argue that, although the critical framework that positions new-build gentrification as an expression of neoliberal militarization of space raises important questions about privilege, exclusion, and privatization, the experiences of these environments in everyday life do not necessarily reflect a revanchist value system.

Furthermore, gender mediates these experiences in perhaps unexpected ways. While conventional gender stereotypes suggest that women would express more fearful and revanchist attitudes shaped, in part, by their gendered vulnerabilities, I found that women, while largely appreciative of many of the security measures in their condominiums, were also keen to claim their autonomy, freedom, and fearlessness even in borderline neighbourhoods. In fact, this was one way that women constructed their identities as city dwellers. Geographers Anna Mehta and Liz Bondi (1999), in their examination of the construction of gendered identities in relation to fear of violence in urban spaces, suggest that women may assert fearlessness, in part, due to a desire to appear rational and autonomous rather than passive or paranoid. Women thus simultaneously resist and conform to patriarchal norms around fear. Wilson's (1991) discussion of gendered urban subjectivities draws attention to the multiple ways that women use urban space to undermine or move outside of patriarchal norms around women's feelings and behaviour. Wilson's theories continue to resonate in the context of neoliberal urban revitalization. Redeveloped urban spaces such as condominiums still reflect, and indeed explicitly draw upon, gendered ideologies around safety and fear; however, women are not passive subjects who uncritically accept the boundaries constructed for them.

Nonetheless, neoliberal ideals are expressed in many ways through condominium development. For example, the emphasis on security in the private space of the home is particularly interesting, given that women are deeply socialized to feel fear in public urban spaces. In part, this shift has occurred because many condominium developments are located in areas of the city that have little established residential community and are thus isolated from the sense of safety that comes from busy streets and a plethora of neighbours. However, this does not fully explain why the discourse around gender and urban safety now emphasizes the need for women to secure their safety within their homes rather than on the streets. This shift to focusing on safety in private space may instead be a result of the shift towards a neoliberal ethic of individual responsibility and the commodification of social objectives. Atkinson and Blandy (2007, 444) argue that, as ideals of individual responsibility are elevated during the neoliberal restructuring of governance, there is "an imperative for the control and handling of domestic territory that seeks autonomy and refuge from dangers, as well as [a connection] to prevailing ideologies that celebrate personal autonomy and control." It may also reflect a desire for a sense of enclosure and privacy rather than public freedom. As urban theorist Mike Davis (1991, 224) suggests:

> "Security" becomes a positional good defined by income access to private "protective services" and membership in some hardened residential enclave or restricted suburb ... "[S]ecurity" has less to do with personal safety than with the degree of personal insulation, in residential, work, consumption and travel environments, from "unsavory" groups and individuals, even crowds in general.

Problematically for feminist urban activism, the emphasis on private security provided by condominium developments is premised on the notion that women's safety is a personal lifestyle choice rather than a political issue that must be pursued collectively. Safety, if it is seen as a private choice exercised in private space, becomes a function of privilege (Kern 2005; Day 1999) rather than a good available to all women. In Toronto, safety has long been a primary motivation for women's urban activism (Andrew 1995; Whitzman 1992, 2002; MacGregor 1995; Wekerle and Whitzman 1995). In an urban environment increasingly comprised of private, gated spaces, where safety is seen as a commodity that can be chosen and purchased, there is little political motivation to pursue collective action to ensure that all citizens, in both private and public spaces, have access to security. As Bashevkin (2006) notes, women's actions on safety have become increasingly marginal in Toronto since the restructuring of urban government and a renewed interest in urban revitalization strategies.

Indeed, safety concerns may be deliberately evaded by policy makers seeking to attract homeowners and, in particular, young women homeowners. For example, Brownlow (2006) exposes how police statistics on sexual violence in Philadelphia were deceptively labelled to avoid portraying the city as dangerous for young, middle-class, white women. These strategies – privatizing safety, producing militarized urban spaces, and making safety issues invisible – are decreasing both the perceived need for collective action on safety and the amount of public space available for the all-important meeting of strangers or eyes on the street (Young 1990; Jacobs 1961).

Conclusion

For the women condominium owners interviewed here, safety was one dimension of the choice to buy a condominium, and, in a city that has allowed women's safety to drop off the public agenda, it seems to be a legitimate concern. However, the ways in which safety is understood, and the ways in which women gain access to it, suggest that our notions of the public and private dimensions of safety are shifting in a manner that emphasizes the increasingly private nature of city life within enclosed condominium communities. Security features illustrate the literal and symbolic boundaries of community in ways that suggest that condominiums are not fully expected to become part of the wider community that may exist in the neighbourhood. For condominiums located in less established areas, or in areas that have yet to be fully revitalized, security functions to distinguish the condominium community from the surrounding area. For women condominium dwellers, the boundaries are not absolute or impermeable, but the presence of security mitigates certain insecurities and provides a sense of personal safety and control in the home. Security thus mediates the relationship between condominium dwellers and the surrounding neighbourhood. Furthermore, security features illustrate one of the ways in which gender ideologies are not only central to city building practices but also shape the kinds of urban communities that are desired and expected to exist under the conditions of urban revitalization.

The notion of security is, interestingly, woven through both issues of condominium ownership and condominium community. This suggests that an integral, if often implicit, part of the neoliberal urban revitalization agenda involves fostering different forms of personal security. In the context of home ownership, financial security is a key factor; in the context of constructing condominium communities, personal security is emphasized. The emphasis in both cases on individuals privately securing themselves in these different ways articulates with the broader shift from welfare state responsibility for the security of citizens to neoliberal state withdrawal from responsibility by reorganizing governance in ways that make individuals responsible for securing themselves. This shift is accomplished, in part, by conflating security with autonomy and freedom, even if this appears somewhat paradoxical (Foucault 1997). For women, autonomy and freedom from patriarchal norms and expectations come through the search for, and attainment of, security in various forms: financial, personal, physical. Condominium ownership and condominium living are ways that women can pursue these goals in the context of urban revitalization.

Moreover, gendered narratives are deployed by city building agents such as developers to normalize the securitization of urban space. However, the everyday lives of many of the women I interviewed challenged some of the gendered stereotypes that ostensibly legitimate the security both within and around condominiums. In a surprising way, fear is tied to wealth accumulation and profit-making for women: if they are willing to risk safety and discomfort in dodgy neighbourhoods, they will likely be vindicated through greater resale profits. For many women, the gates of the condominium were certainly permeable – for some, even unnecessary – and they felt an affinity for the wider neighbourhood beyond. Notably though, the permeability of the gates works only one way – other city dwellers have restricted or no access to the enclosed spaces within, even the quasi-public shared facilities. This creates an urban fabric where either spaces for interaction are increasingly limited or the ability to initiate interaction is in the hands of the privileged.

The issues raised in this discussion are implicated within a wider concern for the remaking of the city and the reshaping of people's relationships to urban living. In the following chapter, I continue to explore how condominium living mediates the urban way of life in the contemporary postindustrial city by shifting the focus of my analysis to women's life worlds within the city – their experiences of working, playing, consuming, and socializing in Toronto.

5

A Date with the Big City
Gendering the Myth of Urbanity

Here we have, apparently, "City Living at its best," and residents enthusiastically describe their experience in these terms. There is pride in being "downtown people," condescension for "suburbia." This seems to celebrate the interpenetration of work with leisure, the rejection of "separate spheres," the pleasure of feeling boundaries melt away. Of course, the appealing urban landscape of Fairview and False Creek conceals as much as it reveals. But for those in a position to take advantage of it the blurring of real and imaginary is an agreeable condition.

– Caroline Mills, "Life on the Upslope"

In vital respects, modern property entrepreneurs are part of the culture industry; they seek to produce, advertise and sell not just functional spaces but desirable places for everyday life. As much as housing, their product is lifestyle. Like the rest of the culture industry, though, they cannot invent the desires they commodify but need to extract them from living culture.

– Jon Caulfield, "'Gentrification' and Desire"

> Captivating. Seductive. Exciting. Romantic. Artistic.
> Cosmopolitan. Where else in T.O. can you find a lifestyle
> with so many adjectives?
>
> – Ad for Malibu Condominiums

The discourses of urban revitalization in Toronto turn us clearly away from the promised calm idyll of suburban life and towards a rediscovered – and reinvented – ideal of urbanity: an urban way of life and an urban way of being. In order to challenge and complicate the celebratory narrative of a new "back-to-the-city" movement that "evicts" (Slater 2006) critical perspectives on the resurgence of interest in city living, I problematize the construction of this ideal in the context of new-build gentrification and unpack the gendered assumptions that shape, and are shaped by, contemporary norms of urban life in the postindustrial city. What, as geographer Caroline Mills (1988) asks, is concealed by the revitalized urban landscape?

The narrative that Mills labelled the "myth of urbanity" is drawn from an array of sources. These include early urban sociologists like Georg Simmel (1971) and Louis Wirth (1938), who theorized the construction of new identities and new ways of being within the industrial city. Contemporary urban gurus like Richard Florida (2002) are rapidly reinvigorating this discourse, promoting the idea that successful cities will use culture, the arts, and diversity to attract the creative class. Current city planning policies, including Toronto's, have adopted and promoted this reconstituted ideal of urbanity to support a vision of reurbanization. The promotion of this ideal is also essential to the success of the condominium boom.

In positioning the notion of contemporary urbanity as a myth, I draw attention to the ways that certain ideals about urban life are commodified, repackaged, and sold under the rubric of revitalization. This is not to suggest that urban identities and ways of life are fantasies; rather, I highlight the ways that these are socially constructed and, more important, drawn into the sphere of neoliberal urbanism. The elements that are particularly significant to this discussion are the packaging and promotion of integrated work/play/dwelling spaces in the downtown core; the focus on conspicuous consumption, entertainment, and leisure; the valorization of certain areas of the downtown core at the expense of other neighbourhoods; and the mobilization of the notion of the authentic urban dweller. These elements of urbanity and, in particular, their gendered dimensions are effectively neoliberalized (commodified, privatized, and securitized) and sold as a neat package to urban dwellers. This process reaches its height in the marketing and development of urban condominiums and in the notion of the urban condominium lifestyle.

The introductory quotations from Mills and Caulfield, each of which is over twenty years old, illustrate that the myth of urbanity, and its production and marketing, are not terribly new. The myth has certainly been deployed repeatedly in the context of gentrification and new residential development. Notions of lifestyle, the rejection of suburbia, the desire for diversity – these tropes continue to circulate in the contemporary revitalizing city. As Caulfield (1989, 1994) suggests, the condominium development industry not only benefits from the increasing interest in the notion of city living but is also active in *creating* and propagating reinvented myths of urbanity. Embedded in this notion are normative and practical ideas about the personal and social benefits of city living, about the practices that constitute city living (or lifestyle), and about the desired subjects of this new urbanity.

Ideals of urbanity, and ideas about urban condominium living more specifically, draw on a symbolic system of imagery (Baudrillard 1988) that shapes the practice of aesthetics, social location, and lifestyle (Podmore 1998), and they are deployed in specific spatial contexts that produce local variations on the myth. Geographer Mark Davidson (2007) argues that capital is now central to this process: while, in the case of London, gentrifiers help shape market demand, the construction of gentrified urban space originates with residential property developers. I would add that urban policy and planning documents also draw upon and reproduce ideals about the contemporary urban way of life (Kipfer and Keil 2002). Thus, the contemporary (and local) myth of urbanity is produced and propagated by a variety of sources across different scales.

In deconstructing some of the mainstream gendered discourses around city living in Toronto, I want to challenge the seduction of the narratives of "latté urbanism" (Slater 2006) by arguing that its appeal is based on a consumer model of urban citizenship, which represents a lot of froth and foam layered over neoliberal processes of privatization, securitization, and commodification. I argue that the re-emerging association of women with a primarily consumption-oriented model of city life is highly problematic. Far from fostering a non-sexist public realm, the revitalized city of leisure, consumption, and lifestyle represents a space where particular women are drawn into the neoliberal ideal of entrepreneurial citizenship. Instead of women being understood as an "irruption in the city, a symptom of disorder, and a problem" (Wilson 1991, 9), women, at least middle-class women in the gentrified city, are a symbol of the success of revitalization with regard to purifying and aestheticizing the city. Here the neoliberal city co-opts and commodifies feminist visions of interconnected spaces of production, social reproduction, and consumption to sell the revitalized city to gentrifiers and investment capital, while simultaneously denying this connectivity to poor and marginalized groups who cannot afford central city living. The celebration of Toronto as a city of culture, leisure, and interconnectedness masks an agenda of competition, entrepreneurialism, and spectacle. Under the current rubric, conflict and difference in the city, once seen as engines of democracy and political action (Holston and Appadurai 1996), are commodified and aestheticized into a purified spectacle for consumption (Zukin 1997, 1998). These reinvented, re-aestheticized city spaces facilitate the intensification of a consumerist model of citizenship, wherein the right to make claims on the city is performed through acts of consumption (MacLeod 2002; Bell and Binnie 2004; Isin 1998, 1999).

My analysis thus reveals a troubling rearticulation of patriarchal, bourgeois gender norms and gender relations in the urban realm, now deeply intertwined with neoliberal agendas. Many of the experiences articulated by women condominium dwellers point towards the emancipation of middle-class women from the oppressive role of the suburban middle-class housewife/homemaker under Fordism, who was more isolated from public space, burdened with reproductive and consumptive work, and economically dependent on the family wage (Hayden 2002). Although the women condominium dwellers of the postindustrial city have greater access to public life, less reproductive work, and less dependence on a male breadwinner, their place and role in the revitalized city do not fundamentally challenge many of the traditionally accepted places and roles for women in the city. I am particularly interested in questioning how daily practices of city living articulate with both mainstream ideas about urbanity in the global, postindustrial city and with critical, feminist perspectives on the gendered benefits of city living and a vision of the "non-sexist city" (Hayden 1980; MacGregor 1995).

Reurbanizing Toronto: Quality of Life or "Urbanism Lite"?

In order to operationalize Toronto's plan for reurbanization, the city has to facilitate the creation of new spaces for living, working, and playing. Those who brand and market the city must also promote Toronto as a desirable place to live. In the context of a metropolis in which suburbanization has been the dominant trend for many decades, this is a major ideological undertaking. In a background document to the city's *Official Plan* (City of Toronto 2002), Bourne (2000a, 76) notes a shift in values, which he describes as

> changes in the relative images of the suburbs and the central area as places to live. The suburbs for many are seen not only as distant and inconvenient, but as boring and uninteresting, living spaces that discourage social interaction and a sense of community, and based on a road system that is increasingly congested.

He compares this to conventional images of the central core as solely a place to work or visit and as congested, dirty, polluted, and crime-ridden. Bourne also notes that this residential revitalization is an important way to sell the city and the region abroad. This notion is echoed by city planners and the *Official Plan*.[1]

Defining Quality of Life

I asked city planners for their perspectives on why residential intensification was seemingly a successful policy in Toronto, in the context of the recent condominium boom. They raised the notions of quality of life and quality of place, ideas that are also present in the *Official Plan*. As well, the idea of an interconnected live-and-work lifestyle was an important aspect of their responses.

> But it's also based partly on the quality of the place and the quality of the neighbourhoods and all that goes with that. The quality of the place to live. So if there are nice places there, there are good neighbourhoods, there are vital streets, there's good shopping, there are good schools for your children, you can get proper health care when your mom gets sick, there's a seniors' place that she can conveniently live in. All of these things, and it's not that one comes without the other, it's more like a cycle, and they all reinforce each other. And so for us to continue to be the economic engine, really for the country, we need to continue to build good communities and to make high-quality places. *(Planner interview, 18 July 2005)*

In this narrative, quality of life and quality of place are linked to economic growth and inter-city competition. However, quality of life is also joined here to the idea of an integrated lifestyle – that is, access to shopping, schools, and seniors' homes. Interestingly, this planner is describing what might typically be understood as women's everyday lives and needs. This description of urban quality of life resonates with feminist discussions of the benefits of city living and of women's needs in urban environments (Wekerle 1984; Rose 1984; Rose and Villeneuve 1993; England 1991; Hayden 2002). Given this, a city plan that encourages the interpenetration of these activities might benefit women in particular. Nonetheless, the current *Official Plan* contains no explicit references to women or gender (Bashevkin 2006).

The planner continues to describe quality-of-life issues:

> Now which is where I come in. I'm a community-builder, I'm a
> place-maker. Great streets, lovely quiet leafy neighbourhoods,
> bustling shopping streets. Grand institutions, campuses – you
> know, all of these different kinds of places that make up a diverse
> metropolitan area like Toronto. We need to rediscover what we
> have, reinforce it, and build more of them, because – and better
> ones, we're always looking for the best. You know, so it's really
> about keeping the engine firing on all cylinders so we all ultimately
> can continue to be both attractive to settle here because of the
> quality of life, but will continue to live here because of the quality
> of life, and it's all kind of mixed in around this idea of quality of
> life. *(Planner interview, 18 July 2005)*

Again, quality of life is linked to growth and redevelopment through the metaphor of an engine (the growth machine, perhaps?). Problematically, there is no mention of quality of life as a social justice issue. Likewise, although the *Official Plan* mentions diversity, inclusivity, and equity, the bulk of it is concerned with improving the city's look and feel. And, through this process, it is assumed, the values of diversity, inclusivity, and equity will somehow be realized.

Feminists and others concerned with quality of life as a social justice issue must, however, ask *which* women will be able to benefit from the lively, mixed-use neighbourhoods. Terms and phrases such as "liveability" and "quality of life," in the context of entrepreneurial growth and redevelopment agendas, become effectively depoliticized and coded to mean the

production of landscapes suited to the tastes and desires of young gentrifiers. In the case of women, these young gentrifiers may be professional,
childless women for whom the notion of mixed-use is related to work and
entertainment rather than to the tasks associated with social reproduction.

The second planner was more specific about the city's desire to have
people work and live downtown:

> Well, it's kind of a double-edged sword. Where we do want to
> attract a critical mass of people down there, because we are re-
> vitalizing our waterfront, we do want to bring people down there,
> but the other side of that is that we also want to bring jobs down
> there. And right now, with so much of a concentration on residen-
> tial development, oftentimes – although we've been encouraged by
> some of the studies that have been done, particularly by our trans-
> portation section in terms of split, like, who lives and works down
> there, we have found that, surprisingly enough, there are a number
> of people who live in the Waterfront who also work in the down-
> town. So that's definitely very encouraging, because that's what we
> are trying to encourage. But more often than not, people hop in
> their cars and drive to get out to the 905 [i.e., the suburbs] ...
> We've got the residents now, now we have to start getting the
> restaurants, the cafes, the cleaners, the supermarkets – that's what
> we need. And we're a little bit slower in catching up on that as
> opposed to the residential development. *(Planner interview, 22
> July 2005)*

The city wants to make it possible for new condominium residents to find
work in the city, but the dominance of residential over commercial development in the past decade has created a tension here. The vision, though, is to
promote more interconnected lifestyles. There is an implicit rationale of
progress (or a logic of highest and best use) underlying these policies:

> When it's finished there will be a new restaurant, there will be a
> bakery that will serve a kind of croissant that you've never had
> before, and a kind of pastry that you've not had, and there will be
> new people who will come to your church and help keep it open.
> With development there is – I guess it's my human nature, I'm an
> optimist ... You know Yonge Street now in the evening, it's lined
> with restaurants, it's happening ... In ten years this will be a major

regional destination. People will come to this part of Yonge Street
[in North York] for restaurants and nightlife. It's happening. It's
just happening. Every second store is being renovated into a high-
end Asian fusion restaurant with fancy martinis and all that stuff.
(Planner interview, 18 July 2005)

This narrative essentially describes the process of commercial displacement
that often accompanies new-build gentrification (Davidson and Lees 2005).
It also resonates with developers' accounts of change and progress in "up-
and-coming" neighbourhoods (see below). There is no question, in these
accounts, of the inherent good of high-end Asian fusion restaurants. Nor is
there any mention of how these changes might negatively affect current
residents.

I mean, as a Torontonian, it's very expensive for me to live here.
But if I were to come from elsewhere, then it's like, "Wow, what
a deal." I was just reading an article this morning about how the
New York Times is going to be writing an article on Toronto
restaurants and how cheap and how excellent they are. Like,
"Torontonians, you don't know how good you have it." *(Planner
interview, 22 July 2005)*

Who, then, is the typical citizen imagined for this vision of urbanity, this
form of quality of life? Although the planners describe many qualities of city
life that feminist geographers suggest will be particularly beneficial to
women, it is clear that class will largely define the ability to gain access to
this lifestyle. As critical urban scholars have suggested, this vision translates
urbanism (as a politicized way of being) into "urbanism 'lite'" – a process
wherein quality of life becomes synonymous with quality of lifestyle, and
social justice concerns are drained from policy and development.

The *Official Plan* has codified this ostensibly social vision into an economic strategy that will shape Toronto's future for many decades. In the
Plan, the interpenetration and concentration of specialized services are
celebrated as part of the city's economic strength. The *Plan* lists the variety
of urban amenities and services to be found in the downtown core:

Government offices; arts and cultural venues; entertainment activities and
sporting events; destination and speciality retailing; lively restaurants and
food markets featuring Toronto's diverse cuisines; major tourist attractions

and convention facilities; concentration of print and broadcast media; higher education; and research and health services. (City of Toronto 2002, 15)

> Toronto is an interesting and cohesive city that offers a dynamic mixture of opportunities for everyone to live, work, learn and play. As in nature, diversity is key to our social, cultural and economic life. Diversity is our strength because it means vibrancy, opportunity, inclusiveness and adaptability – it is a fundamental building block for success. (City of Toronto 2002, 3)

The notions of clustering and cohesion, diversity and vibrancy, are seen as the foundation for Toronto's competitiveness in the region and beyond. The *Plan*, as a "vision" document, works to induct city dwellers into a set of beliefs around the natural and right form of the city and model of city living. Davidson and Lees (2005) found similar rhetoric in London policy documents from 1999 to 2004. They suggest that these celebratory discourses of culture, vibrancy, and community serve to neutralize a program of state-led gentrification, justifying public expenditure and/or support for the redevelopment of spaces and services that meet the demands of the new middle class.

Place marketing and branding campaigns echo this discursive regime, lauding the revitalized city. Toronto's recent marketing strategy, *Toronto Unlimited* (launched in 2004-5 but somewhat short lived), described Toronto's attributes on its website in the following ways:

> What makes Toronto such a uniquely interesting place is answered by a constantly growing list: its innovative architecture, its theatre district, the hundreds of ethnic restaurants, the character of its neighborhoods, its accepting legislation, a multi-talented workforce, museums that are themselves works of art, the stories of its street corners, its cleanliness, the International Film Festival, the parks, the lake, the celebration of humanity.

Texts such as the *Plan* and the branding campaign portray the visions of city planners and city boosters, who seek to "imagineer" the city in line with particular economic ideals (Short 1999). Here the imagined lifestyle of the city dweller is centred upon the consumption and enjoyment of difference and spectacle, which is easily facilitated by the clustering of work, home, and leisure. Atkinson (2006) maintains that these policies provide spaces geared to affluent groups, promoting a concept of liveability that is increasingly isolated from the problems of the wider city.

The official vision of urbanity promises development that, on its face, appears to be socially equitable and concerned with quality of life – for example, by promoting the kind of connectivity that could support women in their multiple roles across sites of production, consumption, and social reproduction. The end result, however, is based on a conflation of quality of life with economic goals, and this leads to the creation of spaces that facilitate the lifestyles of the affluent. As MacGregor (2002) points out in her gender critique of eco-city policies, a feminist definition of "sustainable" communities does not imply isolated, upper-class enclaves that are segregated from vulnerable and marginalized populations; rather, it is meant to serve these populations (see also Torre [1999] for a similar gendered critique of new urbanism). Despite the rhetoric of liveability and quality of life, planning and marketing visions of sustainable communities appear to be founded upon an imagined consumer citizen.

In the context of neoliberal urban agendas, these planning accounts and documents constitute discourses that reframe our understandings of social concerns and collective matters by rearticulating them as economic issues and individual choices. They work to shape values in the sense that they deploy the rhetoric of choice, progress, and opportunity, which is mirrored in the kinds of subjects that are imagined and desired for the revitalized city.

Developers: The Pied Pipers of a New Urbanity?

City builders have a major role in the reinvention and propagation of the myth of urbanity (Fincher 2004; Fainstein 2001; Davidson 2007; Mills 1993; Lorimer 1978; Podmore 1998; Zukin 1982). Their texts and ideas are more widely and directly disseminated than planning documents. Caulfield (1994) interprets their role as one of capital manipulating the genuine desires of potential city dwellers for alternatives to modernist planning and suburban conformity. From a feminist perspective, Fincher (2004) suggests that developers also draw on assumptions about gender relations to create a narrative that justifies the sudden appearance of high-rise condominium developments. Developers, therefore, both tap into, and actively construct, ideas about urban living that will appeal to their desired consumers.

Condominium developers in Toronto viewed themselves as pioneers leading the public towards a new urban lifestyle by bringing the people to the city and by bringing culture and cosmopolitanism to the people. These pied pipers of urban living are also active producers of the very notion of urbanity upon which they seek to capitalize.

> We purchased a parcel of land, and this was at the time when the Etobicoke Waterfront was all seedy motels. So this was back, like close to ten years ago. And so we were the pioneers. We were thinking that, you know, "We can bring residential to this neigh-bourhood," 'cause the waterfront is such an integral part of Toronto, people want to live on the waterfront, and at the time we were pioneers. *(Developer interview, 5 July 2005)*

> Traffic congestion in the GTA is becoming a major issue. How do you want to spend your time? If you work downtown, do you need to be commuting an hour and a half to get to work? So those begin to drive some of those choices. I think we're becoming socio-culturally more sophisticated as an urban centre as well. When you look at the development of arts, theatres, events in the city overall, over the course of the last fifteen years we've become far richer on that end as well, so it's giving people a reason to stay within the downtown hub. *(Developer interview, 21 June 2005)*

Developers seem to perceive a shift in values among Torontonians, a move away from a suburban, commuter-based ideal of living to a more urban-centred ideal. The developer interprets this as progress, a notion echoed in the following narrative, where the developer lists some of Toron-to's attributes but notes that we still "have a lot of work to do":

> Toronto is viewed internationally as a really great place ... Toronto is also just a really happening spot. You know, I think you walk downtown at night, there's all the talk about it, it's a very safe city, to be able to enjoy yourself ... I think we as a city have a lot of work to do, by way of cleaning it up, and making it perhaps more walkable, and cleaner, and a higher sense of civic pride, that it once had, that hasn't been there for a number of years. *(Developer interview, 28 July 2005)*

If revitalization is seen as a work in progress, there are then more opportun-ities for development and growth.

Developers shared how they carefully choose their locations based on existing infrastructure and local amenities; however, they also recognized that condominium development effectively encourages new businesses to locate in these neighbourhoods, spawning a process of "cleaning up," which is also clearly interpreted as a beneficial change:

> The best spots. By a subway station. We always look for – like the waterfront properties – it's great, everyone loves it. But they're right by the subway station as well. Major highways, shopping malls ... We just launched a new site in Scarborough. It's right beside the Scarborough Town Centre. *(Developer interview, 28 June 2005)*

> We look at locations that are up and coming, that we know where the growth is going to be happening in the next few years. For instance, at our College Park site, when we started five years ago, no one would go to College Park. It was considered the seediest area in the city. After we started construction there, Great West Life, who owns College Park, they leased out their retail in there. We've got Dominion [grocery store] in there, the Carlu event theatre is coming there, and the whole area is getting completely intensified. All the shops along Yonge Street are getting changed and they're getting updated. *(Developer interview, 5 July 2005)*

The pioneer theme continues, and we see as well the ways in which developers can portray themselves as visionaries who have the ability to look at "the seediest area in the city" and see its potential as a residential, retail, and leisure centre. Here the notion of upgrading, and potential displacement, is explicitly described through the trope of the "up-and-coming" neighbourhood and the updated shops. The phrase "up and coming" is also an important signifier of the capital accumulation processes at work here. It signals to both developers and condominium purchasers that they are buying low, with the potential to sell high. In this way, the notion of the pioneer is connected to the notion of the city or neighbourhood as a frontier that can be exploited by those who are entrepreneurial, visionary, and pioneering enough to take the risk. While this position has typically been taken up by predominantly male figures – venture capitalists, financiers, developers, and landowners – women, as homeowners, are increasingly identifying with this entrepreneurial position.

The developer continues to describe other challenges and successes in up-and-coming areas:

> There are challenges for up-and-coming neighbourhoods, and at
> those points it's really important to stress what the future growth
> for those neighbourhoods is. Even at King West, I mean six, seven
> years ago no one would have thought King West. King was an
> industrial zone ... and now that people are moving into King West
> it's exploded. There's so much condominium and town home
> development. So I think you've got to really present to people
> what the future is for the neighbourhood. *(Developer interview,
> 5 July 2005)*

Consumers need to be led to such areas based on a vision of the future, one that sells the urban lifestyle and the future of the neighbourhood. This raises questions around the extent to which the city's ostensibly new neighbourhoods are shaped by developers' visions of the future rather than by community groups, residents, public participation processes, or even the city planners. If it is up to developers to identify and lead this growth, then whose interests are such spaces likely to reflect? Whose visions are absent? In this process, current residents and the existing shops, businesses, and public spaces are likely to be seen as part of the problem, as features that require "updating" in order to bring the neighbourhood in line with the vision of the revitalized city. In contrast, it is the presumed needs and desires of incoming residents that will shape the way that "up and coming" is operationalized on the ground.

Vancouver's Downtown Eastside is undergoing an extreme version of this process, where the fifteen-year battle between community/anti-poverty activists and the city/developers over the redevelopment of the Woodward's building has been resolved in favour of the condominium developers Concord Pacific Group Inc. (see Blomley [2004] and Lees, Slater, and Wyly [2008] for more on this story). This news article clearly positions the developers and potential buyers as daring pioneers:

> One of Canada's largest real estate developers believes it has struck gold in
> the nation's most wretched neighbourhood, with plans to build a new condominium project for the moneyed – and the daring. Despite opposition
> from local activists and community groups, Concord Pacific Group Inc. is
> moving forward with construction of a 154-condominium complex in the

heart of Vancouver's notorious Downtown Eastside, an open drug and sex market that for decades has been a home of last resort to the down and out ... It's not a pretty place. But a sustained real estate boom combined with a shortage of available land has made the neighbourhood irresistible to developers. And, it seems, to buyers, who just a few years ago would not have set foot in the area, let alone live there ... He [the developer] has no doubt that all 154 units inside the Greenwich will sell quickly. (Hutchinson 2008)

In these narratives, condominium development is positioned as a natural progression, one that cannot be stopped by the social justice claims of community members. A similar story is told in Toronto about a developer (nicknamed the "Lord of the Junction" by the reporter) who has tackled the revitalization of the industrial Junction neighbourhood with several condominium projects:

Tom Falus dreams big. A man with a vision, this developer is slowly transforming an area in Toronto's west end, reshaping industrial boneyards into housing ... The project is being forged into an example of the new urbanism embraced by both Toronto and the provincial government. Bryan Levman of Guidelines Advertising Ltd., who is marketing the project, says of Falus: "He must have been prescient. With the Liberals in power, this is the exact kind of direction they've given the whole development industry. They want these old industrial areas changed into residential ... The future's here now and everybody's scrambling, looking for sites like this." ... The development process for Davenport Village has been anything but painless ... A major stumbling block was a resin plant, operated by Chemerico Chemicals, which was incompatible with residential use ... With homes in the area selling for $300,000, Phase I's starting price of almost $170,000 is drawing a wide range of buyers, including single women and first-time homebuyers. (Laporte 2004, P01)

In this heroic story, the developer takes on the challenge of polluted industrial lands (associated with "death" through the boneyards metaphor) in a working-class neighbourhood, despite opposition by local residents who fear that the construction process will create air and water contamination. Buyers, including single women, are similarly positioned as pioneering individuals for their willingness to assume the risk of living on contaminated lands. This tale prompts me to ask, at what price comes the dream of urbanity and home ownership?

Developers have fairly clear ideas about what the needs and desires of their consumers are, and, although these may differ from project to project, neighbourhood to neighbourhood, it is these ideas that play a role in shaping the spaces and subjects of the revitalizing city. In the comment below, the developer notes that people already want the downtown amenities: they know what this lifestyle entails and what they want from it (consumption and leisure in the city). For this developer, the city (as an "amenity") is an integral part of his firm's developments.

> People living downtown, they live downtown because they like
> the amenity of downtown, not because they want to be cooped up
> in their own building. And they'd rather not pay the fees to have
> excessive amounts of things in their building ... So they prefer that.
> They prefer to just spend their money on those types of things.
> *(Developer interview, 21 June 2005)*

Other developers actively promote the integration of work, leisure, and home life at the intersection of condominium and city living.

> I mean for condo buyers, the two things that I have found, that are
> really irregardless of the products, is, like location is number one.
> How does this location work in relation to where your employment
> is? And how does this location work in terms of your personal
> network of family and friends? *(Developer interview, 19 July 2005)*

> Well, it's all related to neighbourhood. I think that transportation
> is a key thing. Where do they work? Where do they play? We've
> had a tremendous amount of success in the entertainment district,
> 'cause we were able to put all of those components together.
> People worked in that area, they liked to visit there, you know,
> on evenings and weekends, and so we created a home for them.
> *(Developer interview, 2 August 2005)*

The idea of bringing people to culture and entertainment reappears in these narratives; developers are leading this shift towards urbanity and are enlightening consumers about the virtues of particular urban neighbourhoods. Significantly, the idea of neighbourhood promoted here is one of neighbourhood as consumption niche. Marketing the loud and rowdy entertainment district as a residential zone means drawing upon its proximity to work and leisure, and being specific about the target consumer. Fincher's (2004, 332) research with developers in Melbourne found that downtown developers articulated a lifestyle of "high-consuming mobility, or 'portability' as one had it, one is here and there, out and about, 'eating out and jetting off.'" This resonates with my research on Toronto, suggesting that the re-articulated myth of urbanity is surfacing in remarkably similar ways in postindustrial cities across the globe (N. Smith 2002). Developers can position themselves as heroes for their vision and leadership in identifying and providing spaces for the enactment of this lifestyle.

One developer explicitly stated that young or single women would actively seek out this interconnected, high-consuming, portable lifestyle.

> Definitely [this project] was where a lot of single women
> purchased. They want to be in King West, because King West has
> everything from the restaurants, the clubs – you know, the whole
> heart of, gamut of what it means to be downtown. They work
> downtown, in the centre. They could easily take TTC [public
> transit] from the site there. *(Developer interview, 5 July 2005)*

In this ethos of development, a feminist vision of urbanity (proximity to work and transit) is co-opted, commodified, and transformed into a postfeminist version of urbanism lite, focused on consumption and instrumentalized to legitimate the goal of opening up devalorized spaces to redevelopment. The ability of a relatively new group of housing consumers, young and/or single women, both to afford to own a home downtown and to enjoy the amenities of the city due to reduced restrictions (i.e., less need to pay for child care and transportation, less housework) is capitalized upon to fulfill the promise of the up-and-coming neighbourhood.

Condominium advertising also reflects these ideals. Although such advertisements are arguably ephemeral and their effects depend upon a particular reception by a particular audience, I highlight their significance as cultural products that may shape behaviour by encouraging consumers to identify with the subjects and lifestyles portrayed within. The emphasis in these advertisements is on choice, freedom, opportunity, and autonomy – all experienced through modes of consumption. It is possible to identify two central categories of advertisements that represent the intersection of gender, condominium living, and urban lifestyles. The first category comprises advertisements that focus on leisure, pleasure, and consumption; the second, advertisements that use women's bodies to represent the city and/or condominiums as objects to be consumed. Through these advertisements, women's role in the city is seemingly recast as one of consumer, in a way that recalls nineteenth-century bourgeois gender roles (Domosh 1996; Wilson 1991; Bowlby 2001; Rappaport 2001; Valentine 1999). Moreover, different female urban archetypes are circulated that position women as conspicuous consumers; stylish flaneuses; elegant, culturally savvy urbanites; or eroticized figures that help developers to conflate sexuality and city life.

In selling new-build gentrification, images of women and women's bodies are used in ways that seem to signal both women's place in the city and a mapping of the city onto the female body. They also signal a rather narrow definition of the idealized city dweller in terms of age, class, occupation, appearance, and ability. The use of women's bodies in this way raises significant questions about the presumed role(s) for women in revitalization projects and about the gendered dimensions of the process of taking or claiming the city through gentrification (N. Smith 1986, 1996).

Women's enjoyment of city life is essential to the successful marketing of the city. Ads often portray women shopping, exercising, dining out, drinking, laughing with friends, and embracing male partners. The images are often accentuated by terms such as "victory," "liberty," "freedom," or "stimulation," words that, in some cases, also serve as the name of the condominium project. In Figure 6, a young white woman in a cocktail dress sips a coffee drink perched atop a bar, situated graphically inside the V of "Victory." The slogan maintains that "life is too short to live anywhere else." In a similar print ad for the same development, the woman glances left to where the same bar is awash in red, and the printed text incites the viewer not to "miss your chance to be among the first to achieve Victory in downtown Toronto!" The ad invokes the twenty-four/seven lifestyle available in the downtown bars and cafés, one that should appeal to the single, twenty-something, middle-class woman. The message is clear: downtown condominium living is a victory for women.

Figures 7 and 8 depict social scenes with women as the foci of the ads. In Figure 7, two women enjoy cocktails while a smiling bartender watches and mixes drinks. The women are staring at one another, suggesting either bonding on a girls' night out or a mutual attraction. Even though a masculine figure is present, the women are foregrounded, and their shared gaze indicates that they are the central story in this image. This scene is positioned above an image of Milano, an upscale restaurant located near the condominium's future site. The text calls on the consumer to "feel the energy" – the energy of nightlife and perhaps sexual attraction. This ad features

FIGURE 6   *Victory.* Billboard for Victory Condominiums, Adelaide Street, Toronto.

three non-white individuals and, as such, may serve to challenge the over-whelming whiteness, as well as the heteronormativity, of most public condo billboards. Given the other marketing images for Vibe, which include pre-dominantly white people but also, in one case, an interracial couple, I do not think that Vibe is marketed at one particular ethnic group. The developer's strategy may be more inclusive and represent an attempt to appeal to differ-ent demographic groups. The use of people of colour may also signify the commodification of diversity and multiculturalism, an important selling point in a city that prides itself on such qualities. The "difference" repre-sented in this ad may be something to consume in much the same way that the young women are positioned within a consumption and leisure-oriented urban lifestyle.

Figure 8 portrays a similar dynamic. Although a man and a woman are present, he is not facing the camera, and his attention is focused on her. She smiles widely at the viewer, assuring the audience that she is fulfilling the goal of "living totally downtown," as the slogan suggests. While the no-tions of stimulation, energy, and excitement have long been part of the ap-peal of urbanity (Wirth 1938; Simmel 1971), the sensual stimulation offered to particular women here is based on elite consumption activities and the women's ability to play (in contrast, presumably, to the need to work, care for children, etc.). City and condominium living are portrayed as appealing due to their association with physical pleasure and attraction embodied in women's enjoyment.

In these ads, women's enjoyment of the gentrified city – their freedom, their victory, their embodied pleasure – is the ultimate symbol of

FIGURE 7   *Feel the energy.* Billboard for Vibe Condominiums, Liberty Village, Toronto.

its success. Indeed, the revitalized city seems to be the city of and for women, where gendered norms of city life are reworked to serve the interests and comfort of women gentrifiers. A feminist lens, however, impels us to question women's role as consumers, the equation of consumption and freedom, and the invisibilized exclusions around race, class, sexuality, and ability.

FIGURE 8   A date with the city. Billboard for LTD Condominiums, Bathurst Street, Toronto.

FIGURE 9   *Sexy.* Billboard for Charlie Condominiums, King Street, Toronto.

In the second category of advertisements, the spaces of new-build gentrification are eroticized through their conflation with (parts of) the female
body, in much the same way as, centuries ago, were colonized lands (Mc-
Clintock 1995) – as places of seduction, pleasure, and availability. In Figure
9, the condominium project named "Charlie" is signified by an image of a
woman in a slinky silk gown, simply labelled "sexy." Here the female body –
white, able-bodied, middle-class, thin – is conflated with the condominium
development itself. Rather than picturing the architecture, the billboard features a female form. Most of the ads for Charlie on billboards and in print
feature women, which suggests that the developer anticipates a female buyer and that, furthermore, "Charlie" is a woman. In this case, it seems that the
woman buyer is expected to identify with, or desire to become, the "sexy"
subject that is embodied by "Charlie." At the same time, her direct gaze may
function as a challenge to the male consumer, who is invited to desire, own,
or take possession of the feminized condominium/city.

In Figure 10, a segment of the female body represents the three-word
mantra of Liberty Market Lofts: "Live. Work. Create." The tattooed back of
the headless, topless figure (again, white, thin, and able-bodied) exists as
a canvas upon which the condominium dweller can construct her or his

FIGURE 10   *Live. Work. Create.* Billboard for Liberty Market Lofts,
Liberty Village, Toronto.

identity, and the tools of this transformation are offered up from her back-
side pocket. Although it is tempting to read female agency in this ad, where
the woman is the artist, the display of her naked back as a sexually (ex)posed
canvas and the lack of a face suggest that she takes a more passive role in this
imagery. This particular ad is displayed repeatedly around the recently in-
dustrial-turned-residential Liberty Village area, perhaps amplifying the
masculine gaze and the social exclusion of women from particular urban
spaces (Rosewarne 2005).

Feminist theorist Elizabeth Grosz (1995, 108) writes that the city is

the site for the body's cultural saturation, its takeover and transformation by images, representational systems, the mass media and the arts –
the place where the body is representationally reexplored, transformed,

contested, reinscribed. In turn, the body (as cultural product) transforms, reinscribes the urban landscape.

The use of very particular women's bodies to both feminize and eroticize condominium development and urban living suggests that what is being re-inscribed in the landscape at the moment of urban revitalization through various images of the female body is a notion of the city as a commodity, available twenty-four/seven for pleasure and waiting to be possessed and consumed. At the same time, this imagery reinscribes a gendered social or-dering in which women's place is defined by consumption: both her own consumption activities and her consumption as an object of desire. Women are simultaneously cast as seduced by the city and as the seducers.

In these texts and images, the city is presented as always available, seduc-tive, and waiting to be explored and consumed by the culturally savvy urban dweller. The condominium is not the only desirable commodity: the city it-self is a product to be consumed. The advertisements convince potential buyers that the city is waiting to be claimed. Such texts suggest that there is an endless possibility for the individual pursuit of pleasure in the limitless city. While Neil Smith (1996) notes that the concept of the urban frontier may have particular resonance in the United States, it is clear that condo-minium advertisements in Toronto also draw on the notion that the elite and professional classes have a right to the city. This right is radically re-articulated in terms of a right to consume the city – in some cases to *be* the city – in contrast to Lefebvre's (and other critical) uses of the term. City life is being sold to new residents as a spectacle, a tourist attraction to which they have continuous access.

Overall, the advertisements are almost disciplinary in their invocations of the good life, defined specifically in an urban context. They are designed to manipulate the consumer's distaste for suburbia and desire for conven-ience, variety, and diversity into a desire for a lifestyle promised by the com-bination of condominium living with city living. They also read as manuals for the creative class, texts that literally tell the condominium buyer how to experience this reinvented urbanity in the revitalized city. For women, some of these ads seem to promise a sense of autonomy, opportunity, and choice through consumption (often illustrated through the trope of sexual free-dom), conflating urban quality of life with quality of lifestyle.

For middle-class women, this model of engagement with the city harkens back to nineteenth-century ideologies about the place and role of women in the urban landscape (Domosh 1996; Wilson 1991; Bowlby 2001; De Grazia and Furlough 1996; Glennie and Thrift 1996), when it was as consumers that women could legitimately experience the public spaces and public freedoms of the city. Of course, women were also part of the visual spectacle of urban life, and their role is also to be watched or consumed in this context. In contemporary Western cities, women are again expected to find freedom and fulfillment through their leisure and consumption activities, which are facilitated by the proximity provided through condominium living. This seems to represent a symbolic shrinking of the public sphere for women, wherein public space is not the space of work or politics but, rather, the space of shopping, dining, and entertainment. Moreover, it may indeed be a re-emergence of mid-twentieth-century gender ideology about consumption. In this period, the suburban housewife was responsible for the mass consumption that would fuel the postwar Fordist economy (Hayden 2004). In the postindustrial period, perhaps it is the young female city dweller who is expected to fuel the new model of consumption: flexible, footloose, and service-based. I argue that the myth of urbanity, in the context of Toronto's revitalization through condominium development, subverts a feminist vision of women's freedom and women's choices by focusing on a very narrow set of choices and freedoms that effectively depoliticizes the practice of city living. The sexualization of women in this context also points to the ambiguous nature of emancipation in this regard.

A Date with the Big City: Women's Experiences

The individual agency of gentrifiers, as well as their affective experiences of city places, are critical to understanding the interactions between individual choice and structural city building processes. As geographers Liz Bondi and Damaris Rose (2003) note in their review of feminist urban geography, women's affective experiences of urban space have often been understood as marked by fear, exclusion, harassment, and constraints. Feminist urban scholars have, at other points, discussed women's feelings of pleasure, power, safety, and confidence in the city (Koskela 1997; Kern 2005; Wilson 1991; Brewis 2004). In speaking to women condominium owners, I also attempt to understand the ways that they construct meaning in choosing a city life and how they connect condominium ownership to their everyday urban experiences. Thus, I ask to what extent the myth of urbanity is just marketing rhetoric and to what extent it resonates with women's actual feelings and experiences. Moreover, can condominium-based urban living be understood as emancipatory for women from a feminist perspective? Or are these lifestyles effectively depoliticized?

"Taking Advantage" of the City

In reading and rereading the interview transcripts, I was struck by the similarities in the women's experiences and in the ways that they framed the
meanings and practices of urban living. Geographer Joanna Brewis (2004),
in her study of London women's aspirations around city living, also found
that her respondents presented rather homogenous accounts of metropolitan life. This homogeneity highlights the need to understand both the extent to which women's attitudes about urban life are shaped by dominant
discursive regimes and the extent to which urban life simultaneously re-
sponds to real gendered needs and desires. In this analysis, I point out some
of the different nuances within women's accounts of city life, but I also consider it important to emphasize the broad similarities that I found across the
interviews.

When asked why they chose city living, or what they enjoyed about living
downtown, women emphasized the interconnected and tight proximity of
work, leisure, shopping, and friends. In this context, walkability and/or public transit access was also important to most women, although three drove
to work regularly.[2]

> You just walk, you know, it's walking distance. A lot of the suburbs
> ... it's not really street-friendly walking. There's usually the neigh-
> bourhoods with the houses, and then there's usually a lot of empty
> space between that and the commercial. I really like how down-
> town, it's really integrated together ... You can just walk down the
> street to the grocery store, it's not like you're walking down a
> highway. *(Nadia, age 25, lives alone)*

Nadia contrasts the integrated, pedestrian-friendly spaces in the city with
the zoned, car-oriented suburbs. Interconnectedness was a key feature that
served to distinguish city living from suburban living for many of the women
interviewed in *Sex and the Revitalized City*, several of whom indicated that
they had grown up in the suburbs.

> I picked this one because the location, I wanted to be close to
> school. It's right across the street from campus. I wanted to be
> downtown. 'Cause I don't drive, and I don't cook so much either,
> so I wanted to be close to a lot of restaurants. *(Rose, age 22,
> lives with roommate)*

I think it's a fantastic location. I can walk to absolutely anything
I could ever want to do in the city. Inconveniently, my boyfriend
lives at Yonge and Lawrence, which is entirely the other end of the
city. But aside from that, like everything, I can walk to work, I can
buy groceries like five minutes away. *(Sandra, age 28, lives alone)*

Convenience, I would say, mostly. I don't like to waste half of my
day on commuting ... I could never be one of those people, so the
convenience is probably the most important thing to me. And the
fact that you can walk to the grocery store, you can walk to the dry
cleaners, you can walk to a pub, or there's so many options of
where to eat, there's so many options of where to shop, so everything is right there. I think those are the most important things.
And a lot of my clients live – not downtown, but at least either
east of me, west of me, not too far by TTC or a short bike ride or
something. *(Naomi, age 29, lives alone)*

For Rose, Sandra, and Naomi, walking, cycling, and taking public transit allow them to connect their work, school, and social lives without lengthy car
commutes, a factor that seems important to their perceived quality of life.
Colleen, below, iterates the specific desire not to own a car. Clearly, she feels
that there would be little benefit, or "joy," in car ownership in the city.

Being across from the subway station – key. Being right on Yonge
Street, I can walk to everything. Which was – I want to be able to
walk to things. I don't want to have to buy a car. Because of the
expense. After parking expenses – really, where's the joy? *(Colleen,
age 28, lives alone)*

These women describe a desire to walk to work, school, and social activities. Many contrast this walkability to life in the suburbs, where it is difficult, sometimes impossible, to walk to satisfy all of the different needs and
desires of daily life. This resonates with Wekerle's (1984) account of the ways
in which cities, in contrast to suburbs, could support women's multiple
roles. Unlike Wekerle's argument, however, which was centred on the city's
supporting the needs of low-income women, older women, and single
mothers, the lifestyles described by the women in *Sex and the Revitalized
City* clearly reflect their positions as, for the most part, young, single, and

childless women. Their desires for interconnected work, leisure, and home lives reflect a relative lack of constraints. Even the inability to drive or lack of a car was viewed as a positive aspect of their lives rather than as a deficiency (see Zielinski 1995; Wekerle 2005).

The ability to get to work efficiently and conveniently was a major aspect of my respondents' decisions to purchase condominiums in particular locations. Proximity to employment is a key dimension of feminist thought on why city living can be advantageous for women, and most women here expressed this as a major reason for living downtown, although three commuted outside of the core (to Etobicoke and North York).

> Basically I targeted an area that I wanted to be in, and that was in the downtown area. I didn't want anything that was too far away from the subway system because I have to get up to North York to work. *(Alicia, age 30, lives alone)*

> I wanted to be close enough to campus that I could walk. Other than that, I didn't really care whether I was north, south, whatever. *(Rachel, age 21, lives alone)*

> It had to be on the subway line, and the closer to work the better. I mean, I could have been on the subway line, but out at Islington, but then I would have had an hour's commute every day. So now, where I – being right here right on the Yonge line, it's twenty minutes to work every day. *(Colleen, age 28, lives alone)*

> For me, I don't drive, I can't drive, and I don't have a good sense of direction. I like to live close to where I work and that I can walk, so I can also avoid the commuting hassle, and that's it basically. I don't also have time to go exercising, the gym. Walking to work is my only form of exercise ... so I don't feel guilty about binging or eating junk, because I know I'll be walking home anyway later! *(Jaime, age 33, lives with roommate)*

The experiences of these women suggest that perhaps condominium living has brought Toronto to the promised land in terms of creating a culture where people actively prefer walking, cycling, and public transit over driving. This would fulfill many of the goals of the *Official Plan*, not to mention the wildest dreams of anti-modernist urbanists such as Jane Jacobs (1961).

This seems like a significant success, especially given that many of these women were not forced to walk or take public transit because of low income; on the contrary, they actively chose and claimed a preference for alternative forms of transportation. Their accounts may reflect the ways that the anti-sprawl discourse has shaped the terms of debate; however, walking is indeed a major part of their daily lives.

My concern here, though, is that, in interpreting these women's experiences as preliminary evidence of a revival of walkable urban environments, I am ignoring critical questions about *which* areas of the city are havens for walkable lifestyles and about *who* has the privilege to live and work in such spaces. The women whom I interviewed were employed in professions that dominate the postindustrial city: cultural production, law, financial services, education, design, and marketing, for example. Thus, their ability to connect home and work is predicated, in part, on the specific types of work that they do. Gentrification researchers have often found that women gentrifiers expressed a strong relationship between their desire to live in the city and their need to work there; for many central city dwellers, convenience and lifestyle are linked (Karsten 2003; Tallon and Bromley 2004). What is not sufficiently problematized in these accounts is the unevenness in the ways that the convenience of city living is distributed. For women and others whose work is not in one of the specialized sectors that are increasingly centralized, or who cannot afford the rising costs of living in the core, walkability and proximity are scarce commodities.

The social lives of the women condominium owners seem to further support the notion that new-build gentrifiers desire instant access to the city's amenities and, moreover, that these functions of the city are very important for women. Downtown condominiums were viewed as living spaces that facilitated their ability to "take advantage" of these aspects of city living.

> I think for me it would just be the fascination of – you know, I
> have the whole city to myself. Whatever I choose to do I can go
> and do it. That sort of thing. Kind of like going on a date with a big
> city. You can go anywhere, just have like a really fabulous time.
> *(Jillian, age 30, lives alone)*

> I like the noise. I like the amount of people, most of the time. And
> just the fact that I can pretty much do what I want, when I want.
> Everything's available to me. I think that's what I like. *(Hope, age
> 29, married)*

I want to experience all the city has to offer. A lot of events that go
on, I try to attend those. Whatever there is to do, I want to do it.
(Colleen, age 28, lives alone)

Work brings me into the city, and while I'm here, I've learned to
love it and I might as well take advantage of it ... For me the reason
for living downtown is because you're so close to everything.
(Amanda, age 29, lives alone)

Such narratives suggest that women condominium owners are eager to
participate in the spectacle, excitement, and freedom of city life. The downtown condominium functions as a base from which to pursue various activities; in this regard, the home's value is assessed, in part, on its ability to allow
one to take advantage of urban amenities rather than on its ability to connect one to neighbours and community. The women's comments resonate
both with critical accounts of the urban pioneer's experience in claiming the
city (N. Smith 1996) and with feminist accounts of the ways in which the
ability to participate in the carnival of city living is itself liberating (Wilson
1991; Karsten 2003). However, this model of liberation is focused on leisure,
entertainment, and consumption:

My number one pastime is shopping, and number two would
be movies, and they're both available. *(Jaime, age 33, lives with
roommate)*

I made the decision last summer to try to look at Toronto as a
tourist would and check things out. So last summer I started going
to, like, the Bata Shoe Museum. I've been to the ROM [Royal
Ontario Museum], I've been to the AGO [Art Gallery of Ontario],
went over to the Islands ... I started to make a concerted effort to
actually see things in the city and indulge in this stuff. *(Stephanie,
age 35, lives alone)*

Jaime and Stephanie make focused efforts to seek out activities that they
enjoy. In contrast, Lynn, Ava, and Jillian describe the accidental nature of
social interaction in the city:

I just like being where things are happening. Because I'm still single,
most of my socializing is hanging out with friends, and most of my

friends live downtown. So it's easier to see them. And just the fact that you can go out and do things and you don't need a car, you don't have to drive, you don't have to worry about that. I like having access to all of the different kinds·of culture, and cuisine, and all the different sort of shops and the arts scene, the music scene. It's just nice to live somewhere where things happen all the time, and you don't have to hunt them down, they're just all around you. You can sort of pick and choose. *(Lynn, age 28, lives alone)*

A lot of it has to do with the fact that there are actual public spaces. The public is pretty ... Proximity, I don't have a car, I like to walk. And just the kind of accidental nature of living in the city, your plans could change at a moment's notice, when you run into some-body. There's a kind of vitality, and everything is right there. *(Ava, age 32, lives alone)*

You know what – good food, kind of checking out good restau-rants and new restaurants, that sort of thing, and being close to downtown, finding little treasure shops, on Queen, stuff like that. I love walking around, kind of exploring, that area's really – you know it's a really up-and-coming area, King West, as well [as] just blowing up with restaurants and clubs, that sort of thing. It's a relaxing area, and if you're off on your own, you can spend the entire day just walking around and kind of getting to know the area. The thing with my friends, they lived here for thirty years, and there's still spots downtown they've never been to. It's always exciting, it's always new. *(Jillian, age 30, lives alone)*

These accounts suggest a flaneuse-like experience for women who enjoy the uncontrolled and unplanned aspects of city life, the excitement of dis-covering new places and meeting different people (D'Souza and McDonough 2006). They suggest that there is a value in the less-ordered spaces and ex-periences of the city. This was also reflected in the responses to questions about visiting major city attractions and high-profile revitalization projects like the ROM, the AGO, and the new ballet/opera house. These places were much less important in women's typical experiences of the city, a point that calls into question the value of such attractions and their impact on the urban experiences of Toronto's inhabitants.

I haven't [visited cultural institutions] much lately. At first when I
moved I did. A friend and I were visiting every area because there's
so much to see. The novelty really does sort of wear off. I haven't
really done anything overly cultural in a while besides maybe
eating at a Chinese restaurant! *(Alicia, age 30, lives alone)*

No, I mean the closest I would come is I'd say the theatre. I love
going to the theatre. You know, I don't live in the city for the
theatre, because it's not really in my budget to go more than on
occasion, but museums and art galleries? God, I'd love to say that
I make more, or take more advantage of that. You know, you see
all the cultural events in the paper that are so close by, that I just
don't ever take advantage of. So I'd say out of all of that my biggest
interest would be the theatre, but rarely – maybe once a year.
(Caitlin, age 31, lives alone)

Funny thing is I never seem to explore those museums where I
live, but I go to museums in Montreal, Quebec, when I travel. But
when I'm here, I never go. *(Jaime, age 33, lives with roommate)*

As important as leisure and consumption are to the enjoyment of city life,
people are not necessarily attracted by the most spectacular examples of
revitalization efforts. One concept that does filter through all of these accounts, though, is that of choice. Women express a desire to choose among
a wide range of options for activities and to express identities.

I think when you live downtown there's a lot more culture that's
just sort of easily accessible. Like the film festival or theatre and
stuff like that. I like all of the goings on. I like the vibrancy of it.
Sometimes you're like, "Aah, I gotta get out here," but most of the
time I like the pace, and I like the options, the variety. *(Sandra,
age 28, lives alone)*

I like the energy of it, and that there's always stuff going on. It's like
Tuesday, and they're all out for dinner, and they're all at the bars.
It's easy for people to get together. I don't know, I just find that you
can walk to all these places. I think it's just the sense of diversity. I
think out in the suburbs, you have to stay in the line of how you

live, and here, people do whatever they please. Sure, we're supposed
to be stylish or whatever, but there's lots of people – they don't care,
they just do whatever they want. It's creative. *(Samantha, age 33,
lives alone)*

I love getting together with friends and trying different restaurants. Growing up in a small town – the town I grew up in, nine
thousand people, all white – needless to say there's been a lot to
learn in Toronto. My first time in an Indian restaurant, or eating
Thai food. I want to experience all the city has to offer. *(Colleen,
age 28, lives alone)*

These women describe the pleasure of diversity, its connection to choice,
and the ways that this kind of space opens opportunities to be creative, original, and less conformist. The experiences described here also reflect a
sense that the city's amenities are, and should be, available to be used at any
time. The fact that women feel confident to claim this right in the city suggests that they feel a sense of ownership and belonging in Toronto. However, the claim that is being staked here is founded on the desire to consume
as an integral element of the ability to find or make a place for oneself in the
web of interconnected city services. The ability to make this claim is predicated on a certain class position that mediates women's gender-based exclusions in urban space.

I want to complicate this, however, by noting that, for women condominium owners, the cost of living in the city was sometimes a constraint that
limited their ability to "take advantage" of all the leisure and consumption
activities being offered.

I would like to spend a lot, because that's the whole point of living
downtown, but I can't. *(Ava, age 32, lives alone)*

I'm trying to stay away from the shops, 'cause of my bank account.
(Jillian, age 30, lives alone)

I love to travel and I don't have any money anymore – but I'm a
wanderer, you know? ... So that's what I like about the city as well.
And Toronto is a great walkable city. Entertainment, I don't know
that I have money to do any kind of entertainment, but you know

my favourite restaurant is Jamie Kennedy, which is the next corner
over. Restaurants, there's a movie theatre right there, which I
actually go to anyways, because it's like $4.25 matinees. *(Stephanie,
age 35, lives alone)*

Stephanie's decision to buy a condominium as a single woman had left her
without a great deal of disposable income and an inability to pursue one of
her favourite activities – travelling. However, her flaneuse-like attitude towards city living allowed her to find ways to enjoy Toronto as she might a city
she was visiting for the first time. Stephanie, Jillian, and Ava point out a key
tension, though, in the narrative of freedom, choice, and leisure in the city
as connected to condominium living. For women who may be somewhat
marginal housing consumers in terms of their ability to afford mortgage
payments, property taxes, monthly fees, and other expenses, the pleasures
promised by the myth of urbanity may always be a little out of reach.

   This discussion of interconnected lifestyles, leisure, and choice highlights
critical issues that need to be considered in the context of debates around
the neoliberal city. In positioning the experience of interconnectivity as a
dimension of liberation or freedom for women who live in the city, we must
consider what lies in the shadows of this story. Critical perspectives on new-
build gentrification argue that the integrated spaces of redevelopment are
potentially exclusionary, allowing the affluent to maintain what Atkinson
(2006) calls a cloaked presence, slipping easily between home, work, and
leisure in areas that make urban problems, disorder, and difference invisible.
Similarly, feminists noting the positive association of urban living with
choice for women have also problematized the depoliticization of choice
and the threats to choice from processes of increased social polarization
(Darke 1996). The question raised, then, is whether the interconnected lifestyles described here by the women condominium owners are implicated in
broader processes of exclusion, privatization, and purification.

   In the last chapter's discussion of security and community, I note that
some of the women interviewed in this book described a desire to be insulated from certain types of disorder and deviance in their neighbourhoods.
For the most part, however, the women did not actively express a need for
clear boundaries between themselves and, for example, homeless people,
strange behaviour, or prostitution. Nonetheless, the kinds of spaces that
are set up to attract young women as consumers of goods and entertainment are likely to be those purified glamour zones that are implicitly, and

sometimes explicitly, exclusionary, thanks to techniques such as surveillance, privatization, or simply cost of entrance. The choices offered to women as consumers, and the convenience that comes with being a downtown condominium owner, are offered in ways that may work to limit the choices and conveniences available to other city dwellers who are less welcome in, or who are unable to pay for access to, the spaces of interconnectivity, freedom, and choice. The spaces of the revitalized city are purified in these ways, in part, as a response to the need to attract young women, who, it is assumed, desire clean, orderly, and safe spaces in which to conduct their lifestyles (Latham 2003).

Everyday City Lives

Asking women what they enjoy about city life does not necessarily give us a picture of how their actual day-to-day lives articulate with the lifestyles that are promoted and encouraged in the context of urban revitalization and new-build gentrification. In order to understand how women's everyday city lives are enacted, I asked women to describe typical weekdays and weekends in order to clarify the relationships between gender, work, and urban spatial structure (Bondi 1994; Saegert 1981). Here I include five responses to questions about everyday life that illustrate the ways that spatial and social interconnectedness function for these women and that highlight the relationships between work, social, and domestic lives.[3]

> [Weekday]: I walk to the subway. I take the subway to work. I generally read on the subway. I get to work, work 'til, I don't know, about four o'clock or so, then come home. Well, I might not go straight home. I often socialize after work with people from work. After work I might get together with a friend. If I don't, I will sort of putter around, clean up, maybe watch television, maybe read and go to bed. That's about it ... [Weekend]: Well, I might, it might sort of be the time that I've designated for housework, so I can spend about four hours cleaning, and then maybe read the paper and that's the day! I like to go to the St. Lawrence Market on Saturdays a lot, that's nice. I like to go over there and wander around. Weather dependent too, so I might wander over to the Eaton Centre. At night, I might get together with friends, or I might just stay in and have a quiet night in by myself, have a glass of wine. *(Alicia, age 30, lives alone)*

Alicia's description of life as a single woman condominium owner suggests a relative lack of obligations outside of work and weekly domestic chores. However, these obligations are not insubstantial: there are daily housework chores and several hours of cleaning to be done each weekend. Outside of these tasks, she is free to wander, experiencing the life of the flaneuse and the joys of visual consumption of the city. Alicia is also free to make plans after work as well as to enjoy contemplative time by herself. Her narrative suggests a tension between the freedom of the flaneur (as imagined by early-twentieth-century writers like Walter Benjamin) and the obligations of the single woman homeowner. The flaneuse may only be able to commence her wanderings after the dishes are done.

Hope also describes some contemplative time, and time for aimless wandering and visual consumption, after obligations such as work and making dinner.

> [Weekday]: I get up, take the subway to work. Streetcar and then the subway. Work, come home. Come home, make dinner. Eat. After dinner go for a walk. Come home and read a book, sit on my balcony if it's nice and read a book. That's pretty much it ... [Weekend]: I like to go walking up to Queen Street, and then walk along maybe to the Eaton Centre. Walking along Harbourfront, sort of see everything. It's funny, we leave the city a lot. We go out to Mississauga or something. We go shopping a lot for our house right now, and all the big box stores are out there ... We go out to restaurants, we have people over occasionally. Mostly go out to dinner. *(Hope, age 29, married)*

Hope draws attention to shopping and dining out as central activities for her and her partner; interestingly, they leave the city to go shopping at suburban big box stores, an activity that suggests that interconnected urban living does not fulfill all the needs and desires of the condominium owner.

Ava also describes the rather mundane obligations that compete for her time.

> [Weekday]: Okay, but it's going to make me look really old. I get up in the morning and go to work ... I walk to work. I agonize over the lunch that I didn't make. I'm supposed to be saving. On horrible days I'll actually take a cab. [Some days] I'm not going home, I'm going out to dinner or whatever. If I don't have plans, I'll be heading

home, making dinner, eating, watching TV. Or being next door at
my neighbour's house ... [Weekend]: Well, unfortunately, there's,
like, the must activities, like the laundry, and grocery shopping,
and dry cleaning. That kind of has to be done. By the time that's
done, there's not much of the weekend left. And then I might
actually have to visit my family or my grandmother, I've got family
that lives out in the suburbs. Um, and then the remainder of the
time would either be spending time at home, or whatever, or seeing friends ... It often revolves around food. Whether it's a dinner
party or a restaurant. You know, films, whatever. There are certain
parts of the year when there are a lot of interesting lectures on
urban stuff. *(Ava, age 32, lives alone)*

Ava expresses a concern that perhaps her life is not exciting enough or not
living up to the ideal of youthful urbanity promised by downtown condominium living. This is influenced by her work schedule, her financial situation, and other obligations such as domestic tasks and visiting family.
Nonetheless, she is relatively free to do "whatever," suggesting a lack of daily
obligations beyond work. Her comments raise the question of how the ideal
of city living is perceived by new city dwellers: is it "disciplinary" in the sense
that it promotes a lifestyle that few (and perhaps, in particular, few women)
can afford or manage? Or is it liberating, allowing women the permission to
be wanderers or flaneuses and do "whatever"?

Rose, a graduate student and one of the younger women whom I interviewed, is quite enthusiastic about the variety of social activities in which
she is able to participate due to living in central Toronto.

[Weekday]: Probably get up at around seven-thirty, eight, get ready
for work, go to work, come home, make dinner. Either go out for
dinner or make dinner, or hang out in the house. Or I'll be out to
about nine or ten ... [Weekend]: Mm, I don't know. Going out!
Parties, bars, clubs. When I'm in school sometimes I spend the
whole weekend working, depending on what's going on. Lately,
since I've gotten together with my boyfriend, we do all sorts of
stuff – like, he does Dragon Boat racing, so we went out to Centre
Island. He's racing this weekend, so I'll be out there. We've gone
flying. Cottaging in the summertime ... I love the festivals. I would
go to like every festival. Some of us went to Winterlicious [a two-
week event featuring discount menus at top restaurants], we love

that. Gay Pride parade, I'm always there for the whole weekend ...
The film festival, next week. All those little festivals that go on in
downtown. Most of them are downtown, so I try to go to all of
them. We always try to go to Dream in High Park [an annual
outdoor production of a Shakespeare play]. *(Rose, age 22, lives
with roommate)*

Unlike Ava, Rose seems able to fulfill the requirements of the creative urban
lifestyle (Florida 1998). Downtown locations are pivotal for her in that they
provide an array of possible options for consumption and entertainment.
Rose's ability to live this lifestyle is likely predicated on her status as a student, her age, and her lack of family and household obligations.

Amanda also has an active lifestyle, but her narrative exposes, again,
some of the mundane aspects of life as a condominium owner.

[Weekday]: I'll get up. I'll have, you know, breakfast. Or if I'm
feeling really responsible and energetic I'll actually go down and
do some yoga or something. And then I get the paper delivered, so
I read the paper, and then I make my way into work. At work until
five, five-thirty, and then I'll have an evening activity. Like I might
go straight from work to play soccer, or I'll have classes, so I'll go to
one of those. And then get home, little bit later on in the evening,
and eat dinner, have dinner at eight-thirty, nine, something like
that. And just unwind. Do a little tidying up or do the dishes and
go to bed ... [Weekend]: On the weekend, I might, on a Saturday, if
I'm in the city – most of the time I'm out of the city on weekends
– so, like, last weekend was the first time I was in the city since
May. In the summer I was at cottages, or I'll be travelling. But in
the winter, a weekend if I'm in the city will be, I'll go to maybe the
market, the St. Lawrence Market. Go there in the morning on
Saturday. Try to get together with some friends. Maybe do some
household things, cleaning up. I might go see a movie. Just general
– I'll use my condo more as a home base, I might go back and
forth out in the morning, afternoon, evening. *(Amanda, age 29,
lives alone)*

Amanda's lifestyle involves several outdoor activities, and she pursues these
outside of the city on many weekends. On weekdays, however, she tries to

make use of her condominium's gym to do yoga, if feeling "responsible and energetic." This phrase suggests that Amanda feels as though she *should* engage in these activities, invoking, again, the question of how certain attributes of the downtown condominium lifestyle become viewed as imperatives or as necessary to the good life. Her account also explicitly notes the way the downtown condominium can be used as a home base from which to launch into different activities in and around the city. The condominium's location facilitates her ability to do a variety of different activities in one day, without necessarily having to plan each of these in advance.

Women consume the spaces of the city in a multitude of ways: through walking and wandering, eating, shopping, attending events, going to movies. What these narratives cannot show is that "the contemporary urban woman is both consumer and consumed ... she remains an object of consumption at the same time as she becomes an actor" (Wilson 1991, 139). Like her Victorian counterparts, the middle-class woman of the postindustrial city pays for her freedoms by becoming part of the spectacle. Today, the spectacle is revitalization, gentrification, and redevelopment, although in some ways this is not entirely new. Novelist Emile Zola (1984) was eerily prescient in his novel *Au bonheur des dames* (*The Ladies' Paradise*, originally published in 1883), in which the construction of the great department store for bourgeois ladies destroys an old neighbourhood of local shops and artisans, and the women who work in the department store are controlled like prisoners (Wilson 1991). Not only are middle-class women, as consumers, drawn into the spectacle of the revitalized city, but this so-called emancipation rests upon the low-status labour of other women. I question, then, the extent to which the revitalized city has relinquished the traditional patriarchal desire to survey, control, and restrict the movements of women in public space. In a shift that reflects the move to governance through autonomy and freedom, rather than directly repressive practices, women's urban lives are policed through a governmentality that positions consumption as freedom and fulfillment.

The women condominium owners interviewed here also mention more mundane aspects of daily life, such as housework and grocery shopping and, of course, paid employment. The tone and rhythm of their narratives evoke the routine predictability of many of these obligations. In some respects, their daily lives, with multiple roles facilitated by interconnectivity, seem to exemplify a feminist vision of how the city can work for women; however, there are important caveats to examine before making such an enthusiastic claim. First, it is interesting to note some of the activities that are absent from these accounts. None of the women mentioned community-based activities such as volunteer work, attending religious functions or spirituality-centred events, membership in organizations, extensive family engagements, or any other types of explicitly community-oriented work. I am not suggesting that these activities are essential to a *feminist* vision; however, their absence highlights the somewhat narrow range of lifestyles that may be encouraged at the nexus of condominium and city living.

A second, related, point is that these are primarily young, childless women who are professionally employed; therefore, their ability to enjoy this inter-connectedness in the ways that they do is not constrained or mediated by the need to juggle multiple roles in the context of financial deprivation.

Third, buying a condominium is a way of literally buying this proximity. Although proximity would presumably be available to renters in the same areas, the massive amount of new condominium development in the down-town core means that these benefits are primarily geared towards, or used as marketing points for, downtown condominium owners. Proximity and inter-connectedness are therefore not necessarily part of a broader right to the city that is guaranteed to all who inhabit it; rather, it is increasingly based upon a particular type of inhabitance – ownership within the downtown core.

In the revitalized, entrepreneurial city, women's presence functions as a symbol of the success of residential and commercial gentrification. Geographer Alan Latham (2003) asks whether the spaces of redevelopment within gentrifying neighbourhoods will potentially facilitate the creation of a new public culture amenable to women. In presenting the narratives of women and men living in gentrifying neighbourhoods in Auckland, New Zealand, he argues that, although the daily routines described by women gentrifiers represent mundane tasks as much as any sense of urban glamour (a point that is echoed in my findings), their leisure activities mark a break with some problematic urban traditions. In the New Zealand context, Latham suggests that women's use of cafés, bars, and shops works to break down the aggressively masculine pub culture of the city at night. While Latham wants to avoid suggesting that gentrification is equal to a straightforward feminization of urban space, he does note that the spaces created by redevelopment and commercial gentrification are often more welcoming and comfortable for women, particularly women unaccom-panied by men (and often for gay men as well). Latham (2003, 1712) inter-prets this as "a sexual polymorphisation of public space," in which both women and men can experiment with identities outside of gender norms.

FIGURE 11   Live the life of a flaneuse. Billboard for King West Condominiums, Strachan Avenue, Toronto.

This reworking of gender within contemporary spaces of revitalization is an important facet of the process that needs to complicate the story of class-based exclusion. Although women do actively appropriate such spaces to their life worlds, their presence here acts as a benchmark of the success of "latte urbanism." In this way, women's supposed emancipation is instrumentalized to produce an image of the revitalized, beautiful city (see Figure 11).

Problematically, though, as Peck (2005) suggests, there is a swelling but unacknowledged group of low-waged workers that is spawned by the creative city dweller's desire for self-validation and a twenty-four/seven lifestyle. The creative city strategy leaves "unanswered the question of who will launder the shirts in this creative paradise" (757). Although this is posed as a question of class, there are also gendered implications. As the daily routines of women condominium owners suggest, domestic chores do not disappear in the convenience-oriented world of condominium and city living. In *Sex and the Revitalized City*, some women suggested that they would use outside help for housework if their financial situations allowed. This illustrates the interlocking systems of privilege and oppression that are manifest in gentrifying cities: as the privileged women of the new middle class work and wander, immigrant and working-class women will perform the domestic tasks that they leave behind (Sassen 1998).

The daily routines described above also reveal traces of the regulatory and disciplinary (i.e., governmental) effects of the myth of urbanity at the intersection of city and condominium living. The particular subject that is promoted in this myth – a subject that is always consuming, enjoying, choosing – is internalized in the ways that women describe a sense of how they feel they *should* be behaving in the city. Larner (2003) suggests that, in such mundane practices, we can see the techniques of neoliberalism and the ways in which they constitute particular subjects. Urban living, in this sense, has become a site of self-governance in which subjects are expected not only to construct their daily lives around specific ideals but also to understand this regime of daily life as an imperative (and as a source of freedom). Moreover, the subjects of the urban lifestyle, including women condominium owners, are asked to identify with these ideals and to internalize them as part of their sense of self.

City Girls: Identity and the City

Beyond questions of how women engage in various aspects of city life is the question of what the city means to women, how they define it and themselves in relation to one another, and what the implications of this definition are for women's engagement with, and attachment to, the city. Contemporary cultural representations of women's urban lives also seem to address these questions, particularly with respect to the issue of how women manage their demanding multiple roles in urban contexts and how the city is central to their professed identities.[4] In this book, the urban was considered a crucial dimension of personal identity for many, although not all, of the respondents. For some women, the urban is positioned as an intrinsic facet of their identities, while for others their identification with the city is contingent and temporary. In either case, the ways in which women city dwellers conceive of their relationship to the city have important implications with respect to the ways in which contemporary urban revitalization projects shape the city.

One of the most striking notions to emerge from the interviews came from women who described a very narrow sense of the geographic boundaries of the city. While other women maintained connections to many areas of the city and surrounding suburbs, there were some who indicated extremely tight personal and work-related networks and a tendency to define the city in relation to their own lives. Although these comments do not represent a majority of responses, I think that they raise important questions for further studies of the relationships between cities and the residents of new-build gentrification projects.

> My sister lives in Bloor West Village and I'm sorry, that's not Toronto to me. It's not. Because she, you have to take the Bloor [subway line] to Runnymede Station, then you have to walk another twenty or thirty minutes just to get to her house, down one of these side streets. And it's like, "Sorry, you're not in Toronto." ... I was looking at some [condominiums] close to Yonge and Bloor, and I was with my realtor, and we were driving up there, and I was like, I wrote it off before we even got there, simply because it took another thirty minutes to get just from this area, you know, King and Yonge, to Hayden Street, which is south of Bloor. And I'm like, "Sorry, but no way would I ever live up here, because I would have friends slitting their wrists before they even got to my place." *(April, age 37, lives alone)*

> I would never live outside the GTA, well not even GTA, but Dufferin, Mount Pleasant, I'm willing to go as far as Mount Pleasant, and then Eglinton and Lakeshore ... Like, my family is mostly north of Steeles, so I don't visit them that often, because I almost feel claustrophobic when I go outside the city. *(Chloe, age 23, lives with partner)*

> I mean, I go and visit my sister sometimes. She's at Bathurst and Wilson. I'm sorry, but I could not live out there. You could not get me out in Scarborough. You just could not get me out. Anything north of Bloor to me is just, forget it. Really out there. *(Leigh, age 46, lives alone)*

> And actually when I was looking the agent was trying to convince me to live in South Etobicoke, because you get more for your money. But I'm like, "Yeah, then I have to spend sixty dollars on a GO [commuter train] pass to get to work, and there's probably not a grocery store on the corner and places to walk to." *(Stephanie, age 35, lives alone)*

Ironically, the very interconnectedness that seems to support women's multiple roles and to offer women choice and opportunity in the city functions here as a way of cognitively narrowing their understanding of what (and perhaps, implicitly, who) constitutes the city. Does this attitude hinder a sense of intersubjectivity in the city or affect the way that gentrifiers relate to other city dwellers? Who counts and whose interests are privileged if the city becomes functionally defined as a narrow area of the downtown core (the interconnected, purified, urban glamour zone)? Defining the city in relation to one particular manifestation of urban identity means that other identities may be increasingly excluded. This is related to the process described by many scholars of gentrification, wherein city dwellers attempt to distinguish themselves from suburbanites. In the examples presented here, however, it is interesting to note that the areas described as "out there" are not even as far as the suburbs.

This process of creating distinctions between urban and suburban people is a key part of constructing an urban identity for many of the women here.

> Commuting ... I don't know how people do it. That is such a waste
> of life to me. But yeah, I like walking everywhere. I would hate to
> be out in the 'burbs somewhere. I can't stand it. *(Leigh, age 46,*
> *lives alone)*

> I'm a big city girl. I love being in the centre of the whole city, where
> I can move around easily, the subways, streetcars, buses, can take
> me anywhere. So I like the fact that I'm living in the centre of the
> city. So I don't see, I don't know any disadvantages. *(Jaime, age 33,*
> *lives with roommate)*

> I don't think I could live anywhere but downtown. *(Naomi, age 29,*
> *lives alone)*

> Actually, I don't like to be down on people who choose to live in
> the suburbs. But I can't stand it. It creeps me out, actually. Like, all
> the houses that are cookie cutter and they all look the same, and
> there's no trees. *(Sandra, age 28, lives alone)*

These accounts express a feeling of being connected to, and belonging in, the city. This is framed in contrast to the "creepiness" or disconnectedness of suburban life. Nadia and Ava, below, present slightly different accounts, connecting their experiences of city living to their positions as single women. Nadia suggests that an urban lifestyle mitigates some of the potential loneliness or lack of sociability that may come with being single, particularly with being a single woman in a suburban context.

> Well, I like to be around like a lot of people. Like, you walk outside and you don't feel like you're in an isolated area. I like the feeling that you know that you're in the centre of it all, especially being a single girl, you know, it's kind of depressing. Because sometimes you feel like nothing's happening, you work long hours, you feel like you're missing out – so for sure, that's like a huge appeal. You come home from work, it doesn't matter what time, you get home at ten, you know, there's always stuff going on outside, it's motivating, and it's more uplifting. And for sure, any day, I would choose, like, a little shoebox in the middle of the city over, like, some huge house in Aurora or something. *(Nadia, age 25, lives alone)*

Ava notes that many of the men she meets do not share her desire to stay downtown, which suggests that the ideal of suburban family living is still strong among many young people.

> My intention is to always live in an urban environment, whether it's Toronto or somewhere else. But interestingly enough, I find that it's a problem when you're dating, because a lot of guys that I've dated, they're first of all shocked that I live downtown, and the common question is "Why do you live there?" And their ambition is to live in the suburbs, not the city. So it's actually harder to find someone that shares that same ideal. *(Ava, age 32, lives alone)*

Both Nadia's and Ava's comments recall my suggestion that condominium ownership, and indeed city living, may function as a replacement for the traditional step of marriage or other partnership for women in their twenties and thirties, or as a substitute for other patriarchal relations, such as those found in the family home. As Jillian notes, it's "like a date with a big city."

The explicit rejection of suburbia and suburban identities is certainly a characteristic commonly associated with gentrifiers and, more recently, with the creative class. Is the rejection of suburbia necessarily a politically progressive or socially critical stance, even among young women who may be rejecting socialization that often directs them to seek out stable and family-oriented suburban life? It is incumbent upon gentrification scholars not to make this bald assumption: rejecting suburbia does not necessarily mean embracing social justice issues or politically progressive ideals.

In contrast to many of the women above, who made their identities as city girls quite clear, others expressed an enjoyment of city living that was simultaneously contingent upon future family situations.[5]

> I don't know. Yeah, I'm kind of undecided at this point. I think it would depend on whether or not I decide to go the route of having kids. I think that would be kind of the driving force. Like, I don't think I would want to raise children downtown. It's just too risky with all the traffic! Yeah, I think that's what would really be the final deciding factor on whether or not I ever would move out to a suburb. *(Amanda, age 29, lives alone)*

> I imagine that if I have kids at some point, I would probably want to leave the city, because I think all of the things that I enjoy about the city are probably – I mean, I know a lot of kids grow up in the city but it's a little too much. I grew up in the suburbs and I think that it's just slower and quieter and, you know, maybe you can be a kid a little bit longer in the suburbs, so, or in the country. So if I were to actually have a family, at some point, then I might be either moving out of the city or at least moving further out, like away from the downtown area. But as long as I'm on my own, you know, or even if I get married, if my partner doesn't mind being downtown, then I think that, yeah, you know, I love it downtown. *(Lynn, age 28, lives alone)*

> It's hard to say. I definitely see the advantages of living in the suburbs. However, at this point in my life, it just makes more sense to be in the city. Plus the cost of living in the city is so much more. So it's really hard to say. It depends what happens with my work, and, you know, whether or not I get married, and – so I don't really know. *(Alicia, age 30, lives alone)*

These respondents held fairly traditional ideas about the innocence of the suburbs and their suitability for children and families. It seems that, for these women, embracing the city is situational. City living fits with their current social position and seems to form part of their identities, but there is a sense that this may change over time or with specific events during the life course. These responses raise critical questions about the long-term effects of planning and development policies and practices that work to attract mainly young people as residents in the central city. The desire for suburban living has not been completely stamped out by popular anti-sprawl and pro-urban discourses; therefore, we must ask whether these gentrifiers form the basis for a stable, long-term pattern of urban resettlement or whether the city will be dependent on continuous waves of new young gentrifiers to fill the vacated condominiums, cafés, bars, and doggy spas – in short, can we sustain the spaces of revitalization? Moreover, as Fincher (2004) suggests, when development is designed to attract a fairly narrow demographic, the spaces and services that help support families with children are often excluded from planning. Even for women who choose to stay in the city through partnership and parenthood, the city may not support their needs. These policies also work against previous planning rationales in Toronto, where housing and neighbourhoods were designed to support a whole lifecycle and encourage community stability.[6] The city is thus increasingly being shaped in the image of a specific subset of the population in ways that run counter to feminist and other social justice visions of liveability.

Another way that many of the women whom I interviewed connected their identities to city living was through a sense that they were being socially and environmentally conscious citizens by choosing urban living in the form of being a condominium owner. This connects to the co-evolving discourses of urbanity and anti-sprawl, wherein a growing concern for the social deficits and environmental costs of exurban development feeds into a desire for urban ways of life, which ostensibly include values such as greater social diversity, better health, and less pollution. The discourse about the environmental benefits of city living has been transformed into a sort of moral imperative, or regulatory regime, through a process that environmental studies scholar Stephanie Rutherford (2007) has labelled "green governmentality." Discourse about social diversity as the "strength" of the city, for example in the *Official Plan*, functions in a similar manner. These shape ideas about appropriate behaviour and mobilize a particular subject who believes her- or himself to be making the right choices about where and how to live.

> I hate driving in the city. I just think it's better for the environment, better for my own health, if I walk places and stuff, so. I

mean I walk to work and back most days, it's under half an hour, so. It's very convenient. *(Sandra, age 28, lives alone)*

Well, I don't drive, so for me I need to be able to walk everywhere. Also doing photography. And I prefer city life. I cannot stand suburbia. And, like I say, just the whole thought of spending that much time in your car to me is complete and utter insanity. These people think that they're saving money. They're really not. Because they're paying for it in environmental costs, because they're polluting the environment. And, like I say, the sanity costs, because they're getting stressed beyond belief. *(April, age 37, lives alone)*

I think a lot of it had to do with just not wanting to have a car. I mean I do have a driver's licence, I just don't like driving, and I don't really want to do it in the city, and I don't want to drive every day into work. I just thought, that added stress is just not what I need, and I'd rather spend the money that I would spend on the car and go travelling somewhere. So it was more of a lifestyle choice. I just want to be in the city because it's convenient. I can get around without the car, I can save a lot of money by not having the car, and I can use that for something else. *(Amanda, age 29, lives alone)*

Sandra, April, and Amanda connect their ability and desire to walk or use public transit to health, sanity/stress, and pollution concerns. These narratives serve to position them, I suggest, as responsible citizens who govern themselves appropriately in accordance with the ideals of anti-sprawl discourse.

Yeah, and in terms of, like, one big thing now is to do with energy efficiency. And things like that, that you're not going to get even if you do a lot of renovation work in some older homes. You're not going to get it to that level. *(Molly, age 33, married, one child)*

Molly is pleased with her choice to buy a condominium partly because the new construction is more energy efficient than that found in some older Toronto homes, suggesting a concern with the environmental effects of inefficiency.

Maya, below, expresses the value of diversity in ways that suggest identification with the socially progressive ideals of multiculturalism that are embodied in downtown living.

> You have different age groups, single people, people with kids, older people, there's still a mix of socio-economic status too ... So it's more of a mixed neighbourhood. So that's what I like. I guess that's the other thing I like about living in the city, is the diversity. You're going to get that in the 'burbs now, but that's not enough reason to live in the 'burbs, you have to drive everywhere. And it's far away from stuff. But living in the country, outside of the city, is still not very diverse. So yeah, I want to stay in the city pretty much. *(Maya, age 30, lives alone)*

For women condominium owners, the rhetoric of social and environmental responsibility appears to be one dimension of both their choice to buy a condominium in the city and their rationale for choosing to construct an urban lifestyle. It contributes to the process of how and why they identify themselves as city dwellers, and it also helps to structure certain enactments, or performances, of urbanity (e.g., refusing to own a car or walking to work). Feminist constructions of the non-sexist eco-city also value social diversity and interconnectedness (Eichler 1995), and the women in *Sex and the Revitalized City* appear to articulate their lives to this vision. The accounts presented here exemplify some of the normative content of current city living discourse and how it works to shape subject positions in the revitalized city. When gentrification is connected to being socially and environmentally progressive, condominiums can be sold as more than investments and lifestyle choices: they can be sold as morally superior choices. Indeed, condominium developers are drawing upon this in the design and advertising of their projects (Saunders 2006). In the context of neoliberal urban agendas, the figure of the environmentally conscious and socially progressive urban dweller can be mobilized to justify spending and policy making that serve the interests of the new middle class. But, as city planners mention in some of the comments presented here, we cannot assume that the hard or soft infrastructure is in place to support reurbanization on this scale. It seems, then, that the environmental and social discourse serves as a way to defuse criticism of development policies that essentially embody the neoliberal goals of opening up more space for capitalist penetration and more opportunities for rapid profit making (Bunce 2004). Geographer Katharyne Mitchell (2003, 400) asserts that, in a neoliberal context, the notion of the cosmopolitan citizen (both multicultural and entrepreneurial) is deployed strategically to serve as "the new, superior foot soldier of global capitalism." Similarly, the progressive urban dweller is mobilized to justify particular redevelopment policies, and the environmentally and socially inflected myth of urbanity supports this process.

City of Women?

I have grappled here with questions of how the rearticulated myth of urbanity is constructed in the revitalizing city, how it is enacted in the everyday lives of women condominium dwellers, and how contemporary urban identities are shaped, understood, and mobilized in relation to the experience and concept of city living. These questions raise critical concerns about the definition of quality of life, about the role of urban citizens in the postindustrial city, about the unevenness of the urban renaissance, and about the desired subjects (or consumers) of this renaissance.

The discourse of liveability – in Toronto's case, shaped by factors such as interconnectivity, walkability, social diversity, and environmental responsibility – as promoted by city building agents works to diffuse criticism of development policies that are aimed at attracting the middle class and at creating new, up-and-coming spaces for capital accumulation. Positioning interconnectivity, for example, as the solution to a variety of urban problems is a powerful way to elide critical questions about which areas of the city are being developed as zones of interconnectivity and which people are able to gain access to these spaces and their benefits. Geographer Gordon MacLeod (2002, 605-6) suggests that "the new urban glamour zones conceal a brutalizing demarcation of winners and losers, included and excluded. Indeed, in some senses we might speculate that the lived spaces of the neoliberal city symbolize an astonishingly powerful geographical expression of the erosion of Keynesian ideals." In the Toronto context, this characterization captures the ways in which the spaces of revitalization and interconnectivity reflect the ability of some to purchase the benefits of urban living and the exclusion of those who cannot afford to live in the core and who are thus forced to contend with the less walkable, less connected inner and outer suburbs. In this way, the ideal of liveability is not connected to social justice or to the even distribution of the benefits of city living; rather, it is a commodity. Liveability thus masks – barely – a creative city

agenda, which, in turn, masks a neoliberal agenda of entrepreneurial revitalization strategies and competition.

What is the role of gender in this process? There is, simultaneously, a
remaking of gender in, and a gendered remaking of, the contemporary
spaces of revitalization. Aspects of various feminist visions of a city designed with women in mind have come to form one of the central pillars of
revitalization policy – interconnectivity and mixed-use. This commodification of feminist urbanity has been stripped of some of the key principles
that would make this policy emancipatory – most notably, any commitment to social justice and the equitable distribution of these benefits of city
living. My analysis points to a potentially profound unevenness in access to
these benefits. For women condominium owners, the ability to "take advantage" of urban amenities is connected to age, relationship/parenting status,
and class. Their everyday lives reflect a relative lack of constraints and a
great deal of freedom to seek out pleasure, consumption opportunities, or,
quite simply, whatever they desire. Perhaps ironically, then, the groups of
people who would benefit most from interconnectivity may find it increasingly difficult to obtain as the spaces of revitalization – condominiums,
shops, restaurants, parks, and so on – are designed to attract and service the
young, mobile, urban professional. Moreover, interconnectivity is tightest
in the downtown core, which is fast becoming a very expensive place to live,
while peripheral, working-class neighbourhoods wait for better transit,
more services, and safer, walkable streets. Women's freedom in the central
city is thus positioned as a symbol of successful revitalization – one that
blinds us to other pressing concerns about inequality, poverty, and marginality in the city.

Conclusion

On a sunny afternoon in 2003, a friend and I leave her apartment to get coffee on Roncesvalles Avenue. I have my camera with me, and we stop at the corner of Howard Park Avenue and Roncesvalles to snap some pictures of three doomed landmarks: a church, a market, and a Kentucky Fried Chicken franchise (see Figure 12). All are slated for demolition by condominium developer Harry Stinson, who has plans to create the High Park Lofts on this unique flatiron-shaped block. It seems timely to capture this rather quirky urban landscape. As I raise my camera, a well-dressed blonde woman in her thirties walks past the buildings. She stops and turns around, walks up to the door of the market, and reads the ad for the lofts, which start at around $200,000. What she does not see – what few see – are the homeless men who sleep in that doorway at night. It strikes us as a significant juxtaposition. The presence of the homeless who occupy the space at night represents the shadow of the story of revitalization, renaissance, and reurbanization. The price of financial security, interconnected urban living, and autonomy in the city for young women is the loss of neighbourhood spaces, the possible displacement of the poor and working class outside of such revitalized areas, and a distinct lack of security, connection, and autonomy for many. In 2009, the High Park Lofts loom over the corner with arguably less charm than the chicken bucket on a pole that had graced that spot five years earlier (see Figure 13). They are not alone: the Sorauren Lofts, Robert Watson Lofts, and Roncesvalles Lofts will provide lots of customers for the recently opened Starbucks up the street. As these spaces form the visible face of revitalization, we need to ask, what spaces, and what individuals, are the invisible shadow in Toronto today?

FIGURE 12   Doomed landscape. The market, church, and Kentucky Fried Chicken franchise will be gone by 2004.

Sex and the Revitalized City seeks to highlight and challenge the ways that the celebratory face of revitalization – with its discourses of emancipation, aestheticization, and intensification – is shaped by other, distinctly less positive, forces that produce divergent outcomes for people and places in the postindustrial city. I argue that, as condominiums are sold as a means to gendered emancipation, feminist and other politicized or social justice-oriented visions of the city are commodified through the increasing neoliberalization of urban space and urban life. This examination of the role of gender in urban revitalization illustrates the mutability and flexibility of neoliberalism, wherein a wide variety of discourses and practices become articulated to processes of commodification, privatization, and securitization. In the case of condominium development, women's financial and personal independence, urban intensification and integration, the notion of community, and an urban way of life are just some of the social and political ideals that are manipulated, subsumed, and transformed under economic imperatives of competition, growth, and entrepreneurialism.

FIGURE 13   High Park Lofts. The imposing structure bears no trace of the previous
urban landscape.

Under neoliberal urbanism, multiple sets of power relations constitute
city building processes, shape everyday lives, and mobilize various subject
positions. Patriarchal power relations are not dismantled in the revitalized
city, despite the freedoms experienced by some urban women; rather, these

relations are integral to the particular contours of neoliberalism as it touches down in contemporary cities. Ideas about gender roles and norms, and about women's needs, desires, and proper places in the city, all work to define the visions behind redevelopment and the actual built environment that results from these visions. My conclusion is that gender is constitutive of the neoliberal city. Gender shapes the geography of urban revitalization, and nowhere is this made clearer than in the case of condominium development. The reinvigoration of patriarchal relations occurs through the property relations, security features, and promotion of consumption-oriented roles for women, none of which fundamentally challenges traditional domestic or public roles for middle-class women. These gender relations are deeply embedded in neoliberal city building practices, in everyday life, and in the mobilization of particular identities. In this way, gender is not just a category through which life in the neoliberal city is experienced; rather, gender informs the visions, policies, and practices that shape actually existing urban neoliberalism (Brenner and Theodore 2002a).

At the same time, neoliberal urbanism, revitalization policies, and condominium development actively produce gender as an identity and a set of social relations. In emphasizing this aspect of contemporary urban transformations, I hope to open space to treat gender as critically as class has been treated in critical urban literature: not as a given category of analysis but as a culturally, temporally, and spatially specific set of ideas, practices, and relationships that order society and sustain hierarchies of groups and individuals. There is still an urgent need for work addressing the constitution of gender in the urban context through sites of discourse and ideology, policy and practices, and the workings of everyday life.

What is the significance of these insights? These broad conclusions stand out in the context of the little literature addressing gender, urban revitalization, and new-build gentrification; however, my intent is to point to their broader implications – beyond women, condominiums, or Toronto – with respect to our understandings and practices of urban citizenship. Here the narratives of those shaping, and living in, the revitalized city tell us a great deal about the ways that the relationships between people and place are being redefined at this political-economic moment. Neoliberal urban policies serve to inhibit or commodify various aspects of everyday urban life that may serve as bases for citizenship claims – broadly defined to include not just political claims but also claims for space, for recognition, and for expression.

Condominium development, as an expression of neoliberal urbanism, defines people's relationships to the city in ways that undermine the notion of everyday life as a foundation for urban citizenship. The narratives that I present throughout this book tell a story of how city lives are shaped by narrow communities that police their boundaries and limit contact with surrounding communities. The shorter-term nature of condominium ownership decreases a sense of connectedness to the home and the neighbourhood, and it limits the development of affective attachments and a sense of belonging. This seems to deter engagement and participation at various scales, from the condominium community itself to the wider neighbourhood and beyond. Instead, participation in city life – the entire notion of urbanity itself – is commodified and centred on capital accumulation, consumption, and individual security and autonomy. The promise of urban condominium living as emancipation is thus radically different from the emancipation that feminist urban scholars hoped to promote, where spaces for alternative lifestyles would flourish; where there would be enhanced opportunities for engagement by women and other marginalized and vulnerable groups; where a right to the city would be centred on inhabitance and everyday life; where the notion of choice would mean more than the freedom to buy and consume; and where the notion of quality of life would be connected to social justice.

What is new about this critique of injustice in the city? In *Sex and the Revitalized City*, I show how various dimensions of condominium development, including tenure, community, security, and urbanity, are part of an accelerated process of commodification, privatization, and securitization that threatens the potential for democratic or equitable citizenship. Home ownership has become more deeply entrenched as the foundation of the right to the city in neoliberal times. Recalling traditional liberalism's focus on the links between private property and political rights, neoliberal urbanism increasingly predicates the ability to participate in urban life upon property ownership. But this is not just about property; citizenship becomes conflated with the entrepreneurial act of investing in, and profiting from, the second circuit of capital (Lefebvre 2003). While once this was exclusively the right of white, bourgeois men, women and other historically excluded groups are now supposed to find freedom, autonomy, and self-sufficiency through this process. The rationality of neoliberalism is thus filtered through condominium ownership into the everyday experience of home ownership and into the construction of enterprising subjects. The implications here are that the conditions of connection, attachment, engagement, and belonging in urban spaces are increasingly privatized and commodified.

The notion of community is a central part of city building, yet it is deployed in the context of revitalization as a foil for exacerbated processes of social and spatial polarization, disconnection, and the development of relations of threat. The community-building rhetoric of planning and development is undercut by an emphasis on private spaces and amenities, the inclusion of a narrow demographic, and the policing of the community by private security. Nowhere does this rhetoric address questions of why security is posited as a necessity, who requires protection, or from whom they are being protected. Gendered vulnerabilities, or the perception thereof, are specifically mobilized to justify extreme and expensive security measures. In a seemingly paradoxical move, the provision of such security allows the expansion of redevelopment efforts into marginal communities. Concerns about safety, then, are subsumed within the logic of the rent gap (N. Smith 1979) and made palatable by the promise of increased profitability.

The movement of the new middle class into so-called borderline neighbourhoods produces yet another contradiction. The elements of urban life that are believed to constitute threat – the presence of homeless people, prostitution, racialized minorities, the drug trade, and so on – also constitute the authentically urban experience. Condominiums resolve this contradiction by providing secure communities in the midst of this perceived disorder. As some of the women condominium owners indicated, the presence of the twenty-four-hour security in their condominiums permitted them to feel safe as they journeyed through threatening surroundings. This passage through danger and disrepute can foster and promote privileged identities for new city dwellers. They can claim an affinity for the borderline, while simultaneously profiting from their willingness to buy a home in such a place. Through this push and pull between community, on the one hand, and threat, on the other, new spaces and markets are opened up for capital accumulation and to colonization by the middle classes.

Feminist arguments about the benefits of city living for women seem to have found some traction in the realm of urban intensification; however, somewhat perversely, the provision of ordered and controlled spaces and roles for women appears to breathe new life into patriarchal urban social structures. In contrast to early accounts of modern city life, where the central subject of the city was explicitly male in most contexts, the postmodern, or postindustrial, city seems to offer spaces within which women can become the subjects of the city, the wanderers, the visual consumers of city life and city landscapes. In some ways, the spaces of revitalization seem to be feminized as they are designed to appeal to women. Cafés that resemble living rooms, wine bars that replace pubs, boutique-like grocery stores, and, of course, retail landscapes are presented as clean, orderly, safe, and attractive places for women, especially women unaccompanied by men. These spaces afford women the comfort to wander, sit, watch, and blend into the urban world. They are not out of place here; rather, they are an integral part of the landscape. But to what extent does this represent a feminist reworking of gendered norms or a feminist vision of women's (all women's) ability to participate in urban life? Are gender norms disrupted in the spaces of revitalization?

As condominium advertisements illustrate, women's bodies are still commodified and consumed in the revitalized city. Women (and, through them, the city and the condominium) are eroticized and objectified. They become part of the spectacle, even as they are told to enjoy it and consume it themselves. In this way, contemporary bourgeois urban women share much with their Victorian sisters. This is also clear in the re-emphasis on women's roles as consumers in the entrepreneurial city. In the modern industrial city, bourgeois women were accepted in the public realm as long as they remained confined to the world of consumption – the shopping arcades and, particularly, department stores were designed as respectable spaces for the female consumer. In the revitalizing city, women are again expected to act as conspicuous consumers, and their ability to do so is positioned as a form of liberation. This is predicated, of course, on having the economic means to engage in consumption practices, and it ignores other dimensions of liberation in the public realm – equality at work, freedom from violence and harassment, and equal political representation, to suggest but a few. Although the postindustrial city is ostensibly less concerned with regulating women's activities and movement, the emphasis on consumption as liberation suggests that patriarchal norms are resurfacing in this context. In defining urban citizenship as consumption, and liveability as access to consumption, the revitalized city circumscribes the potential for feminist visions and social justice.

Such a move also belies the rhetoric of urban sustainability that constitutes part of the rationale for intensification. In promoting and fostering consumption-oriented lifestyles, the city and the city builders do not actually encourage new residents to conserve or to challenge the dangerous effects of our consumption patterns (from the environmental costs of production to the problems of disposal and pollution). This is just one of the ways in which notions of sustainability and environmental benefits are undermined through revitalization policies. Similarly, the environmental and social benefits, including the ostensibly gendered benefits, of a mixed-use, integrated urban realm in which work, home, and leisure are in close proximity have been commodified in the context of massive downtown condominium developments. These benefits are available to those who can afford to purchase or rent a space in the downtown core, while marginalized groups, and the services upon which they rely, are pushed to the far less interconnected peripheries of the city.

This illustrates the extent to which the revitalized city limits the advantages of urban living "to those capable of confirming a financial 'stakeholding' in the new economy of fast capitalism" (MacLeod 2002, 609). Similarly, Wilson (1991, 9) asserts that "we will never solve the problems of living in cities until we welcome and maximise the freedom and autonomy they offer and make these available to all classes and groups ... Leisure and consumption must cease to be treated purely as commodities controlled by market forces." Condominium development produces an uneven geography of freedom and autonomy, making these into commodities available only to those who have the means to buy a stake in the revitalized city.

Wilson's comments are particularly concerned with the exclusion of women from the full experience of urban life, and her exploration of the ways that gender has shaped urban forms since the industrial era still resonates. Gender is a key, though often implicit, component of contemporary city building, and there are surprisingly strong continuities between the gender ideologies that shaped the modern city and those that are currently shaping the postindustrial city. This broad observation, along with the more detailed analyses of tenure, community, and urbanity that emerge in this book, has significant implications for both feminist urban theory and critical urban theory concerned with neoliberalism. It is also important in terms of both public policy and women's urban activism. Perhaps most critically, it is necessary to link these realms, drawing out the connections between discourse, imagery, policy, and everyday life.

For feminist urban scholars, there is much work to be done in expanding and applying a feminist critique of urban revitalization. A feminist analytical approach to entrepreneurial city building demands a reframing of the terms of the neo-Marxist and even Foucauldian dialogue on the processes, politics, and impacts of neoliberal urban restructuring. It is an approach that does not allow for an analytical separation between the study of political-economic rationalities and everyday life; instead, this framework allows for a productive synthesis drawing on the detailed examinations of the shift towards neoliberal agendas and their drastic impacts on cities and on less abstract but highly nuanced accounts of daily life, where the complexities and contradictions of neoliberalism come to light. It is at this intersection that we come to understand the interplay among global economic impera- tives and people's everyday lives. It is at this intersection that claims for citizenship can be articulated.

In bringing the voices of women city dwellers to the scholarly discussion of entrepreneurial urban restructuring, I insert into what has often been a very top-down perspective on political-economic change a commitment to viewing people as knowing and active subjects of the transformations in which they are situated. These voices illustrate the tensions inherent in neo- liberal projects as well as the variations in neoliberal discourses and policies. They also speak back, in a sense, to the discourses and imagery produced by the city and the city builders, reinserting women as embodied and active subjects of the city rather than as objects and instruments in the city's quest for a competitive advantage and a marketable image.

For example, we can begin to see the production of particular subjects through neoliberal city building as a highly differentiated process. There are multiple discourses and ideologies, such as those around gender norms and relations, that mutually constitute identities and city building processes. It is critical to consider how the gendered subjects of revitalization are mobilized and how these subjects enact (or challenge and resist) the new urbanity as it is deployed in the context of neoliberal urban agendas. It is near-sighted to view neoliberalism as a top-down project that uniformly creates particular subject positions and, therefore, subjects who will govern themselves ac- cording to the objectives of neoliberal policies; rather, an analysis of neolib- eralism must consider the role of acting subjects (Larner 2003). In this sense, it is necessary to problematize the ideologies of freedom, choice, and empowerment that are discursively produced in the pursuit of neoliberal urban agendas. I argue that those ideologies are gendered and, thus, work to produce gendered subject positions; women, however, are also acting sub- jects that perform these positions and make their own meanings out of the choices with which they are faced.

Nonetheless, it is critical to ask how subjectivity is constituted through governing practices and what technologies of power are embedded in the notion of urbanity (and the actual spaces of gentrification that are pro- duced within it). As Foucault (1991) argues, the modern state (indeed, all modern techniques of governance) and the modern, autonomous individual co-determine the emergence of one another. In looking at how the everyday lives of women condominium owners in the city articulate with ever-more accepted discourses around city living, freedom, empowerment, and opportunity, I suggest that, in many ways, these discourses operationalize neoliberal ideology by penetrating everyday life. Such discourses promise that freedom will be attained through the practices of everyday life. This notion is certainly integral to the ideal of urbanity as it is promoted by planning, developers, and advertising. It is borne out in the day-to-day lives of women condominium owners, who find meaning in their identities as city dwellers and who connect this to the freedom and empowerment that they feel as they move through everyday life in the city.

Neoliberalism valorizes the self-actualized subject, a position that intersects somewhat paradoxically with critical social practice in that notions of the free, autonomous, self-actualizing individual became widely accepted after they were deployed by counter-cultural movements in the mid-twentieth century (Dean 1999). In the context of neoliberalism, though, the free subject is redeployed as a technical instrument to achieve various governmental purposes; freedom is thus less emancipatory and increasingly oriented to the virtuous, disciplined, responsible autonomy of citizenry. For women condominium owners, city living may in fact be experienced as, or express, a strange hybrid of the critical social practice described by Caulfield (1994), the feminist vision of interconnectedness and autonomy, and the neoliberal consumer citizen. Nikolas Rose (1996, 162) describes the latter position:

> Consumers are constituted as actors seeking to maximize their "quality of life" by assembling a "life-style" through acts of choice in a world of goods. Each commodity is imbued with a "personal" meaning, a glow cast back upon those who purchase it, illuminating the kind of person they are, or want to come to be.

Here the commodities may include the condominium itself as well as the goods and services that are appropriated into the gentrifier lifestyle.

It is critical to question the rights and claims of the consumer citizen and how these shape broad understandings of the right to the city (Isin 1998, 1999). Geographers David Bell and Jon Binnie (2004) maintain that we must also ask: Who is the "other" of the consumer citizen and who is thus excluded from the redefined right to the city? In *Sex and the Revitalized City*, I examine the experiences, identities, and claims of a relatively privileged group of women, and this group certainly does not represent all of the groups of women that feminists argue must be able to find justice, empowerment, and autonomy in the city. In many ways, the claims that they make, the spaces that are created for them and in their image, and the identities that they represent are predicated upon the exclusion of others who will not be able to make such claims, gain access to those spaces, or embody those identities. This approach to studying gentrification – that is, by looking at gentrifiers – has been vociferously critiqued by scholars who argue that we must focus our energies on understanding the impacts of gentrification on the marginalized and displaced (Slater 2006). While I most wholeheartedly agree that this is an urgent project, I also want to challenge the ways that this reasserts class as the only significant dimension of the gentrification debate. Although investigating the lives of more privileged women gentrifiers may reproduce some of the problematic elisions of the lives of those displaced, I argue that this methodology has been effective in exposing the relevance of gender to urban revitalization and in furthering the long-stagnant debate over the ways that gentrification may constitute identities and relations beyond those of class.

In attempting to bring the framework of neoliberalism to bear on the realm of everyday life, and to bring a feminist critique to an analysis of entrepreneurial city building, I hope I have opened a productive space within which different types of questions can be asked of contemporary urban transformations. There are many areas that demand further critical inquiry. In the realm of policy, this book suggests that the draining of social and economic equity concerns from planning in the revitalized city has serious implications. The social and environmental benefits of intensification will not be realized if they are commodified, privatized, and available only to the few who can afford to live or work in the increasingly elite downtown core. Rather than fundamentally altering city life and solving a host of urban problems, intensification may merely alter the geography of those problems, shifting the issues onto peripheral areas where integrated, walkable, safe, and pleasant neighbourhoods are far from the reality. The challenge for planners and policy makers is how to bring the benefits of urbanity to marginalized groups and communities. This cannot be accomplished if quality of life is defined by access to pleasure and entertainment rather than by access to social justice.

The intense focus on residential property development, particularly in the form of ownership housing, also raises disturbing policy issues. Low interest rates and federal mortgage insurance programs have led to the extension of credit to housing consumers who would not have qualified for loans in previous decades. While this has enabled groups like young or single women to enter the home ownership arena, the economic (and, specifically, the credit-related) crisis that was exposed in 2008 has opened profound cracks in many basic assumptions about the structure and ideology of private property. In the United States, the collapse of the sub-prime mortgage market has led to devastating foreclosure numbers, and it is increasingly clear that vulnerable groups (racial minorities, single women/single mothers, the working poor) are the first victims of this collapse (Immergluck 2009). American cities with massive amounts of new condominium construction in recent years, such as Miami, are witnessing foreclosures, defaults, and empty and incomplete buildings (Stellin 2009). Canada has also experienced a slowdown in housing starts and a downturn in most resale markets. While sub-prime mortgages were not as common in the more highly regulated financial industry here, housing consumers who only marginally qualified for loans are suffering. CMHC reports that, compared to a record-breaking level of housing starts in the GTA in early 2008, early 2009 has seen a 33 percent decline (Canada Mortgage and Housing Corporation 2009). In early 2009, reports indicate that the condominium market in Toronto is experiencing a huge decline in sales compared to previous years (Hammer 2009). There are fears that this downturn will become visible on the urban landscape as the "craters" of unfinished condominium projects may leave "enduring pits" in major Canadian cities if the projects cannot obtain financing from creditors who themselves are under immense financial strain (Kirby 2009, 35; Belford 2009; Barber 2008). Perhaps the clearest symbol of this troubling change in fortunes is the halted construction of a luxury tower at Yonge and Bloor streets. The launch of this project was more like a rock concert than a housing sale, with realtors paying citizens to stand in line overnight in the hours leading up to the first day of sales. This event seemed to symbolize the peak of Toronto's condominium success story. Many of the multi-million-dollar units were quickly sold, but the project's financing was jeopardized by the collapse of Lehman Brothers in 2008. The lot now sits empty, and while the developers search for new financing options the site reminds us about the dangerous cycles of capitalist overaccumulation and their dramatic effects on the built environment.

For feminist scholars, these events indicate that we must challenge the perspective that sees home ownership as a form of freedom for women without considering the serious financial risks that might accompany the move to home ownership. Although early home ownership may mitigate women's lower lifetime earnings, fewer investments, and lower pensions, there is also the potential for default or bankruptcy. Long-term studies addressing the sustainability and changing fortunes of developments like condominiums will be needed to help illustrate the successes and failures of residential intensification; in the meantime, feminist housing scholars must draw attention to the tensions and complications in the happy narrative of home ownership.

In placing my analysis of condominium development and city building alongside a consideration of everyday life and identity formation, I hope to highlight the fact that condominiums (and other housing types) cannot be treated simply as physical housing forms or tenure models and that city building agents (like developers and planners) cannot be examined solely in terms of their roles in shaping the built environment. Instead, city forms, and the visions that shape them, affect personal, social, and political engagements with city life and inform identity-building processes. Specifically, I argue that condominiums are made to represent particular notions of urbanity and that they foster specific relationships with the city. This suggests that housing scholars and critics of gentrification must be cognizant of the ways that different housing forms become linked to political-economic rationalities and to contemporary visions of city life. Similarly, researchers interested in the perspectives of developers and other city building agents should pay attention not only to the ways that they construct the rationales behind their developments but also to how the discourses they produce foster and elicit desirable identities and subject positions for consumers and city dwellers.

Although I present a picture of city form and city life shaped by neoliberal ideals and an erosion of social justice and space for alternative urban citizenship claims, there are still entry points for feminist urban activism. The struggles of everyday life have often served as the impetus for women's urban citizenship claims all over the world. In Toronto and other cities enduring the transformations wrought by urban revitalization, feminists can and should demand the extension of walkable, breathable, interconnected, mixed-use, and safe environments in all city neighbourhoods, not just those that constitute the attractive face of the city for tourists, investors, and the creative class. Feminists can also challenge the sexist, heteronormative, and largely white imagery that shapes our collective vision of the desired and appropriate inhabitants of the revitalized city as well as our understanding of who counts as a citizen in this context. In Toronto, feminists have long been involved in movements to support public transit, food security, and environmental sustainability. These will also form key sites for women's activism to make the revitalized city a truly inclusive and liveable place.

Although the politics of urban revitalization move towards the production of commodified and controlled spaces and the self-governance of autonomous and enterprising citizens, elements of the revitalized city can be appropriated and transformed through the practices of everyday life in multiple ways. From anti-gentrification graffiti on condominium ads to the formation of women's networks in condominiums, there are countless examples where the personal and the political converge to alter the hegemonic meanings and practices inscribed in urban space. Despite the rampant forces of commodification and aestheticization, the heterogeneity of city life and city dwellers will not be destroyed by neoliberal urbanism. Many stories of resistance, feminist and otherwise, remain to be imagined, enacted, and written into the new urban landscape.

Appendix A
Selected Characteristics of Women Condominium Owners

Pseudonym	Age	Education	Occupation	Marital status	Ownership
Alicia	30	Master's	Project manager	Single	1st time
Amanda	29	Bachelor's	Project manager	Single	1st time
April	37	Bachelor's	Photographer	Single	1st time
Ava	32	Bachelor's	Urban designer	Single	1st time
Caitlin	31	Bachelor's	Career counsellor	Single	2nd time
Chloe	23	College diploma	Admin. assistant	Single	1st time
Colleen	28	Some university	Call centre super.	Single	1st time
Hope	29	Bachelor's	Project manager	Married	1st time
Jaime	33	College diploma	Administrative assistant	Single	1st time
Jillian	30	Bachelor's	Marketing assistant	Single	1st time
Leigh	46	Bachelor's	Investment analyst	Single	1st time
Lynn	28	Bachelor's	Graphic designer	Single	1st time
Maya	30	Bachelor's	Occupational therapist	Single	1st time
Molly	33	Bachelor's	Law clerk	Married/ 1 child	1st time
Nadia	25	Some university	Real estate researcher	Single	1st time
Naomi	29	Some university	Graphic designer	Single	2nd time
Rachel	21	Bachelor's	Graduate student	Single	1st time
Rose	22	Bachelor's	Graduate student	Single	1st time
Samantha	33	Bachelor's	Marketing manager	Single	1st time
Sandra	28	Bachelor's	HR manager	Single	1st time
Stephanie	35	Bachelor's	Administrative assistant	Single	1st time

Appendix B
Interview Schedules

Women Condominium Owners

- Can you please tell me your age, occupation, and education level?
- Do you share your condo with anyone at the moment?
- When did you buy your condo? When did you move in? What is the name of the condo project?
- Where did you live immediately prior to this home? Did you rent or own?
- Can you tell me how you came to decide to buy a condo?
- How did you choose this particular development?
- In terms of owning a condo, is the lack of maintenance important to you?
- Do you use any of the shared spaces/facilities in the condo?
- Are the security features of the condo important to you? Why or why not?
- Do you participate on your condo board or in condo decisions/meetings?
- Is there a "community" feeling in your condo? Do you feel like you're a part of it?
- Is there anything that you dislike about living in a condo? Any issues with noise, privacy?
- In your unit itself, do you aim for a particular style of interior design? Do you feel that your home expresses your personal tastes and style or other values that are important to you (and your family)? Do you spend much time working on your home? Do you enjoy decorating magazines, TV shows?
- When it comes to your home, what kinds of things do you spend money on?
- Will you do, or have you done, any renovations?
- Do you feel you spend much time on housework? Do you use any outside help for household chores and/or child care? When do you typically find time for housework? Do you share responsibilities with partner, roommate?
- Do you work at home?
- How important is your condo to you as a place to entertain or socialize?
- What does it mean to you to own your own home? Is the investment quality of your condominium important to you?
- So overall, how do you feel about your choice to buy a condo?

- Can you tell me why you choose to live in the city? What do you dislike about living in the city?
- Can you tell me about life in this particular neighbourhood? What do you like or dislike about living in this neighbourhood? Do you feel part of the wider community?
- When you go shopping for things that you want or need for yourself, your home, or your family, what types of places do you typically go to? Is your choice based on cost or convenience?
- Do you find it expensive living in the city?
- What are some of your leisure activities?
- Do you make use of public services, spaces, or events in the city?
- Can you describe a typical weekday? Weekend?
- Is living in the city a temporary or more permanent choice for you? Why? Could you see yourself living in the suburbs or a small town?
- Is living in a condo a short-term or longer-term option for you? Where do you see yourself living in five years? Ten years? Why?
- If you could give any advice to another woman like yourself looking to buy a home, what would you say?
- Is there anything else that you would like to tell me about living in a condominium or any aspect of this discussion that you would like me to emphasize?

Condominium Developers
- How did your firm get into condominium building?
- For developers, what do you think are some of the pros and cons of building condos?
- Why do you think condo development is so big in Toronto right now?
- Do you feel that the city is encouraging condominium development right now? How so?
- What do you think people are looking for in the downtown housing market right now?
- What are some of the key features of your condominiums? Features that you think buyers particularly like?
- Do you market your condos to particular housing consumers?
- What kinds of images and slogans do you use to portray your developments?
- Who do you think are your primary buyers?
- Some recent news articles have suggested that young women and single women are a growing group of condominium buyers. Do you think that young women are a significant group of buyers for you? Why do you think that is?
- What are some of the hot areas in the city right now? Why?
- Where do you see condominium development going over the next five or ten years? More development? Less development? Different types? Different areas?

City Planners

- Can you tell me a little about your role in the planning department?
- How would you describe the goals of the city's latest plan in terms of residential development in the city? Economic goals? Social goals?
- What are some of the wider economic effects that are expected to come as a result of residential intensification (i.e., increased property tax base, increased consumer spending in the core, increased use of public and cultural facilities, attracting capital investment, attracting professional workers)?
- What are some of the goals of the *Plan* in terms of encouraging social mix in the core? Are condos contributing to social mix?
- How is the notion of "liveability" or "quality of life" being addressed with respect to intensifying residential development in the core?
- Is the city actively encouraging condominium development? How so?
- The *Plan* talks about creating a city with competitive advantages over others – does condo development play a role in this process?
- What are condos contributing to the city in terms of urban design?
- What are some of the challenges facing the city based on residential intensification in the core (environmental issues, transportation issues, social issues)? What are some of the most important ways that you think the city will change or develop over the next ten to twenty years?

Notes

Chapter 1: Growing Up

1 In contrast, it is interesting to note that, during the high-rise rental construction boom of the 1960s and 1970s, there was public concern that the city's tenure structure was shifting in favour of renting as it approached 50/50 in 1970 ("Big swing to apartment living in Metro" 1970; "More families live in apartments than in houses in Metro" 1972). There is no public concern over the current shift to increased home ownership, illustrating the differential valuation of these tenure forms.

2 A case in point is the ongoing redevelopment of Regent Park, Canada's oldest social housing project. The massive scheme increases density on the site but does not increase the number of subsidized housing units. Instead, condominiums are planned. The revitalization of this area – including its ability to draw in new services like banks, coffee chains, and grocery stores – is contingent upon its ability to attract the middle classes. Providing home ownership opportunities is assumed to generate this process (Mays 2005).

3 A note about pseudonyms and identity: the women condominium owners whom I interviewed were guaranteed anonymity; therefore, I use pseudonyms throughout. The planners and developers all agreed, in writing, to allow me to use their names in relation to their comments. However, in presenting the data, I have chosen not to identify the individuals by name. This decision is based on the rationale that I am not attempting to analyze individuals or specific corporations and that including names and specific companies might serve to individualize the issues that I raise and critique.

Chapter 2: Troubling Tenure

1 Hulchanski and Shapcott cite a 1996 Cambridge University Study comparing housing policy in twelve industrialized countries (Freeman, Holmans, and Whitehead 1996).

2 Zoning regulations deal with density and site coverage rather than tenure. However, in previous rounds of high-rise construction, various levels of government subsidized the construction of rental buildings. From the late 1940s until 1985, there were a variety of government programs encouraging the construction of private-market rental housing, including the Limited Dividend Program, the Assisted Rental Program, the Multiple Unit Residential Building tax shelter, and the Canada Rental Housing Supply Program (Hulchanski and Shapcott 2004).

3 In the United States, the logic of this choice (and, indeed, the dream of home ownership itself) have been badly shaken by the collapse of the sub-prime mortgage market and the subsequent global financial crisis. In Canada, the recent extension of CMHC's mortgage insurance program to mortgages with down payments as little as 5 percent (in some cases, no down payment at all) raises a concern that we may see increased rates of default here.

4 The advertisements never mention that, in condominium ownership, individual owners are subject to the control of the condominium board and the overall regulatory regime governing condominiums.

5 The outcome of recent debates around conversion to non-rental tenure in Toronto was City of Toronto Bylaw 885-2007, through which the city enhanced its right to protect rental housing from demolition or conversion. Landlords require a permit from the city to undertake demolition or conversion (City of Toronto 2007).

6 It is worth noting that condominiums that start out as affordable (by the 30 percent rule) may become less affordable as property taxes, interest rates, condominium fees, and utility costs rise over time.

7 In 2005, the median net worth of families who did not own their homes was a mere $10,600, compared to a net worth of $217,282 for families who own with a mortgage, and $521,140 for those who own without a mortgage (Statistics Canada 2008b). In breaking down net worth by gender and age, as of 2005, the median net worth for women over sixty-five was just over half of the net worth of men over sixty-five ($204,833 for women, $405,000 for men). For young women, the differential is even greater. For women under thirty-five, the median net worth was $9,600; for men, $28,203 (Statistics Canada 2008b).

8 A scan of twelve random issues of *Condo Guide Magazine* revealed that approximately 83 percent of all advertisements with human subjects included women.

9 Similar trends have been noted in other large condominium markets, like New York City, where a recent news article suggested that women were enthusiastically taking on condominium ownership (Haughney 2006).

10 Rose uses this phrase to invoke the social and economic ideals associated with the regimes of Margaret Thatcher and Ronald Reagan. See also F.M.L. Thompson's *Gentrification and the Enterprise Culture: Britain 1780-1980* (2001).

11 It is worth noting that Jillian's assertion that "anyone can get a mortgage these days" would probably not have rung true until relatively recently. Although Canada does not collect information specifically on mortgage discrimination, data from the United States show that women (among other groups) faced systemic

discrimination in the mortgage market (Ladd 1998; Robinson 2002; Novac, Darden, Hulchanski, and Seguin 2002).

12 Blomley here draws on G.W.F. Hegel's *Philosophy of Right* (1996), wherein Hegel outlines the ways in which the ownership of property and its exchange necessitate a mutual recognition of the rights and subjectivity of each willing actor.

13 In fact, many of the women interviewed here suggested that they would like to hire outside help for housework, if finances permitted. All of the women worked or studied full time and thus found it difficult and unpalatable to make time for domestic work.

Chapter 3: Under Construction

1 Suburban developers have placed even more emphasis on this role, attempting to provide not just homes but total communities (Weiss 1987).

2 Ultimately, these amenities serve primarily as sales features that cater to the original target market. In the long term, the condominium owners continually pay for features that were provided by a developer who is long gone and that may not serve the potentially changing needs of residents.

3 Strahilevitz (2006) notes an extreme example of this type of pre-selection of community, wherein developers circumvent anti-discrimination laws by incorporating amenities, such as golf club memberships, for which all members must pay and that may result in the functional exclusion of racial or ethnic groups.

Chapter 4: Securing Relations of Threat

1 One developer informed me that the twenty-four-hour concierge service was the most expensive item in the monthly budget, a cost that is passed to residents through the monthly fees (developer interview, 19 July 2005).

Chapter 5: A Date with the Big City

1 The current *Official Plan* is certainly not the first to promote city living as a desirable option. Earlier plans also sought to draw and retain residents in the core (Metropolitan Toronto Council 1983, 1994). However, these plans were focused on maintaining stable downtown neighbourhoods, without major amounts of redevelopment. Moreover, they sought to provide housing and services for the entire lifecycle in order to encourage long-term neighbourhood stability.

2 Only seven of the twenty-one interviewees owned a car.

3 I include only five responses here due to space considerations. Like most of the other accounts of city living that I have presented throughout this chapter, the responses that I collected to these questions were strikingly similar in tone and content. This might indicate that women draw, to a certain extent, from a cultural script about city life that reflects cultural norms as much as it does individual practices. It may also be a function of shared social characteristics that shape these women's lives in similar ways. Despite the homogeneity of many of these responses, I attempt to indicate the various nuances and complexities that can be drawn from looking at five narratives.

4 Television series such as *Sex and the City* and *Men in Trees* focus on the identity crises of the modern urban woman; books such as the *Bridget Jones' Diary* series (Fielding 1998, 2000), the Shopaholic series (Kinsella 2001), and *I Don't Know How She Does It* (Pearson 2002) address the lifestyles, identities, and dilemmas of urban working women.

5 About half of the women with whom I spoke were adamant about staying in the city long term; the other half described various scenarios, usually related to family and life course, that would make them consider leaving the city.

6 Although the 2002 *Official Plan* acknowledges the need for housing for people throughout the life course, condominiums seem positioned to satisfy only two stages: young adulthood before children and the "empty nest" stage later in life.

References

Abrar, S., J. Lovenduski, and H. Margetts. 1998. Sexing London: The gender mix of urban policy actors. *International Political Science Review* 19 (2): 147-71.

Abu-Lughod, J. 1960. A survey of center-city residents. In *Housing choices and housing constraints*, ed. N.N. Foote, 387-448. New York: McGraw-Hill.

Andrew, C. 1995. Getting women's issues on the municipal agenda: Violence against women. In *Gender in urban research*, ed. J.A. Garber and R.S. Turner, 99-118. Newbury Park, CA: Sage Publications.

–, and B. Moore-Milroy, eds. 1988. *Life spaces: Gender, household, employment*. Vancouver: UBC Press.

–, and Canada Mortgage and Housing Corporation, International Relations Division. 1994. *Canadian women and cities*. Ottawa: CMHC, International Relations Division.

Atkinson, R. 2000. Measuring gentrification and displacement in Greater London. *Urban Studies* 37 (1): 149-65.

–. 2006. Padding the bunker: Strategies of middle-class disaffiliation and colonisation in the city. *Urban Studies* 43 (4): 819-32.

–, and S. Blandy. 2007. Panic rooms: The rise of defensive homeownership. *Housing Studies* 22 (4): 443-58.

–, and G. Helms, eds. 2007. *Securing an urban renaissance? Crime, community and British urban policy*. Bristol: Policy Press.

Bain, A.L. 2003. Constructing contemporary artistic identities in Toronto neighbourhoods. *Canadian Geographer* 47 (3): 303-17.

Barber, J. 2008. Tremor signals correction in condo city. *Globe and Mail*, 10 December.

Bashevkin, S. 2006. *Tales of two cities: Women and municipal restructuring in London and Toronto*. Vancouver: UBC Press.

Battle in the sky. 1971. *Globe and Mail*, 2 October.

Baudrillard, J. 1988. *Jean Baudrillard: Selected writings*. Stanford, CA: Stanford University Press.

−. 2003. *The spirit of terrorism*. Trans. Chris Turner. London: Verso.

Bauman, Z. 2000. *Liquid modernity*. Malden, MA: Polity Press.

Belford, T. 2009. Gloom lifting, but developers face a new landscape. *Globe and Mail*, 17 April.

Bell, D., and J. Binnie. 2004. Authenticating queer space: Citizenship, urbanism and governance. *Urban Studies* 41 (9): 1807-20.

Berg, B.L. 1998. *Qualitative research methods for the social sciences*. 3rd ed. Boston: Allyn and Bacon.

Bevir, M. 2006. Democratic governance: Systems and radical perspectives. *Public Administration Review* 66 (3): 426-44.

−, and R.A.W. Rhodes. 2006. The life, death and resurrection of British governance. *Australian Journal of Public Administration* 65 (2): 5-23.

Bickford, S. 2000. Constructing inequality: City spaces and the architecture of citizenship. *Political Theory* 28 (3): 355-76.

Big swing to apartment living in Metro. 1970. *Toronto Star*, 12 December.

Blakely, E.J., and M.G. Snyder. 1997. *Fortress America: Gated communities in the United States*. Washington, DC: Brookings Institution Press.

Blandy, Sarah, and D. Lister. 2005. Gated communities: (Ne)gating community development? *Housing Studies* 20 (2): 287-301.

Blomley, N. 2004. *Unsettling the city: Urban land and the politics of property*. New York: Routledge.

Bondi, L. 1991. Gender divisions and gentrification: A critique. *Transactions of the Institute of British Geographers* 16: 190-98.

−. 1994. Gentrification, work and gender identity. In *Women, work and place*, ed. A. Kobayashi, 182-200. Montreal and Kingston: McGill-Queen's University Press.

−. 1999. Gender, class, and gentrification: Enriching the debate. *Environment and Planning D: Society and Space* 17: 261-83.

−. 2005. Working the spaces of neoliberal subjectivity: Psychotherapeutic technologies, professionalisation and counselling. *Antipode* 37 (3): 497-514.

−, and D. Rose. 2003. Constructing gender, constructing the urban: A review of Anglo-American feminist urban geography. *Gender, Place and Culture* 10 (3): 229-45.

Booth, C., J. Darke, and S. Yeandle, eds. 1996. *Changing places: Women's lives in the city*. London: Paul Chapman.

Boudreau, J-A. 2000. *The mega-city saga: Democracy and citizenship in this global age*. Montreal: Black Rose Books.

Bourne, L.S. 2000a. *The future of downtown Toronto: Downtown Toronto as living space*. Background Study No. 4. Toronto: GHK International.

−. 2000b. Urban Canada in transition to the twenty-first century: Trends, issues, and visions. In *Canadian cities in transition: The twenty-first century*, 2nd ed., ed. T. Bunting and P. Filion, 26-52. Oxford: Oxford University Press.

−. 2001. The urban sprawl agenda: Myths, realities and hidden agendas. *Plan Canada* 41 (4): 26-28.

−, and D. Rose. 2001. The changing face of Canada: The uneven geographies of population and social change. *Canadian Geographer* 45 (1): 105-20.

Bowlby, R. 2001. *Carried away: The invention of modern shopping*. New York: Columbia University Press.

Boys, J. 1989. Beyond maps and metaphors? Re-thinking the relationships between architecture and gender. In *New frontiers of space, bodies and gender*, ed. R. Ainley, 203-17. London: Routledge.

Brenner, N., and N. Theodore. 2002a. Cities and the geographies of "actually existing neoliberalism." *Antipode* 34 (3): 349-79.

–, eds. 2002b. *Spaces of neoliberalism: Urban restructuring in North America and Western Europe*. Malden, MA: Blackwell.

Brewis, J. 2004. Sex and not the city? The aspirations of the thirty-something working woman. *Urban Studies* 41 (9): 1821-38.

Brownill, S. 2000. Regen(d)eration: Women and urban policy in Britain. In *Women and the city: Visibility and voice in urban space*, ed. J. Darke, S. Ledwith, and R. Woods, 114-29. Houndmills, UK: Palgrave Publishers.

Brownlow, A. 2006. Risking contradiction: Sexual violence and entrepreneurial ambivalence in Philadelphia. Paper presented at the Annual Meeting of the Association of American Geographers, Chicago.

Bunce, S. 2004. The emergence of "smart growth" intensification in Toronto: Environment and economy in the new Official Plan. *Local Environment* 9 (2): 177-91.

–, and D. Young. 2003. Image-making by the water: Global city dreams and the ecology of exclusion on Toronto's central waterfront. In *Contested metropolis: Seven cities at the beginning of the 21st century*, ed. INURA. Basel: Birkhaeuser.

Burgess, J. 1998. "But is it worth taking the risk?" How women negotiate access to urban woodland: A case study. In *New frontiers of space, bodies and gender*, ed. R. Ainley, 115-28. London: Routledge.

Canada Mortgage and Housing Corporation. 2001. *Households by tenure and condominium status Canada 2001*. Ottawa: CMHC.

–. 2004. *Greater Toronto Area condominium report*. Toronto: CMHC.

–. 2008. Affordable Housing. http://www.cmhc-schl.gc.ca/en/inpr/afhoce/index.cfm.

–. 2009. *Housing now: Greater Toronto Area April*. Toronto: CMHC.

Carroll, B.W., and R.E. Jones. 2000. The road to innovation, convergence or inertia: Devolution in housing policy in Canada. *Canadian Public Policy* 26 (3): 277-93.

Caulfield, J. 1989. "Gentrification" and desire. *Canadian Review of Sociology and Anthropology* 26 (4): 617-32.

–. 1994. *City form and everyday life: Toronto's gentrification and critical social practice*. Toronto: University of Toronto Press.

–. 2005. Toronto: The form of the city. In *Urban Canada: Sociological perspectives*, ed. H.H. Hiller, 312-42. Oxford: Oxford University Press.

Charmaz, K. 2004. Grounded theory. In *Approaches to qualitative research: A reader on theory and practice*, ed. S.N. Hesse-Biber and P. Leavy, 496-521. Oxford: Oxford University Press.

Chien-Yuan, C., and C. Webster. 2006. Privatising the governance and management of existing urban neighbourhoods. *Property Management* 24 (2): 98-116.

Choko, M., and R. Harris. 1990. The local culture of property: A comparative history of housing tenure in Montreal and Toronto. *Annals of the Association of American Geographers* 80 (1): 73-95.

Chouinard, V. 1996. Gender and class identities in process and in place: The local state as a site of gender and class formation. *Environment and Planning A* 28: 1485-506.

–. 2006. On the dialectics of differencing: Disabled women, the state and housing issues. *Gender, Place and Culture* 13 (4): 401-17.

City of Toronto. 2002. *Official Plan*. Toronto: Toronto Urban Development Services.

–. 2003. *Profile Toronto: Toronto's housing*. Toronto: Toronto Urban Development Services, Policy and Research.

–. 2007. By-Law No. 885-2007 Residential Rental Property Demolition and Conversion Control.

Conway, D., ed. 1977. *Human response to tall buildings*. Stroudsberg, PA: Dowden, Hutchinson and Ross.

Cordileone, E. 2002. Single women buying up condos. *Toronto Star*, 16 February.

Cotroneo, C. 2006. Toronto's growing sky-high. *Toronto Star*, 24 September.

D'Souza, A., and T. McDonough, eds. 1996. *The invisible flâneuse? Gender, public space and visual culture in nineteenth century Paris*. Manchester: Manchester University Press.

Darby, C. 1969. Where the frantic frolic. *Toronto Life*, May.

Darke, J. 1996. The man-shaped city. In *Changing places: Women's lives in the city*, ed. C. Booth, J. Darke, and S. Yeandle, 88-99. London: Paul Chapman Publishing.

Davidson, M. 2007. Gentrification as global habitat: A process of class formation or corporate creation? *Transactions of the Institute of British Geographers* 32 (4): 490-506.

–, and L. Lees. 2005. New-build gentrification and London's riverside renaissance. *Environment and Planning A* 37: 1165-90.

Davis, M. 1991. *City of quartz: Excavating the future in Los Angeles*. London: Verso.

–. 1999. *Ecology of fear*. New York: Picador Press.

Day, K. 1999. Embassies and sanctuaries: Women's experiences of race and fear in public space. *Environment and Planning D: Society and Space* 17 (3): 307-28.

–. 2001. Constructing masculinity and women's fear in public space in Irvine, California. *Gender, Place and Culture* 8 (2): 109-27.

De Grazia, V., and E. Furlough. 1996. *The sex of things: Gender and consumption in historical perspective*. Berkeley: University of California Press.

Dean, M. 1999. *Governmentality: Power and rule in modern society*. London: Sage Publications.

Delany, S.R. 1999. *Times Square red, Times Square blue*. New York: New York University Press.

Delap, L. 2006. The new starter home. *Toronto Life*, February.

Desfor, G., and R. Keil. 2003. Ecological modernisation in Los Angeles and Toronto. *Local Environment* 8 (1): 27-44.

–, R. Keil, S. Kipfer, and G.R. Wekerle. 2006. From surf to turf: No limits to growth in Toronto? *Studies in Political Economy* 77 (Spring): 131-55.

Desforges, L., R. Jones, and M. Woods. 2005. New geographies of citizenship. *Citizenship Studies* 9 (5): 439-51.

Devault, M.L. 1999. *Liberating method: Feminism and social research*. Philadelphia: Temple University Press.

Doling, J. 1997. *Comparative housing policy: Government and housing in advanced industrialized countries*. London: Macmillan Press.

Domosh, M. 1996. The feminized retail landscape: Gender ideology and consumer culture in nineteenth-century New York City. In *Retailing, consumption and capital: Towards the new retail geography*, ed. N. Wrigley and M. Lowe, 257-70. Harlow, UK: Longeman Group.

Doolittle, R. 2009. Surveillance camera project wrapping up. *Toronto Star*, 30 December.

Dowling, R. 1998. Gender, class and home ownership: Placing the connections. *Housing Studies* 13 (4): 471-86.

–, and G. Pratt. 1993. Home truths: Recent feminist constructions. *Urban Geography* 14 (5): 464-75.

Duncan, N. 1996. Negotiating gender and sexuality in public and private spaces. In *BodySpace: Destabilizing geographies of gender and sexuality*, ed. N. Duncan, 127-45. London: Routledge.

Durkheim, E. 1964. *The division of labor in society*. Trans. G. Simpson. New York: Free Press of Glencoe.

Eichler, M., ed. 1995. *Change of plans: Towards a non-sexist sustainable city*. Toronto: Garamond Press.

England, K.V.L. 1991. Gender relations and the spatial structure of the city. *Geoforum* 22 (2): 135-47.

–. 2002. Interviewing elites: Cautionary tales about researching women managers in Canada's banking industry. In *Feminist geography in practice: Research and methods*, ed. P. Moss, 200-13. Oxford: Blackwell Publishers.

Evans, G. 2003. Hard-branding the cultural city – from Prado to Prada. *International Journal of Urban and Regional Research* 27 (2): 417-40.

Fainstein, S. 2001. *The city builders: Property development in New York and London*. 2nd ed. Oxford: Blackwell.

Fallis, G. 1995. The social policy challenge and social housing. In *Home remedies: Rethinking Canadian housing policy*, ed. G. Fallis, M. Poulton, L.B. Smith, M.Y. Seelig, and J.H. Seelig, 1-49. Toronto: C.D. Howe Institute.

Federation of Rental-Housing Providers of Ontario. 2005. *Conversions and demolitions policies in Ontario: Myths and realities*. Toronto: FRPO.

Fenster, T. 2005. The right to the gendered city: Different formations of belonging in everyday life. *Journal of Gender Studies* 14 (3): 217-31.

Fielding, H. 1998. *Bridget Jones' diary*. New York: Viking.

–. 2000. *Bridget Jones: The edge of reason*. New York: Viking.

Fincher, R. 2004. Gender and life course in the narratives of Melbourne's high-rise housing developers. *Australian Geographical Studies* 42 (3): 325-38.

Florida, R.L. 2002. *The rise of the creative class: And how it's transforming work, leisure, community and everyday life*. New York: Basic Books.

–. 2008. *Who's your city? How the creative economy is making where to live the most important decision of your life.* New York: Basic Books.

Flusty, S. 2001. The banality of interdiction: Surveillance, control and the displacement of diversity. *International Journal of Urban and Regional Research* 25: 658-64.

Foldvary, F.E. 1992. Public goods and private communities. PhD diss., George Mason University.

Forrest, R. 2004. Who cares about neighbourhoods? http://www.neighbourhood centre.org.uk.

–, A. La Grange, and Y. Ngai-Ming. 2002. Neighbourhood in a high rise, high density city: Some observations on contemporary Hong Kong. *Sociological Review* 50 (2): 215-40.

–, A. Murie, and P. Williams. 1990. *Home ownership: Differentiation and fragmentation.* London: Unwin Hyman.

Foucault, M. 1980. Truth and power. In *Michel Foucault, power/knowledge: Selected writings*, ed. C. Gordon, 109-33. Brighton: Harvester.

–. 1982. The subject and power. In *Michel Foucault: Beyond structuralism and hermeneutics*, ed. H. Dreyfus and P. Rabinow, 208-26. Brighton: Harvester.

–. 1990. *The history of sexuality.* Vol. 1. New York: Vintage.

–. 1991. Governmentality (Lecture at the Collège de France, February 1, 1978). In *The Foucault effect: Studies in governmentality*, ed. G. Burchell, C. Gordon, and P. Miller, 87-104. Hemel Hempstead, UK: Harvester Wheatsheaf.

–. 1997. The birth of biopolitics. In *Michel Foucault: Ethics, subjectivity and truth*, ed. P. Rabinow, 73-79. New York: The New Press.

Freeman, A.J.M., A.E. Holmans, and C.M.E. Whitehead. 1996. *Is the UK different? International comparisons of tenure patterns.* London: Council of Mortgage Lenders.

Freeman, L. 2006. *There goes the 'hood: Views of gentrification from the ground up.* Philadelphia: Temple University Press.

Gans, H. 1962. *The urban villagers.* New York: Free Press.

Garber, J.A., and R.S. Turner, eds. 1995. *Gender in urban research.* Thousand Oaks, CA: Sage.

Gibson, T.A. 2004. *Securing the spectacular city: The politics of revitalization and homelessness in downtown Seattle.* Lanham, MD: Lexington Books.

Gilroy, R., and R. Woods, eds. 1994. *Housing women.* London: Routledge.

Glennie, P., and N. Thrift. 1996. Consumption, shopping and gender. In *Retailing, consumption and capital: Towards the new retail geography*, ed. N. Wrigley and M. Lowe, 221-37. Harlow, UK: Longeman Group.

Gordon, M.T., and S. Riger. 1989. *The female fear: The social cost of rape.* Chicago: University of Illinois Press.

Gordon, T. 2005. The political economy of law-and-order policies: Policing, class struggle, and neoliberal restructuring. *Studies in Political Economy* 75 (Spring): 53-78.

Graham, S., ed. 2004. *Cities, war and terrorism: Towards an urban geopolitics.* Malden, MA: Blackwell.

–, and S. Marvin. 2001. *Splintering urbanism: Networked infrastructures, techno-logical mobilities and the urban condition.* London: Routledge.

Grant, J., K. Greene, and K. Maxwell. 2004. The planning and policy implications of gated communities. *Canadian Journal of Urban Research* 13 (1): 70-89.

Greater Toronto Home Builders' Association. 2007. 2006 a very good year for new home sales. http://www.gthba.ca/media_releases_2007_detail.asp?id=419.

Greer, S.S. 2006. Families matter in these condos. *Toronto Star,* 29 April.

Grosz, E. 1995. *Space, time and perversion: Essays on the politics of bodies.* New York: Routledge.

Hackworth, J., and N. Smith. 2001. The changing state of gentrification. *Tijdschrift voor Economische en Sociale Geografie* 92 (4): 464-77.

Hall, T., and P. Hubbard. 1998. *The entrepreneurial city.* Chichester, UK: John Wiley.

Hammer, K. 2009. Sales of new homes, condos plunge. *Globe and Mail,* 21 April.

Hanes, T. 2005. Europa at home in Little Italy neighbourhood. *Toronto Star,* 22 January.

–. 2006. Where home is a hotel. *Toronto Star,* 25 March.

Haraway, D.J. 1991. *Simians, cyborgs and women: The reinvention of nature.* New York: Routledge.

Harris, R. 2004. *Creeping conformity: How Canada became suburban, 1900-1960.* Toronto: University of Toronto Press.

Harvey, D. 1985. *The urbanization of capital.* Oxford: Blackwell.

–. 1989. From managerialism to entrepreneurialism: The transformation in urban governance in late capitalism. *Geografiska Annaler, Series B, Human Geography* 71 (1): 3-17.

–. 2005. *A brief history of neoliberalism.* Oxford: Oxford University Press.

Haughney, C. 2006. Women unafraid of condo commitment. *New York Times,* 10 December.

Hay, I., ed. 2000. *Qualitative research methods in human geography.* Victoria, Australia: Oxford University Press.

Hayden, D. 1977. Skyscraper seduction, skyscraper rape. *Heresies* 1 (May): 108-15.

–. 1980. What would a non-sexist city be like? Speculations on housing, urban design, and human work. *Signs* 5 (3): S170-87.

–. 2002. *Redesigning the American dream: The future of housing, work, and family life.* 2nd ed. New York: W.W. Norton and Company.

–. 2004. *Building suburbia: Green fields and urban growth.* New York: Vintage Books.

Hegel, G.W.F. 1996. *Philosophy of right.* Trans. S.W. Dyde. Amherst, NY: Prometheus Books.

Helms, G., R. Atkinson, and G. MacLeod. 2007. Securing the city: Urban renaissance, policing and social regulation. *European Urban and Regional Studies* 14 (4): 267-76.

Hipp, J.R., and A. Perrin. 2006. Nested loyalties: Local networks' effects on neighbourhood and community cohesion. *Urban Studies* 43 (13): 2503-23.

Holston, J., and A. Appadurai. 1996. Cities and citizenship. *Public Culture* 8: 187-204.

Hubbard, P. 2004. Revenge and injustice in the neoliberal city: Uncovering masculinist agendas. *Antipode* 36 (4): 665-86.

Hulchanski, J.D. 2006. *OMB witness statement and report Lascelles Blvd.* Toronto: Centre for Urban and Community Studies.

–, and M. Shapcott. 2004. *Finding room: Options for a Canadian rental housing strategy.* Toronto: Centre for Urban and Community Studies.

Hutchinson, B. 2008. Condo developer takes a chance on Vancouver's Downtown Eastside. *National Post,* 23 April.

Immergluck, D. 2009. *Foreclosed: High-risk lending, deregulation, and the undermining of America's mortgage market.* Ithaca, NY: Cornell Press.

Isin, E.F. 1998. Governing Toronto without government: Liberalism and neoliberalism. *Studies in Political Economy* 56 (Summer): 169-91.

–. 1999. Citizenship, class and the global city. *Citizenship Studies* 3 (2): 267-83.

–, ed. 2000. *Democracy, citizenship and the global city.* London: Routledge.

Jackson, P. 2001. Making sense of qualitative data. In *Qualitative methods for geographers: Issues and debates,* ed. M. Limb and C. Dwyer, 199-214. London: Arnold.

Jacobs, J. 1961. *The death and life of great American cities.* New York: Random House.

Jones, A. 1992. Writing feminist educational research: Am "I" in the text? In *Women and education in Aotearoa,* ed. S. Middleton and A. Jones, 18-32. Wellington, New Zealand: Bridget Williams Books.

Karsten, L. 2003. Family gentrifiers: Challenging the city as a place simultaneously to build a career and to raise children. *Urban Studies* 40 (12): 2573-84.

Katz, C. 2005. Partners in crime? Neoliberalism and the production of new political subjectivities. *Antipode* 37 (3): 623-31.

Keil, R. 2007. Empire and the glocal city: Perspectives of urbanism after 9/11. *Studies in Political Economy* 79 (Spring): 167-92.

Keller, S. 1968. *The urban neighbourhood.* New York: Random House.

Kern, L. 2005. In place and at home in the city: Connecting privilege, safety, and belonging for women in Toronto. *Gender, Place and Culture* 12 (3): 357-77.

–, and G.R. Wekerle. 2008. Gendered spaces of redevelopment, gendered politics of city building. In *Gender in an urban world,* ed. J. DeSena, 233-62. Bingley, UK: Emerald Group.

Khosla, P. 2003. *If low-income women of colour counted in Toronto.* Toronto: The Community Social Planning Council of Toronto.

Kingwell, M. 2004. The $195-million scribble and other tales of seduction from our romance with celebrity architects. *Toronto Life,* June.

Kinsella, S. 2001. *Confessions of a shopaholic.* New York: Dial Press.

Kipfer, S., and R. Keil. 2002. Toronto Inc? Planning the competitive city in the new Toronto. *Antipode* 34 (2): 227-64.

Kirby, J. 2009. Attack of the condo craters. *Maclean's,* 9 March.

Klodawsky, F., and S. Mackenzie. 1987. *Gender-sensitive theory and the housing needs of mother-led families: Some concepts and some buildings.* Ottawa: Canadian Research Institute for the Advancement of Women.

–, and A. Specter. 1988. New families, new housing needs, new urban environments: The case of single-parent families. In *Life spaces: Gender, household, employment*, ed. C. Andrew and B. Moore-Milroy, 141-58. Vancouver: UBC Press.

Kobayashi, A., and L. Peake. 1994. Unnatural discourse: "Race" and gender in geography. *Gender, Place, and Culture* 1 (2): 225-43.

Koskela, H. 1999. "Gendered exclusions": Women's fear of violence and changing relations to space. *Geografiska Annaler Series B* 81 (2): 111-24.

–. 2002. Video surveillance, gender, and the safety of public urban space: "Peeping Tom" goes high tech? *Urban Geography* 23 (3): 257-78.

–, and R. Pain. 2000. Revisiting fear and place: Women's fear of attack and the built environment. *Geoforum* 13 (1): 269-80.

Kristenson, G. 1997. Women's economic progress and the demand for housing: Theory and empirical analyses based on Danish data. *Urban Studies* 34 (3): 403-18.

Kruzynski, A. 2005. Women's spiral-like journeys through three decades of community activism in a working-class Montreal neighbourhood. *Nouvelles Questions Feministes* 24 (3): 86-99.

Ladd, H.F. 1998. Evidence on discrimination in mortgage lending. *Journal of Economic Perspectives* 12 (2): 41-62.

Lang, R.E., and K.A. Danielson. 1997. Gated communities in America: Walling out the world? *Housing Policy Debate* 8 (4): 867-77.

Laporte, D. 2003a. Making room for kids. *Toronto Star*, 4 October.

–. 2003b. Sound advice. *Toronto Star*, 26 July.

–. 2004. The Lord of the Junction. *Toronto Star*, 7 August.

Larner, W. 1997. The legacy of the social: Market governance and the consumer. *Economy and Society* 26 (3): 373-99.

–. 2003. Neoliberalism? *Environment and Planning D: Society and Space* 21: 509-12.

–, and R. Le Heron. 2002. The spaces and subjects of a globalising economy: A situated exploration of method. *Environment and Planning D: Society and Space* 20 (6): 753-74.

Latham, A. 2003. Urbanity, lifestyle and making sense of the new urban cultural economy: Notes from Auckland, New Zealand. *Urban Studies* 40 (9): 1699-1724.

Lazerwitz, B., and Y. Ginsberg. 1994. Privatization and public participation in Israeli urban life. *Journal of Urban Affairs* 16 (3): 255-70.

Lees, L. 2000. A reappraisal of gentrification: Towards a "geography of gentrification." *Progress in Human Geography* 24 (3): 389-408.

–. 2003. Visions of "urban renaissance": The Urban Task Force and the Urban White Paper. In *Urban renaissance? New Labour, community and urban policy*, ed. R. Imrie and M. Raco, 61-82. Bristol: Policy Press.

–, T. Slater, and E. Wyly. 2008. *Gentrification*. New York: Routledge.

Lefebvre, H. 1991a. *Critique of everyday life*. Vol. 1. Trans. J. Moore. London and New York: Verso.

–. 1991b. *The production of space*. Trans. D. Nicholson-Smith. Oxford: Blackwell.

–. 1996. *Writings on cities*. Selected, translated, and introduced by E. Kaufman and E. Lebas. Cambridge, MA: Blackwell Publishers.

–. 2003. *Henri Lefebvre: Key writings.* Ed. S. Elden, E. Lebas, and E. Kaufman. New York and London: Continuum.

Lehrer, U. 2006. Re-placing Canadian cities: The challenge of landscapes of "desire" and "despair." In *The Canadian city in transition,* 3rd ed., ed. T. Bunting and P. Filion, 438-49. Oxford: Oxford Press.

–, and P. Gamsby. 2007. Gentrification, neo-liberalism, and the condo boom in Toronto. Paper presented at the Annual Meeting of the Association of American Geographers, San Francisco.

–, and J. Laidley. 2008. Old mega-projects newly packaged? Waterfront redevelopment in Toronto. *International Journal of Urban and Regional Research* 32 (4): 786-803.

Leitch, C. 2004. Getting started: Expert tips on the road to condo purchase. *Globe and Mail,* 3 April.

Lemke, T. 2001. The birth of bio-politics: Michel Foucault's lecture at the College de France on neo-liberal governmentality. http://www.thomaslemkeweb.de.

Letherby, G. 2003. *Feminist research in theory and practice.* Buckingham: Open University Press.

Ley, D. 1996. *The new middle class and the remaking of the central city.* Oxford: Oxford University Press.

Lighthall, W.D. 2004. Artistic, residential mix makes Liberty Village work. *Toronto Star,* 18 September.

Lind, A. 1997. Gender development and urban social change: Women's community activism in global cities. *World Development* 25 (8): 1205-23.

Little, J., L. Peake, and P. Richardson, eds. 1988. *Women in cities.* Basingstoke, UK: Macmillan.

Lorimer, J. 1978. *The developers.* Toronto: J. Lorimer.

Low, S.M. 2001. The edge and the center: Gated communities and the discourse of urban fear. *American Anthropologist* 103 (1): 45-58.

–. 2003. *Behind the gates: Life, security and the pursuit of happiness in fortress America.* New York: Routledge.

MacGregor, S. 1995. Deconstructing the man-made city: Feminist critiques of planning thought and action. In *Change of plans: Towards a non-sexist sustainable city,* ed. M. Eichler, 25-50. Toronto: Garamond Press.

–. 2002. Bright new vision or same old story? Looking for gender justice in the eco-city. In *Urban affairs: Back on the policy agenda,* ed. C. Andrew, K.A. Graham, and S.D. Phillips, 71-92. Kingston and Montreal: McGill-Queen's University Press.

Mackenzie, S. 1988. Building women, building cities: Toward gender sensitive theory in the environmental disciplines. In *Life spaces: Gender, household, employment,* ed. C. Andrew and B. Moore-Milroy, 13-30. Vancouver: UBC Press.

–, and D. Rose. 1983. Industrial change, the domestic economy, and home life. In *Redundant spaces in cities and regions,* ed. J. Anderson, S. Duncan, and R. Hudson, 155-200. London: Academic Press.

MacLaran, A., ed. 2003. *Making space: Property development and urban planning.* London: Arnold.

MacLeod, G. 2002. From urban entrepreneurialism to a "revanchist city"? On the spatial injustices of Glasgow's renaissance. *Antipode* 34 (3): 602-24.

Marcuse, P. 1985. Gentrification, abandonment and displacement: Connections, causes and policy responses in New York City. *Journal of Urban and Contemporary Law* 28: 195-240.

–. 2004. The "War on Terrorism" and life in cities after September 11, 2001. In *Cities, war and terrorism: Towards an urban geopolitics*, ed. S. Graham, 263-75. Malden, MA: Blackwell.

Marston, S.A., and K. Mitchell. 2004. Citizens and the state: Citizenship formations in space and time. In *Spaces of democracy: Geographical perspectives on citizenship, participation and representation*, ed. C. Barnett and M. Low, 93-122. London: Sage Publications.

Matrix. 1984. *Making space: Women and the man made environment*. London: Pluto Press.

Mays, J.B. 2005. A clean slate? *Canadian Architect*, August, 44-47.

McClain, J., and C. Doyle. 1983. *Women and housing: Changing needs and the failure of policy*. Ottawa: Canadian Council on Social Development.

McClintock, A. 1995. *Imperial leather: Race, gender and sexuality in the colonial conquest*. New York: Routledge.

McDowell, L. 1993. Space, place and gender relations. Part 2: Identity, difference, feminist geometries and geographies. *Progress in Human Geography* 17 (3): 305-18.

–. 1998. Elites in the City of London: Some methodological considerations. *Environment and Planning A* 30 (12): 2133-46.

McKenzie, E. 2003. Common-interest housing in the communities of tomorrow. *Housing Policy Debate* 14 (1-2): 203-34.

Mehta, A., and L. Bondi. 1999. Embodied discourse: On gender and fear of violence. *Gender, Place and Culture* 6 (1): 67-84.

Meligrana, J., and A. Skaburskis. 2005. Extent, location and profiles of continuing gentrification in Canadian Metropolitan Areas, 1981-2001. *Urban Studies* 42 (9): 1569-92.

Metropolitan Toronto Council. 1983. *Official plan for the urban structure: The Metropolitan Toronto planning area*. Toronto: The Municipality.

–. 1994. *The liveable metropolis: The official plan of the Municipality of Metropolitan Toronto*. Toronto: Metro Planning, Policy Division.

Mills, C. 1988. "Life on the upslope": The postmodern landscape of gentrification. *Environment and Planning D: Society and Space* 6: 169-90.

–. 1993. Myths and meanings of gentrification. In *Place/culture/representation*, ed. J. Duncan and D. Ley, 149-70. London: Routledge.

Milner, N. 1993. Ownership rites and the rites of ownership. *Law and Social Inquiry: Journal of the American Bar Foundation* 18 (2): 227-53.

Miranne, K.B., and A.H. Young, eds. 2000. *Gendering the city: Women, boundaries, and visions of urban life*. Lanham, MD: Rowman and Littlefield.

Mitchell, D. 2003. *The right to the city: Social justice and the fight for public space*. New York: Guilford Press.

–. 2005. The S.U.V. model of citizenship: Floating bubbles, buffer zones, and the rise of the "purely atomic" individual. *Political Geography* 24: 77-100.

Mitchell, K. 2003. Educating the national citizen in neoliberal times: From the multicultural self to the strategic cosmopolitan. *Transactions of the Institute of British Geographers* 28: 387-403.

Mitrany, M. 2005. High density neighborhoods: Who enjoys them? *GeoJournal* 64 (2): 131-40.

Modan, G.G. 2007. *Turf wars: Discourse, diversity and the politics of place.* Malden, MA: Blackwell Publishing.

More families live in apartments than in houses in Metro. 1972. *Toronto Star,* 11 November.

Naples, N.A., and M. Desai. 2002. *Women's activism and globalization: Linking local struggles and transnational politics.* New York: Routledge.

Newman, K., and E. Wyly. 2006. The right to stay put, revisited: Gentrification and resistance to displacement in New York City. *Urban Studies* 43 (1): 23-57.

Newman, O. 1972. *Defensible space: Crime prevention through urban design.* New York: Macmillan Press.

Newman, Z.G. 2002. Whitening the inner city: The containment of Toronto's degenerate spaces and the production of respectable subjects. PhD diss., Ontario Institute for Studies in Education, University of Toronto.

Novac, S. 1990. Not seen, not heard: Women and housing policy. *Canadian Woman Studies* 11 (2): 53-57.

–. 1995. Seeking shelter: Feminist home truths. In *Change of plans: Towards a nonsexist sustainable city,* ed. M. Eichler, 51-70. Toronto: Garamond Press.

–. 1996. *A place to call one's own: New voices of dislocation and dispossession.* Ottawa: Status of Women Canada.

–, J. Darden, J.D. Hulchanski, and A-M. Seguin. 2002. *Housing discrimination in Canada: The state of knowledge.* Ottawa: Canada Mortgage and Housing Corporation.

Osborne, T., and N. Rose. 1999. Governing cities: Notes on the spatialisation of virtue. *Environment and Planning D: Society and Space* 17: 737-60.

Pain, R. 1991. Space, sexual violence and social control: Integrating geographical and feminist analyses of women's fear of crime. *Progress in Human Geography* 15 (4): 415-31.

–. 1997. Social geographies of women's fear of crime. *Transactions of the Institute of British Geographers* 22 (2): 231-44.

Papayanis, M.A. 2000. Sex and the revanchist city: Zoning out pornography in New York. *Environment and Planning D: Society and Space* 18 (3): 341-53.

Parker, B. 2008. Beyond the class act: Gender and race in the "creative city" discourse. In *Gender in an urban world,* ed. J. DeSena, 201-32. Bingley, UK: Emerald Group.

Pateman, C. 1970. *Participation and democratic theory.* Cambridge: Cambridge University Press.

–. 1989. *The disorder of women: Democracy, feminism and political theory.* Cambridge: Polity Press.

Pearson, A. 2002. *I don't know how she does it: The life of Kate Reddy, working mother.* New York: Knopf.

Peck, J. 2005. Struggling with the creative class. *International Journal of Urban and Regional Research* 29 (4): 740-70.

–. 2006. Liberating the city: Between New York and New Orleans. *Urban Geography* 27 (8): 681-713.

Peck, J., and A. Tickell. 2002. Neoliberalizing space. *Antipode* 34 (3): 380-404.

Peters, E.J. 1998. Subversive spaces: First Nations women and the city. *Environment and Planning D: Society and Space* 16: 665-85.

Podmore, J. 1998. (Re)reading the "loft living" *Habitus* in Montreal's Inner City. *International Journal of Urban and Regional Research* 22 (2): 283-302.

Polanyi, K. 2001. *The great transformation: The political and economic origins of our time.* 2nd ed. Boston: Beacon Press.

Pooley, E. 2005. Pretty cities: Can buildings really boost economic growth? *Canadian Business* 78 (20): 144-46.

Prashad, S. 2004. Young and rentless. *Toronto Star,* 9 April.

Pratt, G. 1990. Feminist analyses of the restructuring of urban life. *Urban Geography* 11 (6): 594-605.

Purcell, M. 2003. Citizenship and the right to the global city: Reimagining the capitalist world order. *International Journal of Urban and Regional Research* 27 (3): 564-90.

Purdy, S. 2003. "Ripped off" by the system: Housing policy, poverty, and territorial stigmatization in Regent Park Housing Project, 1951-1991. *Labour/Le Travail* 52 (1): 45-108.

Raco, M. 2003. Remaking space and securitising space: Urban regeneration and the strategies, tactics and practices of policing in the UK. *Urban Studies* 40: 1869-87.

–. 2007. Securing sustainable communities: Citizenship, safety and sustainability in the new urban planning. *European Urban and Regional Studies* 14 (4): 305-20.

Ramazanoglu, C., with J. Holland. 2002. *Feminist methodology: Challenges and choices.* London: Sage Publications.

Raposo, R. 2006. Gated communities, commodification and aestheticization: The case of the Lisbon metropolitan area. *GeoJournal* 66 (1): 43-56.

Rappaport, E. 2001. *Shopping for pleasure: Women in the making of London's west end.* Princeton, NJ: Princeton University Press.

Razack, S.H. 1998. Race, space and prostitution: The making of the bourgeois subject. *Canadian Journal of Women and the Law* 10 (2): 338-76.

–. 2002. Gendered racial violence and spacialized justice: The murder of Pamela George. In *Race, space and the law: Unmapping a white settler society,* ed. S.H. Razack, 121-56. Toronto: Between the Lines.

Reinharz, S. 1992. *Feminist methods in social research.* New York: Oxford University Press.

Relph, E.C. 1987. *The modern urban landscape.* Baltimore: Johns Hopkins University Press.

Robinson, J.K. 2002. Race, gender and familial status: Discrimination in one US mortgage lending market. *Feminist Economics* 8 (2): 63-85.

Rose, D. 1984. Rethinking gentrification: Beyond the uneven development of Marxist urban theory. *Environment and Planning D: Society and Space* 2: 47-74.

–. 1989. A feminist perspective on employment restructuring and gentrification: The case of Montreal. In *The power of geography*, ed. J. Wolch and M. Dear, 118-38. Boston: Unwin Hyman.

–. 1996. Economic restructuring and the diversification of gentrification in the 1980s: A view from a marginal metropolis. In *City lives and city forms: Critical perspectives on Canadian urbanism*, ed. J. Caulfield and L. Peake, 131-72. Toronto: University of Toronto Press.

–, and P. Villeneuve. 1993. Work, labour markets, and households in transition. In *The changing social geography of Canadian cities*, ed. L.S. Bourne and D.F. Ley, 153-74. Montreal and Kingston: McGill-Queen's University Press.

Rose, N. 1996. *Inventing our selves: Psychology, power, and personhood.* Cambridge: Cambridge University Press.

Rosewarne, L. 2005. The men's gallery: Outdoor advertising and public space: Gender, fear, and feminism. *Women's Studies International Forum* 28 (1): 67-78.

Rutherford, S. 2007. Green governmentality: Insights and opportunities in the study of nature's rule. *Progress in Human Geography* 31 (3): 291-307.

Saegert, S. 1981. Masculine cities and feminine suburbs: Polarized ideas and contradictory realities. In *Women and the American city*, ed. C.R. Stimpson, E. Drixler, M.J. Nelson, and K.B. Yatrakis, 93-108. Chicago: University of Chicago Press.

Sassen, S. 1998. *Globalization and its discontents: Essays on the new mobility of people and money.* New York: New Press.

Saunders, C. 2006. Green inside the box. *This* 40: 19-21.

Secor, A.J. 2003. Citizenship in the city: Identity, community, and rights among women migrants to Istanbul. *Urban Geography* 24 (2): 147-68.

Shim, J. 2004. Strong sales, stable prices spell healthy market. *Toronto Star,* 20 November.

Short, J.R. 1999. Urban imagineers: Boosterism and the representation of cities. In *The urban growth machine: Critical perspectives two decades later*, ed. A. Jones and D. Wilson, 37-54. New York: SUNY Press.

Siemiatycki, M. 2006. *The municipal franchise and social inclusion in Toronto: Policy and practice.* Toronto: Inclusive Cities Canada and the Social and Community Planning Council of Toronto.

–, and E.F. Isin. 1997. Immigration, diversity and urban citizenship in Toronto. *Canadian Journal of Regional Science* 20 (1, 2): 73-102.

Simmel, G. 1971. The metropolis and mental life. In *Georg Simmel: On individualism and social forms*, ed. D.N. Levine, 324-39. Chicago: University of Chicago Press.

Skaburskis, A., and D. Mok. 2000. The impact of withdrawing subsidies for new rental housing: Projections for Toronto and the rest of Ontario. *Housing Studies* 15 (2): 169-94.

Slater, T. 2004a. Municipally managed gentrification in South Parkdale, Toronto. *Canadian Geographer* 48 (3): 303-25.

–. 2004b. North American gentrification? Revanchist and emancipatory perspectives explored. *Environment and Planning A* 36: 1191-213.

–. 2006. The eviction of critical perspectives from gentrification research. *International Journal of Urban and Regional Research* 30 (2): 737-57.

Smailes, J. 1994. "The struggle has never been simply about bricks and mortar": Lesbians' experience of housing. In *Housing women*, ed. R. Gilroy and R. Woods, 152-72. London: Routledge.

Smith, D.E. 1988. *The everyday world as problematic: A feminist sociology.* Milton Keynes: Open University Press.

Smith, N. 1979. Toward a theory of gentrification: A back to the city movement by capital not people. *Journal of the American Planning Association* 45: 538-48.

–. 1986. Gentrification, the frontier, and the restructuring of urban space. In *Gentrification of the city*, ed. N. Smith and P. Williams, 15-34. London: Unwin Hyman.

–. 1996. *The new urban frontier: Gentrification and the revanchist city.* London: Routledge.

–. 2002. New globalism, new urbanism: Gentrification as global urban strategy. *Antipode* 34: 427-50.

Social Planning Council of Metropolitan Toronto. 1973. *Families in high rise apartments.* Toronto: Social Planning Council of Metropolitan Toronto.

Soja, E. 2000. *Postmetropolis: Critical studies of cities and regions.* Oxford: Blackwell.

Southworth, N. 1999. Single women lead charge in house buying. *Globe and Mail,* 12 March.

Starkweather, S. 2007. Gender, perceptions of safety and strategic responses among Ohio university students. *Gender Place and Culture* 14 (3): 355-70.

Statistics Canada. 2003. Census Tract Profile for Toronto CMA, Families and Households 2001 Census. www.statcan.ca/english/census01/data/profiles/ct.

–. 2008a. Census Tract Profile for Toronto CMA, Families and Households, 2006 Census. http://www12.statcan.ca/english/census06/data/profiles/ct.

–. 2008b. Net Worth of Family Units, by Selected Family Characteristics, 1999 and 2005. http://www40.statcan.ca/l01/cst01/famil112c.htm.

Stellin, S. 2009. Miami Beach dodges a cold front. *New York Times,* 1 May.

Stoffman, D. 1973. 30-floor towers plan "insane," but council won't repeal bylaw. *Toronto Star,* 3 March.

Strahilevitz, L.J. 2006. Exclusionary amenities in residential communities. *Virginia Law Review* 92 (3): 437-99.

Swyngedouw, E. 2005. Governance innovation and the citizen: The Janus face of governance-beyond-the-state. *Urban Studies* 42 (11): 1991-2006.

Taggart, W.H.J. 1995. Neighborhood participation: An examination of the relationship between participation, housing tenure, scale of development and community. PhD diss., York University.

Tallon, A.R., and R.D.F. Bromley. 2004. Exploring the attractions of city centre living: Evidence and policy implications in British cities. *Geoforum* 35: 771-87.

Thompson, F.M.L. 2001. *Gentrification and the enterprise culture: Britain, 1780-1980.* Oxford: Oxford University Press.

Tickell, A., and J. Peck. 1996. The return of the Manchester Men: Men's words and men's deeds in the remaking of the local state. *Transactions of the Institute of British Geographers* 21: 595-616.

Timmons, D. 2005. It's not easy to have kids in Canada. *National Post,* 17 January.

Tindal, C.R., and S.N. Tindal. 2004. *Local government in Canada.* 6th ed. Ottawa: Nelson Education.

Toennies, F. 1963. *Community and society [Gemeinschaft und Gesellschaft].* New York: Harper and Row.

Toronto condo sales lift off to new high: 60% of total new-home purchases. 2006. *Canadian Press,* 20 July.

Torre, S. 1999. Expanding the urban design agenda: A critique of the new urbanism. In *Design and feminism: Re-visioning spaces, places, and everyday things,* ed. J. Rothschild, 35-44. New Brunswick, NJ: Rutgers University Press.

Townshend, I. J. 2006. From public neighbourhoods to multi-tier private neighbourhoods: The evolving ecology of neighbourhood privatization in Calgary. *Geo-Journal* 66 (1-2): 103-20.

Turk, M. 2004. The question of rent: The emerging urban housing crisis in the new century. *International Journal of Urban and Regional Research* 28 (4): 909-18.

Vaiou, D., and R. Lykogianni. 2006. Women, neighbourhoods and everyday life. *Urban Studies* 43 (4): 731-43.

Valentine, G. 1989. The geography of women's fear. *Area* 21: 385-90.

–. 1992. Images of danger: Women's sources of information about the spatial distribution of male violence. *Area* 24 (1): 22-29.

–. 1999. A corporeal geography of consumption. *Environment and Planning D: Society and Space* 17: 329-51.

Virilio, P. 2005. *City of panic.* Trans. J. Rose. Oxford: Berg.

Vromen, A. 2003. Community-based activism and change: The cases of Sydney and Toronto. *City and Community* 2 (1): 47-69.

Warde, A. 1991. Gentrification as consumption: Issues of class and gender. *Environment and Planning D: Society and Space* 9: 223-32.

Weiss, M.A. 1987. *The rise of the community builder.* New York: Columbia University Press.

Wekerle, G.R. 1976. Vertical village: Social contacts in a singles high-rise complex. *Sociological Focus* 9 (3): 299-315.

–. 1984. A woman's place is in the city. *Antipode* 16 (3): 11-16.

–. 1988a. Canadian women's housing cooperatives: Case studies in physical and social innovation. In *Life spaces: Gender, household, employment,* ed. C. Andrew and B. Moore-Milroy, 102-40. Vancouver: UBC Press.

–. 1988b. *Women's housing projects in eight Canadian cities.* Ottawa: Canadian Mortgage and Housing Corporation.

–. 1993. Responding to diversity: Housing developed by and for women. *Canadian Journal of Urban Research* 2 (2): 95-113.

–. 1997. The shift to the market: Gender and housing disadvantage. In *Women and the Canadian welfare state,* ed. P.M. Evans and G.R. Wekerle, 170-94. Toronto: University of Toronto Press.

–. 1999. Gender planning as insurgent citizenship: Stories from Toronto. *Plurimondi* 1 (2): 105-26.

—. 2000. Women's rights to the city: Gendered spaces of a pluralistic citizenship. In *Democracy, citizenship and the global city*, ed. E.F. Isin, 203-17. London: Routledge.

—. 2004. Framing feminist claims for urban citizenship. In *Mapping women, making politics: Feminist perspectives on political geography*, ed. L.A. Staeheli, E. Kofman, and L.J. Peake, 245-59. New York: Routledge.

—. 2005. Gender planning in public transit: Institutionalizing feminist politics, changing discourse and practice. In *Gender and planning: A reader*, ed. S. Fainstein and L.J. Servon, 275-96. New Brunswick, NJ: Rutgers University Press.

—, and E. Hall. 1972. High rise living: Can the same design serve young and old? *Ekistics* 196: 186-91.

—, and L. Peake. 1996. New social movements and women's urban activism. In *City lives and city forms: Critical research and Canadian urbanism*, ed. J. Caulfield and L. Peake, 263-81. Toronto: University of Toronto Press.

—, and C. Whitzman. 1995. *Safe cities: Guidelines for planning, design, and management*. New York: Van Nostrand Reinhold.

—, R. Dragicevic, R. Jordan, I. Kszyk, and M. Sorenson. 1980. Contradictions in ownership, participation and control: The case of condominium housing. In *The consumer experience of housing*, ed. C. Ungerson and V. Karn, 170-91. Farnborough: Gower Publishing.

Wellman, B. 1979. The community question: The intimate networks of East Yorkers. *American Journal of Sociology* 84 (March): 1201-31.

Wells, N.M. 2005. Our housing, our selves: A longitudinal investigation of low-income women's participatory housing experiences. *Journal of Environmental Psychology* 25 (2): 189-206.

Werbner, P., and N. Yuval-Davis, eds. 1999. *Women, citizenship and difference*. London and New York: Zed Books.

Whitzman, C. 1992. Taking back planning: Promoting women's safety in public places – the Toronto experience. *Journal of Architectural and Planning Research* 9 (2): 169-79.

—. 2002. Feminist activism for safer social space in High Park, Toronto: How women got lost in the woods. *Canadian Journal of Urban Research* 11: 299-321.

Williams, R. 1976. *Keywords: A vocabulary of culture and society*. London: Fontana Press.

Wilson, E. 1991. *The sphinx in the city: Urban life, the control of disorder, and women*. Berkeley: University of California Press.

Wirth, L. 1938. Urbanism as a way of life. *American Journal of Sociology* 44 (July): 1-24.

Wong, T. 2004. Women lead men as first-time home buyers. *Toronto Star*, 1 September.

—. 2006. Is the sky the limit for condos? *Toronto Star*, 25 May.

Worthington, H. 1973. Apartments with individual touch. *Toronto Star*, n.d.

Yip, N.M., and R. Forrest. 2002. Property owning democracies? Home owner corporations in Hong Kong. *Housing Studies* 17 (5): 703-20.

Yiu, C.Y., S.K. Wong, and Y. Yau. 2006. Property management as property rights governance: Exclusion and internal conflict resolution. *Property Management* 24 (2): 87-102.

Young, I.M. 1990. *Justice and the politics of difference.* Princeton, NJ: Princeton University Press.

Yutangco, P. 2009. GTA murders drop in 2008. *Toronto Star,* 1 January.

Zielinski, S. 1995. Access over excess: Transcending captivity and transportation disadvantage. In *Change of plans: Towards a non-sexist sustainable city,* ed. M. Eichler, 131-56. Toronto: Garamond Press.

Zola, E. 1984. *Au bonheur des dames.* Paris: Bernard Grasset.

Zukin, S. 1982. *Loft living: Culture and capital in urban change.* Baltimore: Johns Hopkins University Press.

–. 1997. Cultural strategies of economic development and the hegemony of vision. In *The urbanization of injustice,* ed. A. Merrifield and E. Swyngedouw, 223-43. New York: New York University Press.

–. 1998. Urban lifestyles: Diversity and standardisation in spaces of consumption. *Urban Studies* 35 (5-6): 825-39.

Index

urban intensification; urban revitalization

Caulfield, Jon, 40

Centre for Addiction and Mental Health, 62

children: appropriating shared spaces of condominiums for, 108-9; children's playgrounds in condominiums, 106; condominiums, as child-averse, 117; condominiums viewed as less attractive option for child-raising, 87, 88; parent network in downtown condominiums, 107-8

cities: gentrification, as global urban strategy, 22; global, definition, 17; as key sites for neoliberal policy implementation, 7; market governance, under neoliberalism, 12-13; municipal government, liberal conception of, 11; responsibility for social housing, 52; as strategic arena for development of citizenship, 11. *See also* citizenship; city planners; gentrification; myth of urbanity; neoliberal urbanism; public space; revanchist city; suburbs; Toronto; urban intensification; urban revitalization

Citizens for Local Democracy, 54

citizenship: cities as strategic arena for development of, 11; condominium buyers, as appropriate citizens of revitalized city, 70; condominium buyers, as entrepreneurial citizens, 55, 58, 60, 79, 90, 125, 202; consumerist model of, 150-51

City of Toronto. *See Official Plan for the City of Toronto* (2002); Toronto

city planners: on city's desire for live-work developments, 154; on commercial displacement by new-build gentrification, 154-55; on condominiums and community services,

95-97; as interviewees, 44-45; on quality of life issues, 152-53. *See also* legislation (Ontario); *Official Plan for the City of Toronto* (2002)

class: and affordability of condominium ownership, 80; creative class/creative city theory (Florida), 24; and gender, 44; and gentrification of central urban landscape, 22, 127; urban restructuring, and polarized labour force, 24, 185, 187; urban revitalization, as beneficial to select group of city dwellers, 25. *See also* gentrification

common-interest developments (CIDs), 37

community: assumptions about creating, 102; condominium, as sites of engagement for privileged few, 124, 125; condominium owners, and surrounding neighbourhood, 86-88, 89, 98, 143, 202; condominium owners, within condominium projects, 102-10, 117; condominiums, as gated communities, 35, 37, 92; definition, 94; gentrification conflated with community, by city planners, 95; marginalized groups, displacement in urban revitalization, 99, 205; multiculturalism, associated with downtown living, 195; sustainable, feminist definition of, 157; undercut by condominium boundaries and narrow demographic of owners, 203. *See also* citizenship; public space

Concord Pacific Group, 160

Condominium Act (Ontario, 1967), 33

condominium corporations: governance, by residents, 118-24; ownership of exterior spaces and structures, 37; responsibility for building management and maintenance, 34, 35, 37; as surrogate husbands regarding

maintenance functions, 81. *See also*
governance
condominium developers: as authors of
articles on condominiums in newspapers, 68; on community development, 100-2; condominium lifestyle
features, based on assumed residents, 103-5, 110; creation and
propagation of myth of urbanity,
157-58; family-averse, 106-7; financial incentives to potential owners,
57, 58-59; gendered commodification of fear and safety, 131-33; as
interviewees, 44-45; marketing to
women, 66-70; narrow vision of
women's emancipation, 10; project
financing and profits, 34-35; promotion of life-work downtown
lifestyle, 162; shaping of image of
desired urban citizen, 3; view of
neighbourhood as consumable,
162-63; view of pre-development
community as problem, 160; view of
themselves as pioneers and visionaries, 158-61. *See also* neoliberal
urbanism; security, condominium
condominium owners: appreciation of
cultural amenities of city, 175-79;
beneficial connections within condominium community, 38; city
living as replacement for partnership or family relations, 191; city
living as situational, depending
upon relationship status, 192-93;
constrained by cost of living in city,
179-80; everyday activities, and
myth of urbanity, 181-85, 207; as
flaneuses, 182, 187f; on identity as
city dwellers, 188, 207; identity
formation, through crossing
boundaries, 139-40, 142, 143-44,
203; importance of walkability and
public transit, 172-75, 194; insulation
from neighbourhood, 180-81; interviewees, 44, 212; majority of female,

one-person households, 39; as
mobile population, 96-97; narrow
sense of city's geographic boundaries, 188-90; resistance to socialization into fear of urban space,
138, 143; target demographic, 36,
107, 108; views of suburbia, 190,
191-92, 193. *See also* citizenship;
condominium ownership; myth
of urbanity; women
condominium ownership: as an investment, 73-75, 76-77; condominiums
as mixed-tenure, limited liability
properties, 36-37; and domestic
services in the home, 83, 85; as
empowerment, 3, 57, 67-70, 73-76,
90; everyday meanings of, 72-73; as
form of entrepreneurial citizenship,
55, 58, 70-71, 79, 90, 125; as form of
governance, 51; as foundation of
Toronto's intensification strategy,
32-33; as freedom from responsibility of physical maintenance, 80-86;
as move towards adulthood, 77-79;
and natural life course, 70, 86-88;
as neoliberal morality tale, 71;
promoted as superior to renting,
57; short span, and lack of connection to neighbourhood, 86-88, 89,
91; viewed as financially responsible, 76-77; as wealth accumulation
strategy, 91, 146. *See also* condominium corporations; condominium developers; condominium
owners; condominiums; governance
condominiums: affordability of, 52,
63; common space, use of, 111-17;
as community, 4, 94, 111-17; as
corporatized urban space, 40;
dead spaces, 109; design, and
urban revitalization, 21-23; and
equity building, 39-40, 52, 55-57;
as gated communities, 37, 92, 98,
125; growth in development of,
1-2; hidden costs, and owners'

McGuinty, Dalton, 19
McLuhan, Marshall, 54
media: articles on young women condominium buyers, 66, 68-69; condominium developers as authors
   of newspaper articles on condominiums, 68; conflation of condominium development with
   revitalization, 99. *See also* advertisements, for condominiums
Mehta, Anna, 144
Mills, Caroline, 149
Mitchell, Don, 12
Mitrany, Michal, 116
Mulroney, Brian, 34
multiculturalism, associated with
   downtown living, 195
myth of urbanity: class, and quality-of-
   life issues, 155; commodification
   of ideals about urban life, 149-50;
   condominiums, and specific vision
   of city life, 4, 170, 210; as consumer
   model of urban citizenship, 150-51;
   internalized by women, 188; out of
   reach for women constrained by
   finances, 180; subverting of feminist
   vision of women's freedom and
   choices, 170-71; as support for
   capitalist penetration of city, 196.
   See also advertisements, for condominiums; class; condominium
   owners; neoliberal urbanism

neoliberal urbanism: cities as key sites
   for neoliberal policy implementation, 7, 12; co-optation of feminist
   discourses of female autonomy and
   freedom, 71-73, 75, 199-201; co-
   optation of feminist visions of
   urban interconnectivity and mixed-
   use, 197; and commodification of
   everyday urban life, 5, 7-8, 201-3;
   and commodification of fear and
   safety, 144, 146; condominiums
   viewed as socially and environment-

ally progressive, 195; condominiums
   viewed as solution to crises of postindustrial cities, 4-5; conflation of
   community with redevelopment,
   98-99; dealing with urban problems
   through regulation of marginalized
   groups, 12; environmental concerns
   as rationale for residential intensification, 20; and internalization of
   myth of urbanity by women, 188;
   liveability as a commodity, 196-97;
   ownership viewed as superior to
   renting, 64-65; participation in
   urban life predicated on property
   ownership, 202; as shift away form
   state responsibility for social and
   economic well-being, 8; and systemic culture of fear, 127; as underlying condominium development,
   2; undermining of urban citizenship, 201-3. *See also* capitalism;
   citizenship; condominiums; consumption; myth of urbanity; neoliberalism; revanchist city
neoliberalism: commodification of
   ideals of gendered emancipation,
   199-201; discourse of social responsibility, as way to defuse criticism
   of policies, 195-96; and Foucault's
   concept of governmentality, 9;
   housing as vehicle for wealth
   accumulation, 39-40, 51; link
   between private property and self-
   actualization, 6, 79; reduction of
   social problems to market-based,
   individual problems, 12; shift of
   governance from state to self-
   governance of individual, 8-9, 64,
   207. *See also* capitalism; Foucault,
   Michel; neoliberal urbanism

Official Plan for the City of Toronto
   (2002): analysis of, including
   background documents, 47;
   definition of successful city, 16-17;

safety: assumption of, for women in
urban space, 30; concern for public
agenda of, in face of private condominium security, 38; women, deliberate evasion of issues by policy
makers, 145. *See also* security,
condominium
security, condominium: boundaries as
marking personal and public space,
130; and commodification of fear
and safety, 131-33, 145; concierge,
131, 132, 133-35; and desire for
personal insulation and privacy,
144; distinguishing of condominium community from surrounding
area, 145-46; and need for protection of women, 3; premise that
women's safety is a personal choice
rather than political issue, 145; use
of gendered vulnerabilities to expand into marginal communities,
138. 203. *See also* safety
Simmel, Georg, 94, 149
Slater, Tom, 62
Smith, Dorothy, 41
Smith, Neil: on gentrification, 61, 127-
28; on residential intensification,
22; on revanchist city, 7, 25; on
urban frontier, 170
social housing. *See under* housing
Sorauren Lofts, 198
Spadina Expressway, opposition to,
54
St. James Town (neighbourhood), 62
Stinson, Harry, 198
suburbs: anti-sprawl rhetoric against,
20, 24, 193; gentrification, viewed
as progressive reaction to suburban
living, 54; low-density zoning regulations, 20; as place to raise family,
87; Toronto, new single-family
housing developments in 1980-90s,
33. *See also* cities
Swyngedouw, Erik, 123

Tenant Protection Act (Ontario, 1997),
61
Theodore, Nik, 7
Toronto: as Canada's global city, 17;
condominium market, 1-2, 15;
increasing discourse around public
violence, 128-29; new condominium
construction since 1990s, 33; objec-
tion to high-rise construction, in
1970s, 21; private partnerships with
investors, 21-22; reasons for intensification, 18; urban revitalization
policies, 17. *See also Official Plan
for the City of Toronto* (2002)
Turk, Michael, 61

urban intensification: advantages to
city, 24; anti-sprawl debate as silencing of discourse on, 93; capitalizing
on demographic effects of urban
restructuring, 24; condominiums,
as shift towards high-density, high-
rise urban living, 16; created by
rental buildings and co-ops, in
1960-70s, 16; greenwashing of,
20-21; as merely shifting the geography of urban problems, 208;
previously involved strong public-
sector participation, 34; re-use of
buildings and disused spaces, 21;
shift towards, 2; through reurbanization, 18. *See also* capitalism;
gentrification; high-rise buildings;
legislation (Ontario); neoliberal
urbanism; urban revitalization
urban revitalization: beneficiaries of,
10, 22, 25; focus on male-dominated
institutions, 27-28; gendered narratives, and social policy, 30-31; label,
as removing problematic aspects of
gentrification from public debate,
124; linked to urban fears, 127;
marginalized groups, displacement
of, 99-100, 198; as opening of new

Printed and bound in Canada by Friesens
Set in Eras and Warnock by Artegraphica Design Co. Ltd.
Copy editor: Joanne Richardson
Proofreader: Dallas Harrison
Indexer: Annette Lorek